PARALLEL HISTORIES

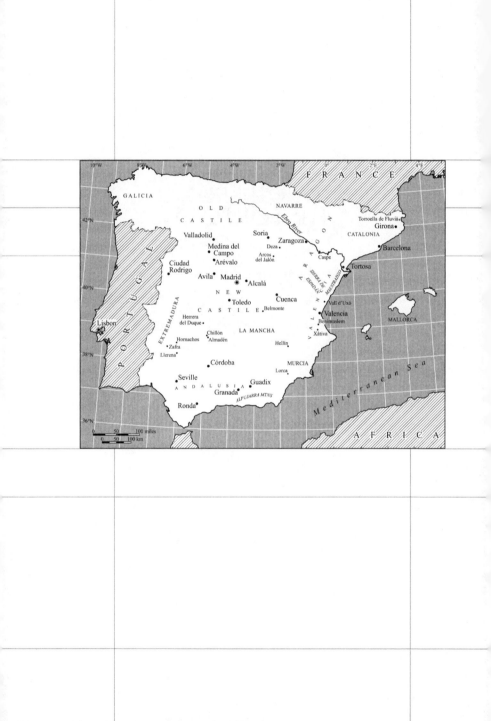

PARALLEL HISTORIES

MUSLIMS AND JEWS
IN INQUISITORIAL SPAIN

JAMES S. AMELANG

LOUISIANA STATE UNIVERSITY PRESS

BATON ROUGE

Published by Louisiana State University Press
Copyright © 2013 by Louisiana State University Press
All rights reserved
Manufactured in the United States of America
First printing

Designer: Barbara Neely Bourgoyne
Typefaces: Requiem, display; Minion Pro, text
Printer and binder: IBT Global

Frontispiece map created by Mary Lee Eggart

Library of Congress Cataloging-in-Publication Data

Amelang, James S., 1952–
  Parallel histories : Muslims and Jews in inquisitorial Spain / James S. Amelang.
    pages cm
  Includes bibliographical references and index.
  ISBN 978-0-8071-5410-6 (pbk. : alk. paper) — ISBN 978-0-8071-5411-3 (pdf) —
ISBN 978-0-8071-5412-0 (epub) — ISBN 978-0-8071-5413-7 (mobi) 1. Moriscos—Spain—
History. 2. Marranos—Spain—History. 3. Muslims—Spain—History. 4. Jews—Spain—
History. 5. Religious tolerance—Spain—History. 6. Spain—History—House of Austria,
1516–1700. 7. Spain—History—Ferdinand and Isabella, 1479–1516. 8. Conversion—
Christianity—History. 9. Spain—Church history. I. Title.
  DP104.A64 2013
  305.6'970903—dc23

                                                                            2013016065

To Sanford Shepard, of blessed memory

What I have, I see as in the distance:
and what is gone, becomes a reality to me.

—Goethe, *Faust, First Part,* dedication
(trans. Abraham Hayward)

CONTENTS

PREFACE

ISCUSSING THE HISTORY of Judaism and Islam in a society that
according to the letter of the law lacked Jews and Muslims may
seem to be a task better suited to Don Quixote than to the present-
day historian. As a challenge it presents both problems and opportunities.
The problems, as will be seen, regard basic historical information, thanks
to the secrecy which shrouded the lives of Muslims, Jews, and their descendants throughout the early modern era. But there are opportunities as well.
Focusing on minorities exposes much that otherwise fails to see the light
of day. It brings into view much of the raw and all-too-revealing underside
of Spanish society, where reality ran roughshod over legislation, and where
ideology did not always trump pragmatism. Above all, it lets the historian
explore one of the most striking ways in which the history of Iberia differed
from that of its neighbors. No other country in early modern Europe could
match Spain in the intensity with which Christianity confronted the Jewish
and Muslim faiths. And in no other country did this confrontation leave
behind such deep traces of coexistence as well as conflict.

The relevance of this story for the history of Spain and, indeed, of Europe
as a whole needs no justification. However, a word should be said about how
this text came into being and why it takes the shape that it does. In regard to
the former, the reader deserves to know that the author is not a specialist in
either Jewish or Islamic history. Rather, I would define myself as a general

historian who is drawn to this theme not only by personal interest but also by recognition of its importance to understanding a distant past that has more than a few links to a difficult present. I do not know Hebrew or Arabic, and I readily confess to hoping that what I lack in expertise can be made up somewhat in other ways. Above all, I trust that something of interest can be said regarding this dual past by a detached if sympathetic observer who looks from outside upon two largely separate historiographies that often seem to be excessively given to sectarian polemics and, what is more, live largely with their backs to each other. These were the very reasons why I decided several years ago to teach a course at my university—the Universidad Autónoma de Madrid—titled "Jewish and Muslim Converts in Early Modern Spain." I was impressed by how much interest it stirred among our students, as well as by—they were the first to admit it—how little they knew about a subject that nevertheless struck them as highly relevant to a wide range of present-day issues. I daresay that some of these students would be amused to find their former teacher confessing to being in the same position they were in. There may be more justice in the writing of history than we find in history itself.

As for this book's structure: it is a synthesis divided into two sections. The main text reviews the history first of the moriscos and then of the judeoconversos, and it closes with some brief reflections on how what I call these two parallel histories both differed from and resembled each other. Then follows a thematic bibliography. One particular feature of this book is that it devotes substantially more space to the history of the Jewish converts than to their Islamic counterparts. Two factors led to this imbalance. The first is the relative length of the two histories. The forced conversion of the Jews not only started a century before that of the Muslims; it also finished at least a century later. This longer historical trajectory affected the other factor in play: the fact that, for various reasons, there are far more extensive sources documenting the *judeoconverso* experience than the *morisco* one. I would by no means say that this longer time span and more varied documentation made for a more complex history. But they certainly contributed to a historical outcome whose twists and turns can be viewed from more diverse angles, as I trust will become apparent.

I close this brief note expressing my gratitude to the many persons who helped make this book possible. I am deeply in debt to a number of specialists in these two fields who generously gave of their time and advice to help improve its arguments and documentation. Mercedes García Arenal not only insisted that I should write this book but also kindly contributed a preface to the Spanish edition. Like her, Miriam Bodian carefully read the entire text; I am grateful to them both for their advice and naturally take responsibility for any errors that remain. I would also acknowledge my other interlocutor on these matters, Stefania Pastore, who despite her youth has done so much to renew our thinking about the intricately related history of these two groups.[1] Lou Rose, as ever, read the manuscript from start to finish and suggested ways in which it could gain in clarity, as did Saúl Martínez. Richard Kagan and his graduate students at Johns Hopkins kindly gave this text its trial run in the classroom, and I am grateful for their suggestions for improving it. Finally, I owe a word of thanks to my students at the Autónoma. Their interest, questions, and papers were of great help as we learned together about these two minorities. Thinking about them takes me back to when I was their age and first read about Jews and Muslims in Spain under the watchful eye of Sanford Shepard at Oberlin College. I cannot help now but feel that a circle of sorts has been closed. Or as Shepard would have put it in his unforgettably kabbalistic style, learning begins when one returns to the beginnings.

PARALLEL
HISTORIES

PARALLEL HISTORIES

T HIS IS A rough sketch of two faiths in a specific time and place. Judaism and Islam, and indeed all religions, tend to have two histories. The first is universal, a "great tradition" in which concrete historical situations take second place to the long sweep of spiritual beliefs and practices as they evolve over the millennia. The other history, a "little tradition" in which the same beliefs and practices are examined in local, particular contexts, often comes across as a lesser story. It does, however, have the singular advantage of avoiding the frequent sins of the long-term, confessional approach: the excess of generalization and the invariably pious cast of a history of belief written by and for believers. If the study of Christianity in early modern Spain is far too important a matter to leave it exclusively in the hands of those who profess it, the same can certainly be said of the religious experience of the persecuted faiths of the minorities.

Medieval Spain was historically the part of western Christianity whose contact with both Islam and Judaism was longest, closest, and most intense. Early modern Spaniards by and large looked on this contact as a fundamental if undesirable legacy, one that played a crucial role in shaping the country's fortunes even after the minority religions had been officially extirpated from the body politic. Studying how persons from all backgrounds grappled with this problematic inheritance from the past teaches a great deal about Spanish society, politics, economy, law, and culture as a whole.

The close study of converts—some of whom were crypto-Jews and -Muslims—reveals much not only about these elusive minorities but also about the Christian majority, and its deeper fears and fantasies in particular. No history of Spain would be complete without keeping the unsure and often puzzling interaction of these three groups in mind.

That said, it must be pointed out that the two minorities have rarely been studied together. That this has not been undertaken until now reflects in large measure the strength of historiographic traditions that have kept Jews and Muslims separate from each other, especially in regard to the postmedieval era. Yet there are compelling reasons for examining these groups together. Both were confessional minorities that wound up being defined in an ethnic and even racial sense, and in some cases in a manner ominously suggestive of the future of European "scientific" racism. And while both housed a wide range of spiritual experiences, they garnered uncommon repute for the suspicion, justified or not, of crypto-religion, that is, secret adherence to ancestral creeds and rites. Finally, the existence of what the Christian majority feared was an underground counterfaith represented the sole fissure in national religious unity within one of the few major European countries that had not witnessed any significant Protestant movement. The otherwise complete triumph of orthodoxy renders the existence of surreptitious dissent—real or imagined—all the more significant.

The two parts of the text follow roughly the same schema. Each opens with an overview of the relations between the majority and the minority in question. Pride of place is given to the more dramatic confrontations that dominated these relations, above all the two expulsions, first of the Jews in 1492 and then in 1609–14 of the *moriscos,* or Muslim converts to Christianity. The less conflictive encounters of daily life, and in particular the long-term assimilation of the converted Jews, also receive attention. Thereafter follow sections on religious beliefs and practices, social and professional characteristics, the construction of collective and individual identities, cultural creativity, the experience of exile, and finally, the sheer difficulties of maintaining orthodox rites and tenets under conditions of persecution. In regard to certain questions, one group inevitably receives more emphasis than the other. Thus, in terms of high politics the moriscos take pride of place, as for various reasons they loomed much larger among the diplomatic and military concerns of the Spanish Monarchy. When dealing with issues of literary expression and promotion of spiritual reform, though, the converted Jews emerge as protagonists, given their far greater presence in the mainstream of Spanish cultural and artistic life. All the same, despite these and other imbalances—many the result of the more abundant documentation generated by and about the descendants of Jews—the overall aim is to examine both groups in the light of often remarkably similar historical experiences. Hence the same, pressing questions, above all the causes and consequences of the forced conversions that converted Spain itself from a haven, however reluctant, of tolerance and pluralism into a society that became a paradigm of a single official religion imposed on all. How and why this new regime took shape through the expulsion of collective difference and the subsequent vigilance of individual nonconformity, defined in ethnic as well as doctrinal terms, is the other major set of questions considered in these pages.

THE *MORISCOS* AND THE END OF MUSLIM SPAIN

CHAPTER I

THE DECLINE
OF COEXISTENCE

T HE RELATIONS BETWEEN the Catholic majority and the Islamic or formerly Islamic minority in early modern Spain ran a lengthy gamut that ranged from episodes of extreme hostility and violence to an impressive degree of coexistence. This was as true of the sixteenth and seventeenth centuries as it was of the Middle Ages, during most of which Islam was the religion of the majority of Spaniards.

Not surprisingly, much of this history has been shrouded in myth. For centuries, the medieval era was uniformly depicted—and by many celebrated—as a "Reconquest," an ongoing crusade during which the various Christian powers drove southward in an unceasing effort to expel the Muslims who had conquered the Iberian peninsula from the Visigoths beginning in 711. More recently a countermyth has appeared. It extols medieval Iberia as a paragon of *convivencia,* the one place in Europe where the three religions of Christianity, Islam, and Judaism thrived together amid peace and prosperity. As is usually the case, the truth is somewhere in the middle and is more complex than either of these myths would allow for. The war logic of crusading was only one of the ways in which Christians dealt with Muslims—and vice versa—in medieval Iberia. Much more common over the long run was some sort of coexistence. It was wary and watchful, to be sure.

It was also for the most part pacific, with a wide range of economic, social, and cultural interactions holding it in place. While it would be stretching the truth to refer to this coexistence as the fruit of a deliberate policy of mutual toleration, elements of such an attitude occasionally made their presence felt. Public recognition of the right of Christians, Jews, and Muslims to practice their religion even when their members were conquered minorities subject to disabilities and discriminations was certainly forthcoming. And it was precisely such recognition that distinguished the Middle Ages from what was to come.

This limited but very real policy of accommodation came to an end following the defeat in 1492 of the last remaining Muslim power in the peninsula, the Nasrid kingdom of Granada. Forced conversions began in the newly conquered territory in 1500–1501. They extended to the rest of Andalusia and the kingdom of Castile in 1502, Navarre in 1515–16, Valencia in the early 1520s, and the rest of the crown of Aragon in 1525–26. While at first official policy closed an eye to the continued use of the Arabic language and a variety of traditional customs, from 1526 onward there was no formal toleration of Islam anywhere within the Spanish kingdoms. By the mid-sixteenth century, escalating pressure on the *moriscos*—the term by which converts from Islam were known—to relinquish their distinctive language, dress, festivities, and other cultural practices led to the second act of this tragedy, open revolt in Granada. The so-called War of Granada, a desperate and merciless conflict waged from 1568 to 1571 in the Alpujarra mountains south of the city, ended in defeat for the moriscos. Thereafter followed their collective exile from the kingdom of Granada beginning in 1569. The finale was the expulsion of the entire morisco population of Spain, ordered by King Philip III beginning in 1609. This drastic measure brought the so-called morisco problem to a definitive end.

When reconstructing this history one needs to avoid reading earlier phases in light of the traumatic finish. While official prejudice against the moriscos was always in evidence, there was no clear long-term state or Church policy toward the converts, nor was there much consistency in legislation and administrative practice. Public handling of these relations evolved in piecemeal fashion, with many of its twists and turns deriving from local initiatives on the part of inquisitors, bishops, lay lords, and others. The interests of these powerful individuals and the groups and institutions they represented did not always coincide. Aristocrats and monarchs alike derived substantial resources from the Muslims: the crown in the form of special taxes—not by accident Muslims were known as the "king's treasure" during the Middle Ages—and the nobles from the ample supply of docile labor which they extracted from those who depended on them for patronage and protection. This important source of income led aristocrats and even on occasion rulers to obstruct the Inquisition's campaigns against what it regarded as crypto-Muslim practices. Many bishops and clerical reformers also rejected harsh measures against the moriscos. Their preference for greater missionary and pastoral efforts to effect peaceful acceptance of Christianity among the converts often put them at loggerheads with the hard-liners in their own camp. Despite its dramatic end, the history of the moriscos meandered along, among false starts, lost opportunities, and puzzling mistakes of perception and policy. Endowed with more than its share of enigmas, it needs to be examined with care.

CHAPTER 2

RISE AND FALL OF
THE *MORISCOS*
A POLITICAL HISTORY

A S THE NORTHERN kingdoms gradually extended their control over the peninsula, particularly beginning in the eleventh century following the collapse of the formidable Caliphate of Cordoba, ever-greater numbers of Muslims fell under direct Christian rule. The victors allowed the continued practice of Islam and officially recognized their Muslim subjects as *mudéjares* (from the Arabic *mudajjan,* "permitted to remain"). Worship tended to be more private than public—discretion was advisable at all times. The faithful gathered in small centers and households, since the larger and more prominent mosques had been converted to use as churches. Still, Muslims were allowed to go about their spiritual business, and their communities included ritual butchers, clerics (known in Spanish as *alfaquíes*), religious schools, and the other personnel and institutions of collective life under their creed.

With the conquest of Granada in 1492 the balance between Christianity and Islam shifted irrevocably to the side of the victors. Seen in retrospect, it was only a matter of time before a militarily triumphant Christianity would put an end to the Islamic spiritual autonomy that it had grudgingly conceded in the past. Yet the conversion of mudéjares into moriscos was not a foregone conclusion, nor was the story a straightforward one. Medieval coexistence had never ruled out the exertion of pressure, much less the exercise of violence, against religious minorities. In fact the Muslims had a long history of paying the price for many of the tensions and conflicts within the society in which they reluctantly found themselves. Thus even before the last of the Granada wars Muslims in more settled areas such as Valencia had been involved in disputes over, for example, boundaries and jurisdictions, irrigation rights, and other bones of contention between towns and rural nobles. While on occasion, as in the city of Valencia in 1455, these conflicts led to the use of force against the Islamic minority, there was little here that departed from medieval patterns of coexistence—a coexistence that by its very nature included sporadic acts of violence among members of different religious groups. The fall of Granada changed not so much the nature of this conflict, as the terms in which it was cast. Clashes for whatever reasons between adherents of different religions soon became contained within a single faith, in the form of disputes over the means and ends of conversion. For after 1492 Queen Isabel and, to a lesser extent, King Ferdinand did not hesitate to favor one among the many available precedents from the Middle Ages: forced baptism of their Muslim subjects. And in the Inquisition, which they had already created in 1480, they now had at their disposal an instrument ready to control and punish backsliders among the newly made Christians.

When the Nasrid rulers of Granada finally surrendered to the besieging Christians in January 1492, they and their subjects were granted liberal terms. The treaty known as the Capitulations of Santa Fe explicitly protected the Muslims' right to practice their religion without hindrance from the Christian authorities. Such generosity on the part of the victors did not last long. Isabel had named as the first archbishop her own confessor, the Hieronymite friar Hernando de Talavera. Talavera, a descendant of converted Jews, was one of the most famous and respected churchmen in Castile. Renowned for his mystic asceticism, he advocated peaceful evangelizing of the Muslim population within his vast archdiocese. In fact, Talavera seems to have bent over backward to respect the sensibilities of his new flock; generations later moriscos still remembered him warmly for his rejection of violent approaches to Christianization. Such a flexible spirit was not unique, and Talavera's gradualist approach found other backers, most notably Iñigo

Hurtado de Mendoza, count of Tendilla and the first captain-general of Granada following the conquest. Their policy of accommodation did not last long, however. Talavera soon ran into trouble of his own with the Inquisition, and even before his death in 1507 Church policy in Granada was decided by the new spiritual leader in the royal court, Fray Diego Jiménez de Cisneros. Cisneros was of a different and much harsher temperament, at least in regard to the Islamic remnant. One of his most notorious acts as royal agent in Granada was to organize the public burning of Muslim books and manuscripts in 1500. Much of the rich cultural as well as spiritual legacy of medieval Andalusia perished in this bonfire. It also inaugurated a new and far less benevolent policy, one that refused to wait patiently for the right moment to usher the Muslims, willing or not, into the Christian fold.

This opportunity was not long in coming. Armed conflict between new and old Christians first broke out in the Albaicín, the heavily populated Muslim quarter of the city on the hill opposite the Alhambra palace, and later spread to the Alpujarra mountains to the south. This "revolt" gave Cisneros the political excuse he needed. Between 1501 and 1502 Isabel presented the Muslims of the kingdom of Granada and then the rest of Castile with a stark choice: convert or leave. While an untold number left Granada for North Africa, most chose to stay. The loyalty to Islam of the small, dispersed, yet locally rooted mudéjar population of Castile had clearly attenuated over time. Centuries of life among their Christian neighbors had led many to resign themselves to what they saw as inevitable. The reasons for conversion of the Granadans differed, but they also reflected a pragmatic wish to avoid the heavy costs of moving overseas. The fragmentary evidence that survives suggests that exile was the option preferred above all by lay and especially clerical elites. The former expected to receive support from their kinsmen and allies elsewhere, while the latter found all professional future in their land of origin closed off forever.

The situation differed somewhat in the territories of the crown of Aragon, even if the winds were blowing in the same direction. In Valencia—which housed the largest concentration of mudéjares after Granada—Muslims lived in larger, more compact, and often isolated communities, usually working as agricultural laborers on the large estates of feudal lords. In the past their dependence on the aristocracy had proved a source of protection. It now meant their undoing. The Christian middle and lower classes had long resented them as competitors who worked for lesser wages, and when they rose up against the crown and nobility during the so-called *Germanies* or "revolt of the brotherhoods" of 1519–22, they obliged many members of the Islamic communities to convert en masse. Additional pressure for conversion came from millenarians who in the European-wide turmoil of the early 1520s looked to mass baptisms as a means of ushering in a new kingdom of the spirit. As in the later Middle Ages, popular resentment of elite exploitation mixed with intense hopes for spiritual reform. The confluence of socioeconomic and religious radicalism resulted in the violent conversion of most of Valencia's Muslims. And after the Inquisition ruled that the baptisms were valid, in 1525 Charles V ordered the conversion of all remaining Muslims in the crown of Aragon. Last-ditch resistance in the inland Sierra de Espadán and elsewhere in 1526 only briefly postponed the day of reckoning. By the end of that year Muslim Spain had officially ceased to exist.

The question now was what to do with these *cristianos nuevos,* or "New Christians." More specifically, how were they to be brought fully to accept the faith they had not embraced of their own will? While open adherence to Islam was not to be accepted, many royal and ecclesiastical officials realized that patience and time would be needed to make effective Catholics of the newly minted moriscos. At least at the beginning, official policy thus discouraged too much activity by the Inquisition. (Large payments by the moriscos also helped buy time.) Meanwhile the Church and the state promoted the same system of fixed parishes that regular clergy on itinerant missions would soon make the norm in dealing with the Amerindian peoples of the New World. Religious rigorists such as the well-known writer Antonio de Guevara, along with fellow clerics and future bishops such as Gaspar de Avalos, Martín de Ayala, and Pedro de Guerrero stood at the forefront of this policy of energetic but noncoercive persuasion. Guevara in fact traveled far and wide throughout the diocese of Guadix in the eastern reaches of the kingdom of Granada to make sure that his orders for making true Christians of the moriscos were obeyed. Yet in the end, few within the Church showed the same eagerness to devote time and above all resources to the task of evangelization. Disinterest on the part of a lax and corrupt parish clergy whose tithes often wound up in the hands of lay patrons or cathedral chapters was more the order of the day. That, and the unassailable reality of stubborn morisco resistance to assimilation, led crown and Church largely to abandon "popular" evangelization. They focused their attention instead on those remnants of the formerly Islamic elites who had not left Spain for northern Africa.

The Jesuits eventually took the lead in pushing this much less demanding strategy. They established several schools solely for moriscos, including one (the "House of Doctrine") within the Albaicín itself. This was largely successful on its own terms, as many members of the morisco upper class did indeed effectively absorb Christianity, for reasons that were not entirely spiritual. (Hence the observation by the chronicler Luis de Mármol that the "stain" of lingering commitment to Islam "was found among the common people, while some nobles who knew what was what—*de buen entendimiento*—came over to the faith, and were willing to become and show themselves to be Christians.")[1] The strategy was nevertheless widely regarded as a failure, in that it did not produce the miracle of bringing the much more reluctant morisco masses over to the Christian side. Both majority and minority could agree on one thing: that the problem was not just one of theology. It was also a larger battle over deeply ingrained customs and behavior. Nowhere was this more visible than in the uniquely conflictive context of Granada.

The moriscos of Granada stood out from their brethren elsewhere in several crucial respects, first of all in sheer numbers. As late as the 1560s the moriscos made up over half the population of the kingdom; here, at least, it makes no sense to refer to them as a minority. Everywhere else the presence of bygone Muslims and their descendants was less pronounced, ranging from over 30 percent of the total population in Valencia and 20 percent in the kingdom of Aragon to the much more negligible contingent in Castile proper. A second crucial difference had to do with land tenure and property structures. In Granada, many if not most moriscos owned and worked their own land, as a sort of independent yeomanry. This contrasted sharply with conditions in Aragon and especially Valencia. There the moriscos constituted for the most part a rural proletariat, a heavily exploited contingent of landless laborers (along with a few artisans) who worked for large, aristocratic landowners. Finally, since Granada was the part of the former Al-Andalus most recently incorporated into Christendom, its moriscos had the most recent experience, and thus freshest memories, of Islamic beliefs and practices. This was particularly true of the converts who lived in the mountain villages between the city of Granada and the coast. There difficulty of access permitted an isolation—and by extension an autonomy—that was much harder to preserve under the watchful eyes of urban Christians.

The difference between country and city would turn out to be a deciding factor in the most dramatic confrontation between moriscos and Old Christians in Spanish history. The armed revolt that began in 1568 was the most important domestic upheaval to occur within the Iberian peninsula between the *Comunero* rebellion of the early 1520s and the Catalan and Portuguese revolts of 1640. It was also, in terms of sheer ferocity, perhaps the most devastating war waged on Spanish soil between the Middle Ages and the Napoleonic invasion of 1808. The conflict itself was deeply rooted in the fate of postconquest Granada as a colonial society, an inland frontier in which a Christian minority lived in continual fear and mistrust of a majority whose subordination could never be taken for granted. The medium-term causes of the war derived from shifts in public policy toward the Christianization of the moriscos. Most royal and Church officials assumed that effective religious assimilation of the ex-Muslims would not happen until they cast aside a host of customs inherited from their Islamic past. Thus, beginning as early as 1508, they decreed the destruction of Arabic-language books and texts, and they limited the use of Arabic itself, first in public venues and later in private ones as well. They also forbade the wearing of "Muslim" dress (including veils for women) and ordered the closure of the public baths where, it was feared, the ritual ablutions of Muslim precept continued to take place. The practice of circumcision was prohibited, along with the ritual slaughter of animals and other dietary prescriptions, and even the traditional music and dances which accompanied weddings and other celebrations. In short, the official point of view was clear: religious assimilation was predicated on the elimination of cultural difference. As long as the moriscos looked and acted in ways that departed from those of Old Christians, they would continue to be Muslims.

Such laws proved impossible to enforce. The crown was the first to recognize the utopian quality of this legislation, and it signed secret agreements beginning in 1526 that assured the moriscos—once again, in exchange for a respectable sum of money—breathing space from the attentions of the Inquisition. Yet the laws remained on the books and could be revived at will. This is indeed what happened in the mid-1560s. In the wake of an archdiocesan synod Philip II issued an order on January 1, 1567, that revived the earlier legislation against morisco dress and other customs. Yet cultural repression was merely one side of the story. The naked economic exploitation typical of colonial societies also played its part in driving the moriscos to revolt. Ever since 1492 the newly conquered population had been subjected to heavy taxation. This contrasted visibly with the experience of the Christian settlers, who were lured southward by a wide range of benefits and exemptions. Four *fardas* or extraordinary tributes were levied on the moriscos, who shared communal responsibility for their payment. At the same time, many individual converts found that their lands were coveted by the Christian pioneers, who used a wide range of tactics, legal and illegal, to force them off their properties. By midcentury the settlers had stepped up their efforts to expropriate morisco lands. In this they were seconded by willing allies in the Chancillería, the court of appeals that functioned as the preeminent legal institution in the south of Spain. The lack of scruples of an especially notorious judge, one Dr. Santiago, led to the confiscation during the 1560s of a growing number of properties of moriscos who were unable to show proper written title—according to the standards of Christian society, that is—to the lands they worked. Simultaneous with the years of economic expropriation, the silk trade—the mainstay of the morisco economy—experienced a disastrous decline, damaged by government measures such as a 1552 ban on exports and a steep increase in taxes in the years that followed. By the mid-1560s, local conditions reached the tipping point.

The revolt began on Christmas Eve, 1568. A group of armed moriscos slipped into Granada and tried to provoke an uprising among their compatriots in the Albaicín. The plot failed, though, and they quickly returned to their strongholds in the Alpujarra mountains. Leadership of the movement fell into the reluctant hands of Hernando de Córdoba, the head of one of the more prestigious of the traditional lineages from old Nasrid Granada. Proclaimed king under the name of Aben Humeya, he found himself in charge of a ramshackle coalition of clan leaders who made decisions on their own with little concern for efforts at broader coordination. The result was a highly localized, guerrilla-style war. At first the rebels enjoyed considerable success against the poorly disciplined Christian militias, more interested in easy plunder than in taking on seasoned warriors in highly inhospitable terrain. The conflict rapidly degenerated into episodes of unspeakable cruelty, including massacres, mass rapes and pillage, and wholesale enslavements of civilians on both sides.

Both sides in the war were deeply divided. Aben Humeya never managed to consolidate his authority as leader of the revolt. After facing challenges from several rivals, he was eventually murdered by one of his followers in October 1569. A principal cause of disunity was the inability of the different lineages to rally behind a single leader in a struggle widely dispersed throughout the kingdom. Even more significant was the lack of support for the revolt among the moriscos living in the Vega, or plain around Granada, and above all in the major cities. Whether this reflected a more realistic appreciation on their part of the local balance of power, the lesser impact of economic crisis in urban areas, or the inroads of an assimilation that may have proved more effective than either side was willing to admit, or all three tendencies, is hard to say. In any event, the gap separating city and country proved damaging to the insurgent cause. So did the lack of help from overseas on which the rebels had so heavily counted. Despite promises to the contrary, the moriscos received only token support in the form of troops and supplies from North Africa and the Ottomans. Without more powerful backing, sooner or later the rebels would be forced to give up their struggle.

Differences emerged from the very beginning within the Christian camp as well, especially over how to respond to the Islamic threat. These disagreements by and large replicated those existing in Granada before the uprising. The main line of division pitted the marquis of Mondéjar, the head of the powerful Mendoza family and hereditary governor of the Alhambra fortress, against Chancillería judges and the clergy, advocates of harsh policies toward the moriscos, whom they saw as obstinate and treacherous crypto-Muslims deserving little charity from king and Church. As part of their more general defense of the status quo, Mondéjar and others like him took a more relaxed attitude when it came to religious matters. Furthermore, they blamed local tensions on the greed and oppression of the settlers whose basic aim was to expel the morisco underclass and seize their properties. Finally, the two conflicting responses to the rebellion reflected distinctive social backgrounds and identities. The upwardly mobile *letrados* or government officials trained in law at the universities were anxious to consolidate the power of the royal and ecclesiastical bureaucracies. Meanwhile, members of older noble lineages such as Mondéjar defended a traditionally paternalistic approach toward their morisco vassals, based on a patron-client relation that admitted little interference from the king and his civil servants.

More personal failings and animosities also threatened unity on the Christian side. Mondéjar, the commander by virtue of his local offices and general prominence, was criticized by his enemies as being too sympathetic to the moriscos. The president of the Chancillería, Pedro de Deza, schemed against him. His first move was to weaken Mondéjar's authority by inviting a rival aristocrat, the marquis de los Vélez, to join the forces pursuing the rebels. The latter's followers proved better at pillaging morisco villages than at locating and fighting the rebels, which only added to the difficulties the Christians faced in the field. These and other sources of disunion help explain what was perhaps the most striking feature of this uprising: how long it took the Christians to defeat the rebels. The back and forth of the initial campaigns and the guerrilla war into which it degenerated would have lasted even longer had it not been for Philip II's decision in March 1569 to order his half-brother Don Juan of Austria to bring seasoned troops from Italy to suppress the revolt. This measure—in itself an index of the desperate situation in which the Christians found themselves outside the cities and the lowland areas—eventually led to the defeat of the rebels, whose strongholds fell one by one to the scorched earth offensive waged by the professional soldiers who replaced the settler militias. By early 1571, after numerous atrocities and widespread destruction, the fighting ended.

The war marked the definitive end of the Muslim presence in what had for centuries been its main nucleus. The Christian victors were willing to hazard no risks regarding the future, and they took the unprecedented step of expelling almost the entire morisco population, loyal as well as disloyal, town dwellers and countrymen alike. Beginning in 1569—that is, well before the revolt was suppressed—a minimum of eighty thousand men, women, and children (some 90 percent of the original morisco population) had their properties confiscated and were forced to resettle in the rest of Castile. The drastic resolution of the "morisco problem" in Granada shifted the spotlight to what was now the largest concentration of descendants of Muslim converts in Spain, the communities of Valencia and Aragon. By 1600 the former comprised well over one hundred thousand moriscos, who lived in numerous rural settlements ranging in size from tiny villages to larger ag-glomerations such as the Vall d'Uxó in the northern part of the kingdom. The approximately fifty thousand moriscos of Aragon reported in a census of 1575 were heavily concentrated in the southern part of the kingdom, in the irrigated lands close to the Ebro river. There they lived to a large degree apart from the rest of society. As will be seen below, these separate patterns of settlement did much to foment mistrust between Old and New Christians.

But the decades after 1560 also saw the emergence of a more immediate source of suspicion: the possibility of political and military disloyalty on the part of the moriscos. For better or worse—usually worse—the latter found themselves in the first line of fire in early modern Spain's general engage-ment with Islam. That they might show more sympathy for Spain's Muslim enemies than for their Christian overlords was hardly out of the question. Especially mistrusted were those New Christians who lived in coastal ar-eas. They were frequently accused of aiding Muslim corsairs from North Africa, as well as the regular navy of the Ottoman Empire. After the latter threat receded following the Christian victory at Lepanto in 1571, France replaced the distant Turks as a more credible threat. Beginning in the 1570s the government in Madrid received what would become a swelling tide of reports concerning plots to forge an alliance between dissatisfied moriscos and Spain's ever-hostile rival north of the Pyrenees. It was moreover feared that the considerable Protestant population of southern France would prove especially willing to join in this unusual alliance against Catholic Spain. Moriscos in the frontier kingdom of Aragon were seen as a special menace. There relations between Old and New Christians deteriorated to the point of open warfare in the later 1580s. Some of the conspiracies the moriscos were suspected of participating in were rather whimsical, but others posed a more serious menace to the Monarchy. As a result, all moriscos fell under a growing cloud of suspicion that they represented a "fifth column," an enemy inside the gates requiring constant vigilance, if not harsher measures.

Repressive schemes and strategies were never lacking. Proposals for a "final solution"—the term is not anachronistic—to the morisco problem included gradual extinction through being confined to ghettos, forcing all adult males to serve in the galleys, or the complete prohibition of marriages among them. In 1587 an unusually imaginative cleric, Martín de Salvatierra, the bishop of Segorbe, proposed deporting all the moriscos to Newfoundland and then castrating the males and sterilizing the women. He was not the only one to contemplate such drastic remedies. In 1588 one Alonso Gutiérrez wrote the king advising him to order the castration of at least some moriscos, while noting in passing that "this is done to slaves in the Indies without much fuss."[2] But what began to loom increasingly large as the most promising solution was the expulsion of the entire morisco population.

The idea of forced removal was born in a committee. In 1581–82 Philip II convened an ad hoc commission in the recently conquered city of Lisbon to discuss the matter of the moriscos. After due deliberation, it eventually recommended expulsion. The king, aware of the delicate international situation and perhaps chastened by the disaster his edicts had provoked in Granada, showed little enthusiasm for the proposal and shelved it. Still, the idea had been broached. When a new king reached the throne in 1598, a growing number of backers seized the opportunity to bring it up again. Ironically, it was the coming of peace to Spain, first through the treaty signed with England in 1604 and then with the Dutch rebels in 1609, that led to the moriscos' undoing.

Several factors joined to narrow the options down to expulsion. One weighty one was the failure in 1601 of a large expedition against Algiers. The fiasco—merely one in a long line of frustrated attempts to capture once and for all the notorious nest of pirates and a key city in the western reaches of the Ottoman empire—proved a humiliating start for the reign of Philip III and his favorite the Duke of Lerma. From this point onward, they were anxious to undo the damage that Algiers had wreaked on Spain's reputation, above all after the defeat of a similar campaign in 1608 against Larache, a city on the Atlantic coast of Morocco. A second contributing element was the consolidation of an internal political coalition that lobbied intensely for this measure. The leading institution committed to the expulsion was the powerful Council of State. Its members—drawn mostly from the higher nobility—were concerned with the possible geopolitical and military threat posed by moriscos working in tandem with the French state, which proved ever more assertive after the new king, Henri IV, brought the Wars of Religion to an end. A handful of eminent clerics also began to mobilize public opinion in favor of this measure. The stridently reformist archbishop of Valencia, Juan de Ribera, wrote two proposals in 1601–2 in the hope of pressuring the Lerma regime to take ever more radical steps. His arguments received a favorable reading at court, and in 1602 the Council of State voted in favor of expulsion, only to have the pope express his opposition. Ribera continued to lobby for exiling the moriscos, and he insisted that pragmatic considerations of "reason of state" should not prevent the king from carrying out a policy that had worked so well earlier with the expulsion of the Jews.[3]

In the end, the final decision to expel the moriscos rested with Philip III, and it is to those who exercised greatest influence on him that one should look to find the key to this extraordinary measure. Philip suffered many scruples of conscience, and arguments by prominent theologians and Church authorities such as Ribera carried much weight with him. His wife, Queen Margarita of Austria, also did her best to convince him to put into effect a program that she saw as cleansing Spain of heresy. She did not live to see what she would have regarded as a happy ending to her efforts, but predictably enough her funeral sermon in 1611 contained praise for her "holy hatred" of the moriscos.[4] In the end, though, the decisive influence was Lerma. Interestingly enough, the king's favorite had previously opposed this measure. Why he changed his mind is not too hard to divine. His main strategic goal was to put an end to the war with the Dutch, the single greatest drain on the Monarchy's resources. This was more easily said than done, however. Lerma found it difficult even to reach a satisfactory preliminary arrangement with the rebels, especially touching the thorny question of religious freedom for Dutch Catholics. His inability to guarantee the interests of the latter, coupled with his decision to go ahead and accept a truce, contributed to his turning to the expulsion as means of compensating for what many would see as an admission of religious as well as political defeat. Removing crypto-Muslims would provide a sorely needed victory for the Catholic faith, as well as a welcome distraction from the loss of face. It was thus hardly an accident that the decision to expel the moriscos was announced shortly after the signing of the truce that brought a (temporary) end to the war in the Netherlands.

The expulsion of the moriscos from 1609 to 1613 represented the largest migration decreed by a state for religious reasons in early modern western Europe. Thanks to it, more persons were removed than in the exile of Spain's Jews in 1492, the population transfers from the states of northern Europe during the confessional adjustments of the sixteenth and seventeenth centuries, or the forced departure of the Huguenots from France following the revocation of the Edict of Nantes in 1685. It is impossible to obtain a precise figure for the number of persons expelled, but recent estimates place it at around three hundred thousand—even more, in other words, than the number of Spaniards who had officially emigrated to the New World to that point. The measure came close to including the entire morisco population. Perhaps one out of every ten managed to melt into the ranks of the Old Christians. A few others, such as Sancho Panza's friend Ricote, who appeared in *Don Quixote* II.54, managed to return years later (see below). That the Inquisition was still persecuting moriscos in the late seventeenth century is a sure sign that some at least had slipped through the net.

The expulsion aroused controversy, and even opposition, both within Spain and beyond. Defenders of the expulsion—and there have been many over the centuries—have argued that the government gave in (quite rightly) to pressure from a number of quarters, ranging from public opinion to the papacy. That this however stretched the truth was admitted even by some of the more fervent apologists themselves. Jaime Bleda, a Dominican from Valencia who knew the enemy firsthand thanks to his service in a morisco parish, endlessly railed against the lack of support for his personal crusade in favor of the expulsion among his fellow clergy, the aristocrats who protected their highly useful vassals, and the curia at Rome. He reserved his greatest vituperation, however, for the "abominable sect of the *políticos*" in Madrid, whose Machiavellian reason of state had until then continually trumped the spiritual considerations that should determine decision-making in a truly Catholic monarchy.[5] In his eyes the expulsion marked a victory for the other side, a righteous remnant that upheld a vision of the commonwealth in which religious concerns took pride of place, and in which heresy could not be accommodated. However, for other, less exalted spirits, it was precisely the religious dimension of the problem that proved so troubling. For unlike the exile of the Jews in 1492, the people now being expelled were at least nominally Christians. Moreover, the refusal of the other European powers to accept them meant that they would surely wind up in infidel lands, particularly North Africa. For many persons, clergy and laity alike, there was little to rejoice over in a measure that not only contradicted standard Catholic theology in regard to the efficacy of baptism, but also delivered hundreds of thousands of Christians directly into Muslim hands.

Much of the opposition to the expulsion derived from what was widely seen as its deleterious consequences for the Spanish economy. One did not have to be a Machiavellian to perceive the damage the removal of a highly productive work force would wreak on a nation already in the grips of demographic contraction and suffering from a downswing in economic activity. Precise assessment of the impact, however, is a difficult undertaking, and students of the period continue to be divided as to its exact effects. Contemporaries such as the reformist author Sancho de Moncada were quick to link economic decline and demographic weakness, and modern historians tend to second their reasoning, even when they note that there is no automatic relation between economic and population change. To begin with, the expulsion was highly uneven in terms of geographic distribution. It clearly affected some regions more than others, and a few not at all. One of Spain's first economic historians, the enlightened intellectual Antonio de Capmany, was quick—too quick, perhaps—to note that neither the expulsion of the Jews nor that of the moriscos had much of an impact on his native Catalonia. In the depressed cities of the interior, however, which had added some of those exiled from Granada in the 1570s to their own population of mudéjar origin, the loss was deeply felt. Such was the case, for example, of the old trading center of Medina del Campo. There the expulsion meant the loss of more than one hundred families, some 10 percent of the local population. Hence the complaint of the municipal council in March 1611 that the city would not be able to pay its taxes, thanks to "the great loss in numbers that has taken place during the past year." For this and other urban centers in decline, the expulsion wreaked as much demographic havoc as the deadly plague of the previous decade.[6]

It is also important to keep in mind that the impact of what Thomas Jefferson later referred to as Spain's "deletion of the Moors" was uneven and differed from one region to another.[7] Valencia was by far the hardest-hit area, as it accounted for at least a third of all moriscos expelled. But within Valencia, the center, including (indirectly) the capital city, registered the greatest losses. The consequences of the expulsion were far less in evidence in the more mountainous, inland areas, such as the Maestrazgo, where few moriscos lived. Even then, apart from some immediate effects such as the foreclosures of loans that came due on properties moriscos had worked, the damage was felt more in the long term than the short. Around 1610 there were still enough Old Christians to occupy many of the niches the moriscos left behind. Rural production stayed high, which would explain the notable stability of prices in the wake of the expulsion. Adjustments included a move away from labor-intensive products such as rice, silk, and sugar toward viticulture and livestock raising, part of a literal "Christianization" of the economy after the departure of a more compact and subservient labor force. The real loss was noticed a decade or so later. The moriscos could have made a significant difference as conditions worsened—and taxes rose—beginning with the European-wide downturn of the 1620s. That the different parts of Spain where they had previously lived and worked were unable to count on their presence meant a relative yet nevertheless very palpable loss. It was future generations of Spaniards who paid the bill for what was in large measure an exercise in demagoguery on the part of a weak king trying to look strong.

Yet in the end the greatest loss involved not so much numbers as the sort of contributions that had been made by those sent into exile. The moriscos were acknowledged by friend and foe alike to be a hardworking and productive sector of the populace. James Howell, a young English polymath whose commercial projects brought him to Spain shortly after the expulsion, remarked that

> 'Tis true that the colonizing of the Indies and the wars of Flanders have much drain'd this Country of People; since the expulsion of the Moors it is also grown thinner and not so full of Corn; for those Moors would grub up Wheat out of the very tops of the craggy Hills . . . so that the Spaniard had nought else to do but to go with his Ass to the Market and buy Corn of the Moors.[8]

There is more than a bit of exaggeration here; Howell offers too simple an explanation of a complex phenomenon. More specifically, the moriscos were never much given to the cultivation of wheat and were much more likely to be found in the (irrigated) lowlands than up in the hilltops. Still, as far as their reputation was concerned, Howell was on the mark. The exile of the moriscos represented not just demographic loss. It also meant the extirpation of an unusually industrious part of the population, and one that Spain in particular could ill afford to give up. The defenders of the edict, such as Bleda, promised that God would compensate Spain for its heroic sacrifice, just as he had given it the Indies immediately after the expulsion of the Jews. Yet no such rewards were reaped the second time around.

The question of why the authorities resorted to such a drastic measure continues to intrigue historians, who are all too aware of its many negative consequences. Contemporary apologists did their best to present the expulsion as the continuation, indeed the culmination of the medieval Reconquest. Now that the Jewish menace had been conjured, and its remnants were under effective control thanks to the Inquisition, it was time to take to the field for the final battle in the centuries-long crusade against the last remaining threat to Catholic orthodoxy. Such a traditionalist case masks the most fundamental feature of the expulsion, its truly innovative character. Rather than hearkening back to the Middle Ages, this precociously modern measure of the use of state power against an ethnic minority actually broke with medieval practice, which was much more given to finding some sort of accommodation instead of waging perpetual warfare between Christianity and Islam. That said, the expulsion was rooted in a number of continuities with the past. The most significant among these was the persistence of the highly negative image of Muslims that had been forged originally during the conflicts of the Middle Ages and was thereafter transferred to their successors, the moriscos. It is among the fears and frustrations that generated such expectations where one begins to find other explanations—social, cultural, even psychological—for the end of Islam in early modern Spain.

CHAPTER 3

IMAGES AND REALITIES

S EVERAL BASIC ATTITUDES dominated Old Christian views of recent Muslim converts. Foremost among these was fear. Catholic Spain perceived various sources of threat in the moriscos. Above all, they were seen as potential allies of their Muslim brethren in North Africa and elsewhere in the Mediterranean. Nor were these fears of "conspiracy and a pact for evil among them" misplaced.[1] The strategic danger of the moriscos was not a fantasy. During the prolonged war with the Barbary pirates—one of the more protracted if least acknowledged conflicts in early modern Europe—moriscos often lent covert aid to their coreligionists. This was particularly true of the coastal areas and islands in the south and east, whose inhabitants had long traded in contraband as part of an intense traffic in goods and persons between the northern and southern coasts. Old Christians in these areas suffered constant fear of surprise attacks and kidnappings, at times of entire villages.

Yet one cannot understand the depths of this very real fear if it is separated from another sentiment, that of contempt. Most Old Christians despised the moriscos. While resenting the Jews as rich, they looked down on the moriscos as poor and lacking in honor, thanks in large measure to their practice of demeaning trades. They also considered New Christians social deceivers, not to be trusted. Thus it was widely believed that while on the outside they feigned poverty, secretly they were quite rich, thanks to their greed, frugality, and penchant for large families. The latter derived in turn from a combination of animal sexuality, their marrying off their daughters young, their refusal to commit any of their members to clerical celibacy, and their lack of public service as soldiers or as emigrants to the New World. This combination of suspicion and rejection was neatly summed up by the following diatribe from a sermon published in 1532 by the reforming cleric Bernardo Pérez de Chinchón, who equated the moriscos with the Turks as "people without faith, without law, proud, barbarous, lustful, bestial, thieves, murderers, cruel, poorly dressed, lacking in the propriety and the good order of honest living, and without fear of God."[2]

These and other complaints represented the usual mixture of fantasy and seeming fact that drew on different sorts of resentment lodged at various social levels. Much of the common image of the moriscos was articulated as charges by unskilled workers and others among the lower classes against their direct economic competitors. Landowners paid morisco agricultural laborers substantially less than they paid Old Christians. Similarly, they preferred to take on moriscos as tenants because they knew they could charge them more in exchange for protection. Much anti-morisco sentiment was nurtured by the obvious fact that the New Christians' acceptance of lower wages or higher leases undercut the rural labor market as a whole. The direct self-interest that motivated much of the contemporary criticism of the moriscos was blatant enough to make its way on occasion into the documentary record. Thus in 1633 one Diego Díaz, an innkeeper from the town of Belmonte in La Mancha, was accused of being a secret Muslim by a former servant and a couple who owned a nearby inn. When Díaz pointed out the latter fact the inquisitors released him, noting "that their being enemies is credible because these others have an inn nearby, and among poor people such situations give rise to envy and plots to have the other thrown out of town."[3]

While economic rivalry played an important role in fanning Old Christian hostility against this minority, the prime mover was the former's unwillingness to accept the latter's sense of cultural difference. Or to be more precise, Old Christians suspected that the cultural differences separating them from the moriscos harbored something more sinister: religious heterodoxy. The moriscos may have been scorned as disloyal competitors, but the fundamental cause of their rejection was their refusal—or lack of opportunity?—fully to assimilate. This led Old Christians to see them as spiritual hypocrites as well as social enemies. And logically enough, one might think, given that most of them had been baptized under pressure if not by force. But how they became Christians was far less under dispute than the question of how Christian they became. In the eyes of the majority, the answer was: all too little.

While it would be difficult to underestimate the depth of hostility to Islam in early modern Spain, it should be stressed once again that this hostility meant in many respects a rejection of a shared and not-so-distant past. A different temper had succeeded the uneasy coexistence of the Middle Ages. Hardened boundaries and a preference for purity of faith over the pollution of contact now replaced centuries of intense personal exchanges and cultural and even spiritual borrowings. This narrowing of options to the crusading vein within medieval religious culture was well underway prior to the Counter-Reformation. Yet while there can be little doubt that the new spirit of militancy that followed the Council of Trent—a warlike fervor which looked on all rivals as enemies—did much to fan the flames of intolerance throughout the Church universal, conditions specific to Spain provide the most cogent explanation of why the crusade against Islam took on deeper roots there than in any other part of western Europe. To be sure, in the sphere of international politics a *modus vivendi* was gradually worked out with the Muslim powers, first with the Ottoman empire in the aftermath of the battle of Lepanto, and then with the diverse kingdoms and city-states of northern Africa. Yet one thing was compromise in the realm of high politics. Quite another was life as lived by average Spaniards on a daily basis. There coexistence ceded pride of place to conflict. Or did it?

Reconstructing everyday attitudes and practices is an extremely difficult undertaking. To begin with, elementary caution warns against confusing official policies and precepts with the realities of local existence. There can be little question that the popular image of moriscos as found in folklore, proverbs, and festive life seems to have been quite negative. Therein the morisco came across as a figure comic at best and decidedly ambivalent even when credited with certain positive traits. One sees this quite clearly in regard to the moriscos' fame as healers. That the New Christians had considerable practical skills in the medical realm was something that only their rivals among academic physicians denied. Yet many Old Christians had doubts about the source of this sort of knowledge and harbored the suspicion that the moriscos obtained magical powers by consorting with the devil. Thus the synodal constitutions of Guadix of 1554—an elaborate program designed by clerical reformers in order to bring the New Christians more closely under Church control—took for granted that numerous moriscos (and especially moriscas) practiced a wide range of magic, including fortune-telling, sorcery (above all the evil eye), superstitious healing, and the use of amulets and talismans. Thus even what was seen as a useful trait could be revealed to have unacceptable, even diabolical origins.

This was serious enough, but far more compromising for the moriscos was the Old Christian belief that as a norm they were both deceitful and menacing. A large part of the responsibility for this can be attributed to the stories told by former Christian captives of Muslim pirates. Some of these woeful tales circulated in written form. This was the case with the lengthy description of Algiers published under the priest Diego de Haedo's name in 1612, or the Carmelite friar Jerónimo Gracián de Dios's contemporary depiction of his imprisonment and ransom in Tunis. The poet and novelist Miguel de Cervantes drew on his own experience when depicting the lives of captive Christians in both short stories and on the stage. Few other major writers shared his misfortunes, but they could easily turn to his and other captives' tales for sources for their own works on imprisonment and slavery in Africa, as did the playwright Pedro Calderón de la Barca in his well-known tragedy *The Constant Prince* (1629). Still, most news of Christian suffering under Islam circulated by word of mouth, in the stories survivors told to their families and neighbors, and in the public testimonies they rendered to the religious orders in charge of ransoming them. The processions undertaken by grateful ex-captives and the numerous ex-votos—including their old chains—left in pilgrimage churches throughout the peninsula provided ample reminders at the popular level of the inhuman treatment awaiting anyone unfortunate enough to be consigned to the "bagnios" or mass prisons of Algiers, Tunis, and other Muslim strongholds in North Africa.

Still, one thing was the persistent strength of the traditional image of the eternal Muslim enemy, and another was the reality of relations on the home ground. Contact between Old and New Christians should not be taken for granted, particularly given that many if not most moriscos lived by and large on their own. Old Christians criticized moriscos for preferring to isolate themselves from others and suspected that the reason for it was to avoid being "true" Spaniards in terms of dress, language, religion, and the like. Spokesmen for the moriscos highlighted other causes of their segregation, above all the multiple types of exclusion to which they were subject. Guild ordinances prohibiting taking on moriscos as apprentices, for instance, made it quite difficult for New Christians to join the stable, respectable reaches of urban society. They were relegated instead to agricultural labor, or to the low-status service jobs of muleteers and long-distance haulers of goods, a specialization that did little to deepen their roots in local communities. The levels of segregation promoted by these policies (or preferences) varied greatly throughout the peninsula. As noted above, they were strongest in Valencia, Murcia, and Aragon, where moriscos often lived by themselves in separate villages with few or no Old Christian neighbors. Thus in the town of Arcos del Jalón, close to the border between New Castile and Aragon, the parish priest refused to administer the Eucharist to any of its inhabitants on the grounds that "all the moriscos who live in this town are bad Christians and never go to mass on Sundays or feastdays."[4] Morisco strongholds could also be found elsewhere, and, as one might expect, in more physically remote locations. The most famous of the latter was Hornachos. A village in the mountainous wilds of central Extremadura, its renown as a shelter for hardy crypto-Muslims led an unknown playwright (Lope de Vega? Francisco Tárrega?) to produce a stage play about these hard-core crypto-Muslim villagers.

Where moriscos lived closer to Old Christians, less conflictive patterns often prevailed. Isolation proved weakest where moriscos were few and far between, as in Old Castile, where prior to the exile of the Granadans in the early 1570s the only Muslim converts were the descendents of the remnant of mudéjares long accustomed to living among Old Christians. In fact, outside the areas where absolute separation tended to be the rule one finds a surprising amount of peaceful interaction between Old and New Christians. To be sure, some of this was mandatory. Synodal decrees, for example, repeatedly required morisco children to have non-morisco godparents. But there was also interethnic contact that went beyond the bare minimum the law stipulated. Some of our best sources for these more discreet forms of unforced sociability come from the Inquisition. A study of some five hundred trials of moriscos charged with secret adherence to Islam in sixteenth- and early seventeenth-century Cuenca reveals varied and numerous contacts between members of what were at first sight segregated communities. Eyewitness testimony eloquently illustrates myriad details of coexistence, as well as conflict, on a daily basis. Work, leisure, worship, and sheer happenstance brought Old and New Christians together, and these occasions naturally produced their share of gossip. The sort that entered the documentary record when the wrong person overheard suspicious statements, or when neighbors quarreled, was along the line that so and so does not buy his meat at the butcher's, but rather kills it at home (that is, he prepares meat according to Islamic dietary laws). Similarly, banter and challenges could get out of hand and degenerate into insults that would lead eventually to denunciations. The same was true with bad jokes, as when Old Christians fed moriscos disguised pork and then waited to laugh at their reaction when the truth was revealed. In short, daily interaction often brought the two groups together. The consequences of this fact of life varied. Real friendships could develop. They could also sour. Inquisitorial testimony clearly shows that what had earlier been said in confidence could later provide Old Christians with ammunition for charges against their former friends.

Also deserving emphasis are the frequent expressions of favorable attitudes toward moriscos. The Jesuit missionary Pedro de León, for instance, contrasted the New Christians' sobriety and willingness to work hard with the much less impressive habits of their Old Christian counterparts. Interestingly, other clerics showed sympathy for moriscos, including those who suffered persecution. In 1596 the Inquisition tried Montserrat Bruguera, the parish priest in the village of Torroella de Fluvià near Girona, for saying "that the moors will not go to Hell nor would be tormented by the Devil, rather they will go to limbo and be deprived of the sight of God because after all they did not promise anything to Our Lord." He went on to say that "he felt very sorry that they would be condemned, and thought that their children would not be punished as much as those who had been baptized and then had left our faith."[5] Bruguera was hardly the only cleric to show sympathy for the morisco minority. The Inquisition investigated a fair number of priests—many working at the more local levels in the countryside—for failing to second persecution of the New Christians or for expressing criticisms of their treatment both on earth as well as in the afterlife.

Even more striking is that some of these favorable attitudes percolated upward and into public circulation as literature. Perhaps the most idiosyncratic form this counterdiscourse took was the so-called "Moorish novel." This genre converted the frontier ballads of the later Middle Ages, which celebrated the clashes between Christian and Muslim warriors, into highly stylized prose. In its best-known embodiment—the *Abencerraje* saga of the Murcian writer Ginés Pérez de Hita (1595)—brave, genteel, and above all worthy Moorish knights and princesses confronted their Christian rivals on the rarefied ground of chivalric romance. The same sort of fantasy seeped into other literary forms as well, such as the overtly pro-morisco tale of "Ozmín and Daraja" which Mateo Alemán interpolated into the first part of his lengthy picaresque novel *Guzmán de Alfarache* (1599). An even more remarkable instance of sympathetic portrayal of moriscos was Calderón's play, *El Tuzani de la Alpujarra*, written around 1633. In it the New Christians appear as heroic victims of the malice of arrogant Old Christians—quite a departure from the standard accounts of the Granada revolt of 1568 which it claimed to portray. Finally, it is worth noting the generally sympathetic portrayal of moriscos throughout the greatest literary work from early modern Spain, *Don Quixote* (1605–15). It too showed Old Christians in an unfavorable light in their dealings with moriscos, as in the "Captive's Tale" of book I, chapters 39–41. And closer to the end (II.54) the novel memorably features Sancho Panza's reunion with a morisco friend, Ricote, who had returned to Spain in disguise after having been exiled in 1609. Cervantes took care to have Ricote defend the expulsion, saying that among the moriscos "some had been true and staunch Christians. But they were so few, that they could not prevail over the others who were not." Still, Ricote proved to be a loyal Spaniard as well as a faithful friend to Sancho, who lamented his former neighbor's fate and promised not to turn him in, telling him "follow your road, and let me follow mine." That popular sympathy for the plight of the exiled New Christians was not just a literary fiction is attested to by an actual letter a morisco in southern France sent in 1611 to an Old Christian back in his hometown of Arévalo. After attributing the expulsion to lies, envy, and prejudice, he sent warm greetings to his "loyal friend" and others this "terrible thing" had forced him to leave behind.[6]

In short, Old Christian attitudes toward New Christians ran a wide gamut, from deep mistrust to genuine instances of what has been called "maurophilia." The norm that prevailed was a cluster of predictable prejudices—predictable in the sense that much of what the Christian majority believed about moriscos has been said about other minorities in other historical contexts. In the end, the single most determining characteristic of the moriscos as far as other Spaniards were concerned was their religion. Did they truly believe in and practice Christianity? Or did they in their heart of hearts worship a different God? These were the crucial questions, and much effort was devoted to finding the answers.

CHAPTER 4

"CHRISTIANS IN APPEARANCE BUT MUSLIMS UNDERNEATH"

RYPTO-ISLAM IS ARGUABLY the most closely studied, as well as controversial, theme in historical writing on the moriscos.[1] Curiously, until recently most speculation on this subject has echoed the two extreme positions of early modern commentators, which asserted that virtually all moriscos were either crypto-Muslims or (less frequently) sincere Christians. Historians today tend to prefer less schematic interpretations and allow room for more mixed experiences. That said, it is clearly harder to study assimilation than nonconformity, as the main sources for morisco history—the trials of crypto-Muslims by the Inquisition—are heavily biased in favor of the latter option. It is true that one can find statements from the sixteenth century itself that take for granted morisco absorption of Catholicism. One example can be found in a 1548 description of Granada by the royal geographer Pedro de Medina, who affirmed that

> although at first some of these new converts were not so upright or attached to the holy doctrine of our faith, as it was something very new to them and which they had abhorred before, but with the passage of time they became very obedient to the holy commandments . . . after overcoming the bad taste in their mouths (*mal resabio*) from before, now they are good Christians.[2]

Still, the vast majority of contemporary comments about moriscos took for granted that their allegiance to Catholicism was lukewarm at best. More nuanced assessment of the religious beliefs and practices of moriscos raises two crucial issues: first, the extent to which members of the group retained their loyalty to Islam (or to ask the question from the Christian point of view, what proportion of the moriscos apostasized), and, second, the contents of their spirituality (or from the Muslim point of view, what sort of Islam did they practice, and why).

As for the extent of allegiance to Islam, the general feeling among Old Christians was that most moriscos remained true followers of their former faith. Luis de Mármol, who had lived as a captive some seven years in Muslim lands, and who felt he knew them better than most, had no doubts on this score. They were hard workers and showed impressive charity among themselves, he wrote. However, as Christians they were heretics, who "pay more attention to the rites and ceremonies of the sect of Muhammad than to the precepts of the Catholic Church."[3] It is not difficult to find instances of moriscos themselves confirming these suspicions. When questioned by the Cuenca Inquisition, one Francisco Ramírez admitted "he had the tongue of a Christian and the heart of a Muslim."[4] According to Ahmad ibn-Qasim Al-Hajari, a Granadan morisco who recorded his escape to North Africa and later career as a diplomat and traveler in a fascinating autobiographical text, the moriscos served two religions: "the religion of the Christians openly and that of the Muslims in secret."[5] In fact, morisco hypocrisy was taken so much for granted that performing all the ritual gestures of Catholicism could be written off as deliberate dissimulation. Such was the fate of the unfortunate morisca whom the Inquisition charged with "taking part in confession and communion only to comply on the outside and to cover up her apostasy by appearing to be a Christian"![6]

The reasons for the moriscos' refusal to accept a new religion which most of them had not freely chosen are not hard to divine. As noted above, the relative isolation of the New Christian communities and their physical separation from Old Christians permitted substantial autonomy in terms of external religious behavior. Furthermore, many moriscos, especially in the eastern parts of the peninsula, received effective protection from aristocratic patrons who had no interest in the Inquisition's or anyone else's interfering with their labor force. One such figure, Don Sancho de Cardona, defended his subjects so successfully that he himself wound up being tried by the Holy Office in 1569. Prosecution testimony revealed that he had gone so far as to counsel his vassals "that on the outside they should fake Christianity, and on the inside be Muslims."[7] With such advice at hand, it was no wonder that most moriscos were regarded as half-hearted at best in their commitment to their new religion.

As far as observance of their old faith was concerned, there is ample proof of morisco adherence to Islam. In fact, readers of Inquisition records may be forgiven for suspecting that *all* moriscos were apostates, so abundant is the evidence of their performance, overt as well as covert, of Muslim precepts. Trial after trial drove home the same message: that morisco attachment to Christianity was superficial at best and the vast majority was merely waiting for an opportunity to return to the ancestral creed. An even greater problem was that many refused to wait. With monotonous regularity moriscos were called before the Holy Office to answer for their lapses into observance of Islam. The charges against them drew on a fixed repertory of ritual actions. To cite merely one example, the major accusations in the Cuenca trials mentioned above comprised the following repeated patterns of behavior:

- fasts, such as those held during solemn holiday periods like Ramadan;
- ablutions, or bathing—called *guadoc* or *alguadoc*—on Fridays and holidays;
- prayers, from simple commendations such as *bizmiley* ("In the name of God") to full recitations of Koranic scripture;
- life-cycle ceremonies, ranging from the *fadas* or naming celebrations following births (which served at least in Christian eyes literally to remove the effects of baptism) to special preparations and rites for burial (washing the entire body, and interring it along with food and other grave gifts in unturned earth);
- dietary prohibitions, above all refusal of pork, wine, and meat and poultry that had not been slaughtered according to established prescriptions.

Some moriscos were even hauled before the Inquisition for explicitly anti-Christian words and gestures. These included jokes, blasphemies, mocking images and crosses as "sticks" and "pieces of wood," and anticlerical statements, as well as speech rejecting concrete doctrines and sacraments, such as the Eucharist.

Once again, this rather surprising degree of open, even casual adherence to Islam was found most often in those areas where moriscos formed a majority or where they lived far apart from their Old Christian neighbors. Elsewhere, such overt practice was less frequent. This was thanks not just to the vigilance of the Inquisition and society in general. One should also recall the long-range consequences of the disappearance after 1502 of the apparatus and personnel of formal worship: mosques, daily calls to prayer by public criers, and the quasi-clerical entourage of judges and other spiritual leaders. In such circumstances, it comes as little surprise to see morisco women stepping in to fill the gap created by the vacuum in male leadership. The Inquisition itself was not slow to recognize the prominent role such *dogmatizadoras*—an eloquent label—played as transmitters of tradition. From 1566 to 1620, slightly over one-fourth of all moriscos tried for Islamic practices by the Holy Office of Valencia were women. What is more, despite the notoriously high rates of female illiteracy, a significant number of these women were charged with owning illegal texts in Arabic. Some of these were full-scale spiritual works: the Koran figured in the case of a woman charged with reading it aloud to others. Other texts stood at a greater remove from orthodoxy. These included the numerous *herçes,* or talismans, often owned by illiterates who looked to the scriptural verses they contained for protection against disease or the evil eye. All in all, women won a hard-earned reputation for their loyalty to Islam throughout the peninsula. One intriguing example was that of Nuzay Calderán, a midwife who traveled widely as an underground teacher of Islam, and who was recorded as giving sophisticated advice on how to interpret the Koran (see below). Hers was, to be sure, hardly a run-of-the-mill case. But it was by no means the only one in which morisco women took upon themselves the task of leading the faithful in such times of duress.

Intermittent persecution had its effects, of course, and over time morisco observance of Islam was gradually stripped down to its bare essentials. The standard trial records of the Inquisition are not the only sources that tend toward that conclusion. One thorough review of a selection of *aljamiado* texts—that is, devotional and other literature written in Spanish, yet transcribed in Arabic characters—has found much the same. Of the five fundamental precepts of Islam—profession of faith, prayer, fasting, alms, and pilgrimage—several were simply out of the question. This was true not just of travel to Mecca. Call to prayer also disappeared, although obviously daily prayers could be performed in private. Other practices, less tied to Koranic precept but considered binding all the same, suffered modification. Daily ablutions, for example, were no longer the slow, limb-to-limb washing of the past. Rather, they were now speeded up, in a quick rub of the body with water. Crypto-Muslims compensated for most of these limitations by making adjustments. They substituted silent for public prayer or put extra emphasis on the duties with which they could comply without calling attention to themselves, such as giving charity.

One particularly revealing text—a formal theological opinion a *mufti* (religious expert) from Oran issued in 1504—stipulated the minimal observances demanded of all Muslims. The lowered standards therein reflect not just a flexible spirit on the part of its author but also his willingness to make enough accommodations to make sure that the moriscos would stay in the Islamic fold. Prayers must be said, he ordered, but some of them could be said in sign language rather than aloud. The traditional *azaque* or alms must be paid, but this could take the form of giving money to the poor. The precept of purification could be fulfilled by bathing in a river or the sea, even at night; if the intention was proper, even ablutions without water (!) would count. If there was no escaping having to pray to idols, one could do so, provided one did not look at them. The same with drinking wine, eating pork, or practicing usury; the important thing was perform them while "distancing oneself from all intention of committing vice." Marrying Christian women was permitted; after all, they too "profess a revealed religion." This unusually liberal spiritual adviser summed up his rules by noting that "God does not pay attention to your external show, but to the intention in your hearts." Still numbered among good Muslims were those whom he encouraged to see themselves as "denying with the heart what they force you to say aloud in words."[8]

There was nevertheless something of a gap between the low bar of requirements for orthodoxy proposed by sympathetic Muslims elsewhere and the persistence of secret belief and observance within a vigilant and repressive Christian society. It thus comes as little surprise to find a broad range of religious opinions among moriscos. A single case illustrates the diversity of spiritual stances even within an isolated and highly compact New Christian community. In 1574 the Valencia Inquisition undertook a tour of inspection of the Ribera Alta district in the Júcar river valley south

of the capital city. After preaching what was known as an "edict of faith"—
that is, a grace period for those who voluntarily denounced their lapses in
Catholic observance—the inquisitor in charge, Pedro de Zárate, received
confessions from slightly over nine hundred local moriscos. Forty-six of
these hailed from Benimuslem, a village made up of twenty-four households,
all of whose inhabitants were New Christians. They were subjected to the
standard interrogation, which included giving information about friends
and relatives, both consanguine and affinal. Nineteen claimed to be good
Christians, and no further questions were asked of them. The other twenty-
seven admitted to different levels of observance of Islam. The nature of local
Muslim practice can be reconstructed from their testimony. It included the
use of Arabic names (instead of the Christian names given at baptism); observance of major fasts, such as Ramadan, as well as (for a few) some minor
ones; knowledge of basic Islamic prayers; and performance (once again,
by a small minority) of ritual ablutions. That Zárate treated them leniently
may seem surprising. It is likely that he saw how weak local Islamic practice
was, at least in comparison with the nearby towns of Carlet or Benimodo,
which boasted some knowledge of written Arabic, as well as the practice
of circumcision. In the end, Islamic observance not only differed substantially within the same village but also varied greatly between villages just a
few miles apart from each other. And one cannot avoid concluding that at
this particular moment, while the Benimuslem moriscos were not yet fully
Christian, they were far from being effective Muslims.

In such circumstances, hybridism, conscious or otherwise, was an altogether predictable outcome. Perhaps the most famous—and without doubt
the most bizarre—instance of mixing religious traditions was the notorious
case of the *plomos* or forged seals of Granada (more on this below). Much
less dramatic instances of absorption of Christian elements by crypto-
Muslims whose departures from orthodoxy became ever more frequent
included the translation and circulation of holy texts from Arabic into
Spanish; reworking of the figure of St. John the Baptist into the precursor
of Muhammad instead of Jesus; transference of the cult of Santiago (the
Apostle St. James) to that of Ali, one of the Prophet's companions who was
transformed during the Middle Ages into a symbol of knightly chivalry;
and even the conversion of Jesus into a distant relation of Muhammad, who
trumped him in a theological debate.

There were limits to what crypto-Muslims could borrow from Catholicism, though. Certain doctrines proved permanent stumbling blocks for
the moriscos and did much to prevent their absorption of Christian teach-
ing. The Trinity was one such construct, as it apparently contradicted the
monotheism that was the very heart of Islam. Catholic reverence of images
proved another obstacle; like the Trinity, it evoked the specter of polythe-
ism, in addition to violating clear Muslim strictures against idolatry. The
autobiography of the ex-morisco-turned-diplomat Al-Hajari identified with
precision the specific elements of Christianity that proved unpalatable to
Muslims. In it the author railed time and again against Christian "pollution."
This he saw as inward (for example, belief in the Trinity and other "absurdi-
ties") as well as outward (these "idolaters," he snorted, never bathed nor did
they perform ritual ablutions. Small wonder then, that their churches were
full of idols and "filth"; they even buried their dead there!).[9] One gets the
impression that in the end he looked on the fact that Christians reveled in
impurity as a sort of blessing. Readers of his text would find it hard to accept
that any Muslim could embrace such a faith of his or her own volition.

CHAPTER 5

COMMUNITIES AND
INDIVIDUALS

R ELIGIOUS LIFE IN virtually all circumstances incorporates personal as well as collective forms of observance. Fulfillment of spiritual obligations under conditions of vigilance and persecution usually tends to favor more individual, and less readily visible, practices. Yet at the same time, external, hostile pressures often foster greater solidarity among members of subordinate groups and wind up intensifying collective adherence to the sort of beliefs and conduct the majority hopes to prevent. This is especially true when the religious minority is also marked as different on other grounds—social, economic, ethnic, or cultural. Such was the case of the moriscos of early modern Spain. They were identified not just as descendents of Muslims and thus potential and real crypto-Muslims. They were also seen as constituting a separate group in other respects as well. In the end these differences were judged to be ineradicable as well as irreconcilable with Christianity. After this most fateful decision in their regard was made, it did not require a great conceptual leap to opt for their expulsion.

Still, the Christian majority did not come to this conclusion immediately. A full century of doubt and debate preceded adoption of this radical measure. During this interval Old Christians forged an image of the moriscos as a social group with recognizable and in some respects unique characteristics of its own.

Perhaps the most prominent feature of this image was the strong solidarity believed to prevail among the converts. Numerous early modern Spaniards repeated the cliché that despite their poverty, one rarely came across a morisco beggar. Whatever their other faults, New Christians were credited with showing enough solidarity among themselves to assure that the poorer among them did not lack for charity. Old Christians attributed the fundamental cohesiveness of morisco society to several factors. First and foremost was segregation. This involved, as has been seen, settlement patterns based on physical separation from the majority in almost all places where the moriscos lived in sizable groups. In some cases the existence of the moriscos as a community apart even found institutional expression. Thus, in the Aragonese town of Caspe in the sixteenth century, Old and New Christians governed themselves through two different municipal councils.

A second factor promoting group cohesion was the relative lack of internal socioeconomic differentiation among the moriscos. In a well-known passage from a brief opposing the expulsion of 1609, the humanist Pedro de Valencia remarked that "the moriscos are for the most part ditch-diggers, reapers, gardeners, foot-couriers, muleteers, blacksmiths, and other trades which involve hard work and effort."[1] In the morisco hamlet of Benimuslem mentioned above, of the twenty villagers examined by the Inquisition whose trades were specified, eighteen were yeomen farmers, one an agricultural laborer, and one a (ritual?) butcher. And of the more than five hundred suspects the Cuenca tribunal tried as secret Muslims during the sixteenth century, not a single one had a university education. In fact, there were only two references to medical personnel among them, a "setter of broken arms and legs" and "a maker of trusses for hernias."[2] This represents a perceptible decline in status from earlier periods, when Muslims and later moriscos won widespread fame for their expertise in healing. Such was recognized even by their bitter enemy Cardinal Cisneros; when he burned numerous Arabic-language texts in post-1492 Granada, he spared a few books of medicine, a discipline "to which that race was always attached, and to great profit."[3] In the hands of the Inquisition, this fame turned to notoriety during the sixteenth century. Moriscos stood out among the best-known cases of healers whom the Holy Office tried for diabolic magic. One famous example was Jerónimo Pachet, who was called to court to heal the eight-year-old Philip III after the learned Christian physicians proved unable to help. Another morisco healer even became something of a folk legend. Román Ramírez was a professional storyteller as well as surgeon who died in an Inquisitorial prison in 1599. The reputation of moriscos as healers even reached beyond Spain's borders. When a London surgeon named George Baker published a medical tract in 1574 he included a discussion of a popular healing oil—called *oleum magistrale*—that he assured readers had been concocted by a morisco empiric in Spain.[4]

That most moriscos were poor and of low status was both cause and consequence of their living as outsiders, if not outcasts, from Old Christian society. It also confers a socioeconomic as well as a religious dimension to another characteristic that contemporaries saw as contributing to their sense of community: marital endogamy. Religious reformers who were genuinely committed to evangelizing the moriscos placed their hopes in intermarriage as the high road—indeed perhaps the only route—to integrating converted Muslims fully into Christian society and belief. Such advocates of gradualist and assimilatory policies did their best to encourage their marrying into Old Christian families. Pedro de Valencia, for example, strongly defended this solution, which he saw as imitating the *permixtión* (mixed marriages) by which the Roman empire made citizens of its subject peoples.[5] Whether this policy ever became a pattern is very much open to question. Once again, the figures from Benimuslem are eloquent. Among the over one hundred morisco villagers, only one was married to an Old Christian. In this case such a high level of ethnic endogamy was not due to refusal to marry outside the local marital pool. Fully one-half of all Benimuslem spouses came from neighboring villages, and one even hailed from the Vall d'Uxó, some eighty kilometers away. Exactly why here and elsewhere so little intermarriage between Old and New Christians took place is difficult to say. Clearly there was strong opposition to it on both sides. Numerous sources document Old Christian rejection of moriscos as demeaning—or as a character in a Lope de Vega play asserted, it was an affront to "honor and decorum."[6] Lack of opportunity was another factor. For such alliances to be formed there had to be prior forms of contact, a shared sociability that would permit the sort of minimally amicable relations that could facilitate marriage unions. As has been seen, such contacts existed only in certain contexts and were limited by and large to areas wherein moriscos were too small in number to live apart from the rest of society.

In the end, however, what contributed most to a sense of community among moriscos were the very characteristics that marked them as different from Old Christians. If the latter felt confident of their ability to detect moriscos, it was because they placed their trust in external signs that set the two groups apart. Foremost among these were "customs," that is, patterned forms of behavior. The most sensitive areas of distinctiveness involved language, dress and bodily hygiene, food, and festive celebrations.

That many moriscos continued to speak Arabic among themselves up until the expulsion is a fact attested to by a variety of Old Christian sources. Nevertheless these sources are reticent regarding crucial issues such as the extent to which Arabic was spoken, or how much it continued to serve as a written as opposed to oral means of communication. One sees in these uncertainties one of the more telling consequences of the post-1492 suppression or exile of specialists in Islamic jurisprudence, history, and other sciences. For throughout the sixteenth century moriscos had few scholars to whom they could turn for instruction in Arabic, even in secrecy. Inquisition documents make sporadic reference to itinerant clerics, some hailing from North Africa, who carried out a quasi-missionary role among their brethren. Yet on the whole it is hard to avoid the impression that while Arabic managed to survive in some areas as a spoken language, the moriscos' ability to read it fell off drastically as the decades went by.

Dress was a different matter. This, along with food habits, was the most visible sign of difference between Old and New Christians, at least in much of Andalusia and Valencia. Contrasts in clothing attracted widespread attention—so much so that a rich iconographic record of morisco dress survives in the present, thanks to the interest of foreign writers and artists in recording the details of "Moorish" garb. What most caught their eye was female dress. This included not just the daily attire of women, above all the silk pants and long veils in which they draped themselves. It also comprised their distinctive *ajuar* or bridal clothing and decorative jewelry, as well as the cosmetics they used. Moreover, the contrast between Old and New Christian bodily habits was not limited to matters of dress. Differences in hygienic practices were also frequently commented upon. Early modern Catholics had lost much of their medieval forebears' habit of frequent bathing—which is most likely yet another sign of their stronger resolve to shun association with anything smacking of Islam. Thus while the Inquisition documents from Cuenca have virtually nothing to say about distinctive patterns of dress, they do register denunciations of moriscos for changing their clothes frequently. That this occurred on Fridays in particular inevitably fed suspicions that even moriscos wearing "Christian" clothes had found a way to observe traditional Muslim precepts of bodily purity. Old Christians did not hesitate to link any form of washing with Islam. Hence one witness in a trial for crypto-Islamic practices remarked with surprise that moriscos "wash out their mouths after eating"![7]

A final area of contention involved leisure. Moriscos celebrated marriages and other festive occasions with *zambras* and *leilas,* that is, rhythmic dances accompanied by drums and other musical instruments of North African origin. Admittedly, such flashy ceremony was more typical of Granada than elsewhere. Not surprisingly, the Cuenca moriscos who were accused of singing in Arabic and playing lutes and reed instruments at weddings tended to be recent immigrants from the south. Once again, in this as in virtually all other facets of daily life, the ethnographic documentation produced by Inquisitorial vigilance reveals a geographical distribution of cultural practices that distinguished southern newcomers to Old Christian ways of life from the more assimilated generations of former mudéjares living in the north.

Both Old and New Christians recognized that the key question was how much religious valence should be attributed to these markers of difference. The former had no problem recognizing and identifying the latter, thanks precisely to the existence of these social and cultural attributes. Philip II's decision in 1567 finally to enforce earlier edicts prohibiting the use of Arabic, separate dress, and the like led morisco apologists to insist that these were traditional customs lacking in theological content. This was especially true of the "memorial" of Francisco Núñez Muley, arguably one of the more interesting anthropological statements in early modern Spanish history. In this text the elderly representative of one of Granada's leading morisco families reviewed item after item of cultural difference, arguing that while some of these practices may have had their origins in Islamic precepts, by this late date they had shed any such association with dogma. The implication was that one could be both culturally "Moorish" and spiritually Christian— doubtless an accurate description of the typical attitude and behavior of the small morisco elite to which he belonged. Núñez Muley's strong emphasis on the religious neutrality of collective traditions was bold enough. Even more unusual was his challenging Old Christians to put themselves in the moriscos' position and imagine how they would feel if they were ordered to wear morisco dress, to listen to morisco music, or to speak and write Arabic instead of Spanish. That this invitation to empathy had scant effect comes as little surprise. After all, even the most tolerant among the Christian conquerors of 1492, Archbishop Hernando de Talavera, had urged the moriscos to give up their food, to sit in chairs instead of on the floor ("as Spaniards do"), and otherwise to become true Christians in behavior as well as in belief.[8]

Still, elementary caution counsels against assuming that the existence of a clear, public definition of a minority means that its members comprise a compact, homogeneous social body. It is important not to overstate the cohesion of morisco communities or their isolation from their Old Christian neighbors. Morisco settlements were subject to many of the same sorts of individualistic pressures and tensions present in all other early modern societies. Not surprisingly, certain moriscos left behind evidence of impressive levels of personal mobility. (This was the case of one Francisco Caffor, who named 964 different persons during the course of his testimony before the Valencian Inquisition!) Others surely found their attachment to family or kin groups, or even to Catholicism, stronger than their obligations to the broader community. Hence the complaint of one morisco in the village of Deza in the later sixteenth century that "all the moriscos of this village detest this witness and his mother because they live like Old Christians and have moved to another neighborhood and live in the Old Christians' quarter." According to his testimony the atmosphere had become so hostile that one day as he was returning from work a group of moriscos threw rocks at him while yelling "scoundrel, son of a whore, you have left a good faith [ley] for one that is much worse"—in itself eloquent testimony both to the strength of community and to the willingness of some members to abandon it.[9]

CHAPTER 6

MORISCO EXPRESSION

T HE CENTURY-LONG HISTORY of morisco Spain left behind relatively little in terms of formal creativity. New Christians continued to transmit the decorative and architectural skills inherited from their Muslim past in those areas where mudéjar and late Nasrid styles were still in vogue. Thus many of the ambitious building projects of sixteenth-century Granada employed morisco masons and other skilled workers. Yet in none of them did New Christians play any but a subordinate role. Architectural treatises such as Diego López de Arenas's 1633 guide to mudéjar building style showed that Old Christians had successfully absorbed many *moro* elements. Framing traditional Islamic decorative motifs and construction techniques within mainstream Renaissance structures, builders in Andalusia and elsewhere consolidated a rich hybrid style that would mark vernacular housing and public architecture in the south in particular for centuries to come.

In terms of written culture, the moriscos produced few authors of renown. Among the few New Christian writers of note was Miguel de Luna, a physician and royal translator from Granada whose fanciful chronicle (published 1592–1600) of the last Visigoth king, Rodrigo, directly challenged the emerging consensus among official historians that identified personal nobility with racial descent from the Goths. A few other writers were reputed to be moriscos. Among them stood out Ginés Pérez de Hita.

Originally a shoemaker from Murcia, he distinguished himself locally as a poet and as a dramatist who specialized in autos and other short religious plays. He then won broader fame for his chronicles of the Granadan wars, both past and present. These included a lengthy account of the Alpujarras revolt of 1568–70, in which the author himself claimed to have fought as a soldier on the royalist side. But he also wrote a true best-seller, the prose romance—Menéndez Pelayo referred to it as a historical novel—titled *The History of the Bands of the Zegríes and the Abencerrages, Moorish Warriors of Granada, and of the Civil Wars which took place there, and the Duels which Moors and Christians Fought outside the City,* which saw its first edition in Zaragoza in 1595. As noted above, this book, more commonly referred to as *El Abencerraje,* marked the beginning of the subgenre known as the "Moorish novel." It was fashionable not only in Spain but also in France, where it helped consolidate the short sentimental novel as a literary form in the seventeenth century. A third contemporary writer who may have been a morisco New Christian was the Granadan priest and mathematician Luis de la Cueva. In 1603 he brought out his *Dialogues of the Notable Things of Granada,* a typical piece of local bombast whose strenuous claims on the behalf of his city's ancient past included the admittedly extravagant assertion that Spanish was an older language than Latin (!). The morisco background of these and other authors, such as the playwright Bartolomé Torres Naharro, has yet to be definitively established. Such difficulties of identification suggest that New Christians generally found themselves at a disadvantage in the sphere of public literature and other forms of learned culture.

Another thing altogether was *aljamiado* literature, which involved transcribing contemporary Spanish using Arabic characters. This highly unusual linguistic register was incontestably written by moriscos, and crypto-Muslim moriscos for good measure. A relatively small number of such texts from the sixteenth century have survived. Some were seized at the time by the Inquisition, while others were later stumbled across in surprising locations, hidden in the flooring or in secret compartments of old buildings. Long the exclusive province of specialists in Arabic literary and linguistic studies, recently *aljamía* has begun to attract broader attention, as transcriptions and translations have made it increasingly available to the reading public at large. When aljamiado works are put alongside writings in standard Arabic that are known to have circulated in Spain during the same period, one gets a vivid sense of the sort of textual resources literate moriscos were able to wield.

At the heart of this corpus was, predictably enough, religion, but other concerns found expression as well. This writing can be separated into five major thematic subdivisions:

- First and foremost came the basic texts of formal Islam: the Koran, the authorized collection of oral traditions known as *hadith,* and commentaries on religious law. Abridgments, anthologies, summaries of basic beliefs, and commonplace books circulated much more often than the original texts themselves, out of elementary regard for caution. Still, it is worth noting that a respectable number of moriscos arrested by the Inquisition owned copies of the Koran, including on occasion the full text itself. That some of these owners were moreover clearly illiterate testifies to the strength of their devotion to their now-illegal faith, symbolized by its central and most binding text.

- The second major body of Arabic-language and aljamiado texts fell into the category of what is best termed popular religion. These included a wide range of spiritual writing for quasi-magical purposes. Particularly prominent were prayers and formulaic invocations destined for use as *herçes* or talismanic amulets against the evil eye and other forms of misfortune. Also much in evidence were *jofores* or popular prophecies, which foresaw the restoration of Islam, the destruction of the Church, and other auguries of the moriscos' collective return to divine and earthly favor.

- A third type of text hovered between these two extremes of canonical revelation and vernacular lore. This intermediary field was inhabited by sermons, commentaries, and polemical literature—that is, literary forms with wide popular appeal, and whose main purpose was to keep morale and observance as high as possible amid admittedly difficult circumstances.

- Fourth, a number of texts partook of what was the most respected intellectual tradition early modern Spaniards in general associated with Islam: medicine. Once again, here one sees continuity with both learned and popular traditions from the past. The former centered around Avicenna, Averroes, and other illustrious medieval Arabic-language interpreters of the anatomical and physiological legacy of classical antiquity, who were now under increasing attack from Renaissance humanistic medicine. The popular side comprised those occasions in which the moriscos' widely acknowledged expertise in applied medical arts reached written form. New Christian healers were known to have frequently used verses from the Koran in *cedulillas* or paper formulas designed to augment the efficacy of their practical skills. Writing in Arabic also marked in recourse to divination, horoscopes, and hermetic lore, which also figured in their arsenal of healing arts.

- Finally, the aljamiado corpus housed a number of more strictly literary narratives. These included more than anything else folktales which centered on heroes—and heroines—who showed courage in the face of injustice and oppression. Yet what is perhaps more anomalous are the clamorous absences within this literature, such as poetry, one of the richest veins of creativity in medieval Islamic Spain, or its close cousin mystic writing (again, which had notably flourished in Al-Andalus).

Amid this varied if fairly small ensemble of texts, one work stands out above all others. It is the *Tafsira* (treatise) of an unidentified author known only as the Mancebo, or Young Man, from Arévalo. Scholars have worked hard to establish his identity, but the truth is that nothing is known of him save that early in life he lived in central Castile. This one firm fact derives from a lone reference to his leaving Arévalo that appears toward the close of the book, which seems to have been written in the mid-1530s or shortly thereafter. The opening pages actually find the Mancebo in Zaragoza, where he attended a meeting of a group of Muslim elders whose conversation he transcribes. The tone is far from cheerful; in fact, the wise men loudly lament the decay in the observance of Islam among the moriscos, which they attribute to the lack of proper instruction in the faith. To remedy this situation they propose that the Mancebo compose a commentary on the Koran that would summarize for his coreligionists the basic precepts of Islam. And this is what he does, in a lengthy and somewhat disordered series of brief chapters on Muslim beliefs and ritual observances.

Most of this involves routine expounding of doctrine. What enlivens the text, apart from the occasional excursus such as a vivid evocation of the (imminent) Final Judgment, is the author's interpolating a handful of entries on how and where he obtained this knowledge. In these passages the text draws inspiration from one of the most prestigious literary traditions in Islam, that of the *rihla,* or relation of a voyage in search of enlightenment. To this end the young scholar criss-crosses much of the peninsula, including both Old and New Castile, Extremadura, Aragon, Valencia, and Andalusia. In these places he manages to study a wide range of texts kept in clandestine libraries. What is more, he comes to know a number of striking individuals, all of whom have remained loyal to Islam. The Mancebo reports in detail their comments and conversations, which focused not only on the present sufferings of the moriscos but also the past glories of Spanish Islam. Several of his interlocutors go out of their way to comment bitterly on the last phase of the Granadan wars, which brought to a humiliating end an Al-Andalus remembered as a sort of earthly paradise. The author also reproduces several exchanges he had with two women. The first is a legendary figure known as the Mora de Ubeda, who was ninety-three years old when the Mancebo visited her in her home near the Puerta Elvira in Granada. While lacking in formal education, she was nevertheless frequently consulted as an expert on the Koran. The other is Nozaita Calderán, a widely traveled midwife (and magical healer?) who was also known for her profound knowledge of the founding text of Islam. The Mancebo's report of his interviews with these two extraordinary (and otherwise undocumented) women constitute some of the most fascinating pages in his entire work.

The treatise is a remarkable text, and it is also a unique one, in at least two respects. First and foremost, it affords the reader an unprecedented look at the morisco world from the inside. Here one encounters voluntary, uncoerced testimony to a secret, parallel society of crypto-Muslims, who stay in touch with each other through an underground system of contacts and hospitality. One is in fact surprised by the seeming ease with which the author wanders from one Islamic community to another, fulfilling unhindered his educational charge. His is a sort of mission in reverse, a specifically Muslim parallel or response to the conversionary efforts that the ecclesiastical authorities had underway at this time, and which would produce more meager results than both crown and Church hoped for. Second, unlike virtually all other aljamiado texts, the *Tafsira* ranges beyond its strictly Islamic roots to draw on other types of sources. To be sure, the vast majority of its citations hail from the main writers of orthodox Sunni Islam. Yet the author also makes strenuous efforts to parade his non-Muslim learning, through allusions to or even interpolations of works from different cultural traditions. Where he is on more solid ground is in Latin, and above all Spanish, a language in which he expresses himself quite fluidly. Brave assertions to the contrary, his Greek and Hebrew appear to be precarious at best. Similarly shaky are some of his claims to have read classic works (even in Arabic) in the original; like many of his contemporaries, he picked up his knowledge of certain authoritative texts secondhand. Perhaps most unusual was his silently inserting some ascetic passages from a standard Catholic source—the late medieval theologian Thomas à Kempis—into his explanation of Muslim doctrine. That the Mancebo was also well versed in nonspiritual Western texts is shown by his (again unacknowledged) citation of the *Celestina*—one of the very first documented borrowings from this early sixteenth-century Renaissance classic.

These and other characteristics serve to remind us what a singular work this is. But even more unexpected is the singularity of aljamiado writing as a whole. Aljamiado texts clearly represented a literature of resistance. What one scholar has written of the Mancebo's treatise—that it was "a desperate attempt to improvise in Romance a religious vocabulary to replace the one that Spain's Muslim community had once possessed, and of which they had been deprived"[1]—could be said of most of the works within this corpus. It was thus hardly an accident that most of the aljamiado texts have been discovered in Aragon. In the main nuclei of morisco settlement, Valencia and (until the 1570s) Granada, Arabic itself was still widely used. Catalonia and Castile represented the opposite extreme; there the ex-mudéjar population had relinquished the use of Arabic generations ago. Aragon represented an intermediate stage of linguistic retention (or loss), in that its moriscos apparently knew enough Arabic *script* to write and read in aljamía, yet lacked sufficient familiarity with the Arabic *language* to allow them to leave behind the Spanish tongue.

Aljamiado works were not only a literature of resistance. They were also a literature of loss, written in anguish over the deprivation not only of public profession of an ancestral faith but also of the language which had shaped all aspects of a centuries-old culture. Hence their frequent evocation of suffering and lament, the sense of impending doom, and the defensive, even plaintive way in which they recorded the steady erosion of the very foundations of Islamic culture. Reading such documents today gives a privileged view into the core of the morisco experience. Indeed, these texts, along with confessions and other statements by defendants to the Inquisition, are without question the most revealing sources for the reconstruction of the historical experience of the moriscos. Yet they represent the point of view not so much of the moriscos as a whole, but of a very special sort of morisco: those who could not only read and write, but could also read and write in Arabic script. As they themselves were all too aware, they were a minority of a minority, and doubtless they felt limited in their ability to reach, much less represent their brethren.

CHAPTER 7

A FINAL BOW

I T IS FITTING to end these pages on the moriscos with a brief glance at an extraordinary episode that took place shortly before the expulsion of 1609. There are admittedly many mysteries in early modern Spanish history, but few have proved stranger or more intriguing than the so-called *plomos,* or lead seals, of Granada. The story began with the demolition in 1588 of the Torre Turpiana. This was the minaret of what had formerly been the city's main mosque, now absorbed into the huge cathedral that was still under construction. Workers at the site dug up a box containing some bones of the early martyr St. Stephen and a piece of cloth that had been part of the veil of the Virgin Mary. Identification of these precious relics was made possible thanks to yet another item in the cache, a parchment containing a hitherto unknown prophecy of the end of the world by St. John. The parchment moreover explained that Cecilio, the first bishop and subsequent patron saint of Granada, had placed the document there in the first century AD. These remarkable finds immediately attracted attention. But the challenge of explaining how they got there, and how the text of the parchment came to be written in large, "Solomonic" letters and in an equally odd combination of Arabic, Spanish, and Latin, had just begun.

Local officials soon took charge and called on various experts, both within and outside the city, to solve the mystery. Translations of the parchment were commissioned from several individuals versed in Arabic, and from two moriscos in particular, Miguel de Luna and Alonso del Castillo. In 1595, however, the mystery took a new twist. In February of that year treasure hunters digging on the nearby mountain known as Valparaíso came across what seemed to be bones from the graves of San Cecilio and a group of other early Christian martyrs, together with a cache of seals made of lead. Between 1595 and 1606 searchers found a total of twenty-two lead plaques on which someone had used an engraver's tool to scratch prophecies and details regarding the early history of Iberian Christianity. The plaques used the same unusually difficult Solomonic script. The 1588 parchment and the later seals provided a heady mixture of prophecy and apocalyptic lore. While their cryptic messages proved hard to decipher, they clearly featured three main figures: Santiago, or St. James, the Apostle who first brought the gospel to Spain, and who supposedly wrote one of the leaden books in a cave outside ancient Granada; Cecilio, his disciple and the founder of Christianity in the city as well as its first martyr; and the Virgin Mary, who had miraculously cured Cecilio of blindness. Her relic (the piece of her veil) turned out to be the most dramatic discovery.

The prominent role of Islam in the texts was not limited to the use of Arabic. In fact, the main common thread uniting the numerous prophecies was their emphasis on the fundamental compatibility of the Christian and Muslim faiths. This was evident implicitly in incidental details, such as the lack of reference to images or to Jesus as the Son of God, both of which Muslims traditionally shunned as offensive. It was made explicit in the accommodation of a wide range of Islamic customs, such as substituting water for wine in communion, the wearing of veils by women, and the prohibition of burials in church. Above all, Mary herself stated that following the Crucifixion God transferred his favor from the Jews to the Arabs and chose to use their language for his final revelation. Hence Santiago took an Arabic text with him to Spain, where it would remain hidden until the time of the Last Judgment, when, in the preceding days, numerous heresies would thrive under the Antichrist.

Granada received all this with undisguised eagerness. Especially important was the warm welcome given the plomos by the newly arrived archbishop, Pedro Vaca de Castro y Quiñones, who had been appointed to the see in 1590. While cautious at first, Castro soon became the leading supporter of the prophecies. He spared no effort to interpret the seals' cryptic messages—he scoured not only Spain but also the rest of Europe for translators and eventually hired nineteen different individuals to work on them—and to collect endorsements of their authenticity. Even before these tasks were completed he held a provincial council in 1600 which declared the relics authentic. Steps such as these proved crucial to shifting debate regarding the prophecies from the relative quiet of scholarly circles to the broader public arena, even if his superiors quickly prohibited discussion of the precise contents of the texts. Finally, in 1609 he began construction of a church on the site of the more recent findings, which was increasingly referred to as the Sacromonte, or Holy Mountain. Masses of Granadans quickly made the spot the object of improvised pilgrimage: in countless processions they marked the hillside site with literally thousands of crosses. It did not take long for miracles to take place, and written statements soon testified to the healing powers of the locale, proof of its sacred character. Within just two years' time archdiocesan officials had gathered from a broad cross-section of the city's population dossiers on the miraculous cures of thirteen men and six women.

Religious authorities elsewhere, however, showed considerably less enthusiasm for the new cult in Granada. Kept informed by its nuncios, Rome was cool from the beginning, and in 1596 the Holy See issued a decree forbidding judgment on the books. The Inquisition scented the possibility of disaster in the extravagant claims made by both the text of the seals—which included the promised unveiling of a fifth gospel!—and the arguments of their supporters. The papacy's insistence that the plomos be sent to Rome for more thorough examination met with stonewalling first from Castro and then by the court in Madrid, which was reluctant to surrender control over such promising spiritual material. In 1642, after decades of stalling, Philip IV finally authorized their departure from Spain. In Rome they were examined with painstaking care by a commission of experts which included the renowned Jesuit scholar Athanasius Kircher. After issuing a preliminary report in 1655, the Vatican finally pronounced the seals (but not the relics) a fraud in 1682 and officially closed the books on the scandal.

What really had happened here? From the beginning some Granadans worried about the possibility of a fraud. The use of the Spanish language in the first century AD naturally raised some eyebrows. Equally anachronistic was the presence of the Arabic language, and involving the Virgin Mary as

a speaker to boot. The appearance of the prophecies in Arabic (and the blatant way in which they favored that tongue), along with their philo-Islamic
reading of Catholicism suggested that the culprits were moriscos. It did not
take long for the first two translators of the Torre Turpiana discoveries—
Miguel de Luna, the historian mentioned above, and Alonso del Castillo,
like him a local morisco physician—to be named as the leading suspects.
On the other hand, sharp-eyed observers would have known that forging
these texts would have required more impressive scholarly credentials in
the field of Christian antiquity than this pair possessed. This meant looking
for additional candidates. Some of these were found among canons from
the cathedral, an institution that stood to benefit from the new attention
showered on San Cecilio, the diocese's first bishop. Other possible suspects
included defenders of the Immaculate Conception, a still-controversial
doctrine deferred to in the plomos' telling reference to the Virgin as "clean
(*limpia*) of sin."

All the same, suspicions of a forgery were easier to find outside Granada,
where the local fervor quickly taught skeptics to keep their doubts to themselves. It has been noted that virtually every Spanish scholar who knew the
three languages in which the esoteric texts were written—Arabic, Latin, and
Spanish—opposed their authenticity at one time or another. Thus Luis de
Mármol, the Old Christian ex-captive who knew both North Africa and the
Arabic language well, was the first to voice doubts after the Torre Turpiana
parchment was found. He also specifically accused Luna and Castillo of per-
petrating the fraud. Beyond Granada, scholars such as the famous humanist
Benito Arias Montano, the Jesuit theologian Juan de Mariana, the clerical
antiquarian (and bishop of Segorbe) Juan Bautista Pérez, and the morisco
Jesuit Ignacio de las Casas all questioned the authenticity of the parchment
and the plomos. The most vocal critic, however, was Arias Montano's disciple
Pedro de Valencia, who later distinguished himself as an opponent not only
of the expulsion of the moriscos but also of the mass trial of witches by the
Inquisition in Navarre in 1610. Valencia wrote a detailed memorandum in
1607 attacking the prophecies on historical and philological grounds. While
he named no names, he did not hesitate to refer to the seals as frauds. He
also berated the Granadans, clergy as well as laity, for their gullibility and
crass indifference to critical historical method.

To this day scholars have argued about the possible authors of these prophecies. While there is still strong disagreement about many of the particulars, a consensus of sorts has been reached on several of the main points of this very twisted tale.

- First, both parchment and plomos were, beyond all shadow of a doubt, forgeries. In fact, this may well have been the single most audacious historical fabrication in early modern Europe. That said, it is dubious that the plomos belonged to a long-term plan from the beginning; the signs of improvised responses to early criticisms of mistakes in the original Torre Turpiana material work against that suggestion. In any event, much thought and effort went into this gamble, which proved resourceful (if not perfectly skillful) in producing a string of texts over a ten-year period.

- Second, the effort probably emanated from a group, some of whose members were almost certainly New Christians. These moreover could have been linked to the handful of elite morisco families who had permission to remain in Granada following the revolt of 1568 and who worried that another round of expulsion would fail to respect their privileges and exemptions. They sought reconciliation, legitimacy, and time for the moriscos. The syncretic vision articulated in the plomos could make Christianity more palatable to their descendents, secure a place for them in sacred history, and hasten their acceptance by Christians.

- Third, Old Christian diehards and the local civic elite soon discarded whatever philo-Islamic elements may have been present within the texts. Meanwhile, Granada's laity showed that it cared very little about the exact wording of the seals, to which it had no access anyway. What most stoked their enthusiasm was the new historical role the prophecies conferred on their city. Granadans who formerly felt the stigma of lacking a solid Christian pedigree during the Middle Ages could now point to their city with pride as the locus of one of the most important revelations since biblical times. The city now boasted a sacred charisma absent during its Muslim past—an embarrassment that conveniently disappeared thanks to the fervor surrounding the discovery of the new site of devotion. If the intention of the forgers was to produce a synthesis of Catholicism and Islam that would facilitate the survival of moriscos within the increasingly hostile local climate following the revolt of 1568, the plan backfired.

The story of the plomos of Granada contains its share of cynicism, to be sure. Yet if in Granada "everyone willingly blindfolded their eyes"—such was the sad verdict of the scholar Nicolás Antonio in the later seventeenth century—it was to a purpose.[1] This peculiar case of "invention of tradition" testifies to, among other things, the strength of localism in early modern Spanish religion. What started as an apparently desperate attempt by moriscos and others to rewrite the religious past of Granada in a light more favorable to New as well as Old Christians ended as a chance for civic glory: the city sought to trade its marginal but accepted presence in Catholic history for a more exalted yet insecure position, one that traced its roots to the apostolic period and challenged the primacy of centers such as Toledo, Santiago de Compostela, and Zaragoza. The interests of Granada's moriscos were shuffled aside in this high-risk game. Only a few years later, the curtain rang down on the moriscos throughout the Monarchy. Muslim Spain had at last reached its end.

CHAPTER 8

AFTERMATH

S O WHAT BECAME of the moriscos? It is a bitter irony that so little is known of their fate following the expulsion. While they do not vanish from the historical record, there can be no denying their growing invisibility as a group, not only within Spain but also outside it. The sources are particularly silent about the most crucial aspect of their experience: their now-permanent and public profession and practice of Islam. For many moriscos the trauma of expulsion had at least one welcome side: it brought them back into the Muslim fold. For many others, however—and we will never know how many—exile not only meant dispossession and the loss of their homes. It also involved adopting (and for many unwillingly) an essentially new religion and identity imposed from without, as both Catholic and Muslim authorities silently colluded in erasing the last traces of Christian belief within the group as a whole.

All this unfolded step by step. The decision to expel the moriscos had been debated for decades, and while the implementation went more quickly, it too proceeded deliberately, one stage at a time. After the Council of State finally cast the die, the New Christians were pushed out one group at a time. It began with the Valencians. The official edict expelling them was issued in September 1609, and within three months well over one hundred thousand moriscos had been forcibly removed. New orders came in December 1609 and January 1610 and decreed the expulsion of the New Christians from the kingdom of Castile; the main areas affected were Andalusia, Granada, La Mancha, Murcia, and Extremadura. Finally came the turn of the Aragonese and Catalan moriscos, ordered out in May 1610. Mopping-up operations continued for some time, and crown authorities did not consider the case finally closed until 1614.

The immediate and, indeed, final destination of most moriscos was North Africa. The Valencian moriscos were shipped by sea to diverse points, though most were sent directly to the Spanish garrison station at Oran. Once the Levant was cleared, the moriscos from the kingdom of Castile were forbidden to enter or transit this area. This meant that those living in Andalusia, Murcia, Granada, and Extremadura had to be similarly shipped out, this time from southern ports such as Seville or Málaga. Many if not most of the moriscos residing in the north (including Aragon and Catalonia) were forced to take the overland route through France. The overall process was hampered by improvisation and poor planning. Likewise, little was done to guarantee the safety of the expelled, many of whom were robbed, extorted, and subjected to violence from beginning to end of this miserable affair.

At first one could detect a certain willingness to retain some moriscos in Christian territory. Both France and western Italy, especially Liguria and Tuscany, showed some initial receptivity to the idea of resettling groups of moriscos. But in the end the morisco New Christians received no warmer welcome from the rest of Europe than they had in Spain, even if Spain's traditional rivals loudly decried the cruel injustice of the expulsion itself. The end result was the triumph of the Old Christian logic that, by proclaiming the deeper Muslim allegiance of the moriscos as a group, now sent them to join their brethren abroad.

The original plan from the initial phase of the expulsion had been to ship the moriscos to Oran. From there the local governor was charged with arranging their passage elsewhere, above all to Morocco and Algiers. This worked at first, but soon the numbers of migrants far outstripped the capacity of reception of all of the local societies. The helpless moriscos soon found themselves at the mercy not only of the Christian oppressors but also Bedouins and bandits who robbed and murdered many of them not only right outside the walls of Oran itself, but also on the beaches where many of them had been hastily abandoned. In the end, however, the majority made their way to safety in a settled society. There they began the slow and for many painful process of adaptation to a new life and, for many, a new religion, Islam.

The later stages of the expulsion were marked by a wider search of destinations to which the moriscos could be taken. Shiploads from Andalusia headed not only toward the other North African ports controlled by Spain, such as Ceuta and Tangiers. They also ranged further eastward, toward Tunis.

In the end, following final transshipment from French and Italian ports, Spain's former morisco population wound up settling in a broad arc along the coast or in the cities of northern Africa from roughly the southern coast of Morocco in the west to Tunisia and slightly beyond in the east. Some of them even made their way to territories directly under Ottoman control, such as Egypt, or even Anatolia. In Istanbul itself, a contingent of moriscos settled in Galata, the part of the city reserved for foreigners, where they immediately appropriated a Sephardic synagogue for use as their mosque, while loudly calling on imperial officials to revenge the affront to Islam represented by the expulsion.

There were three major areas of morisco resettlement. Foremost was the kingdom of Morocco, where earlier generations of New Christians had found employment as artisans and above all mercenary soldiers in the service of the sultan. While the moriscos proved useful as a military force due to their greater familiarity with firearms, artillery, and other forms of western technology, the local rulers soon learned that their loyalty could not be taken for granted. This was particularly true of the rough-and-ready group from Hornachos, the village in Extremadura known for the independent behavior of its inhabitants. The hornacheros turned the port of Salé just outside Rabat into a sort of independent republic from whence they preyed as pirates on Christian and especially Spanish shipping. It would not be until the later seventeenth century that the sultan managed to establish a minimal degree of control over this unusually unruly group of subjects.

The other main locations of morisco migrants were nominally under Ottoman sovereignty. Closest to the Spanish outposts was Algiers, a city-state that since the early sixteenth century functioned largely as an autonomous power of its own. Like Morocco, it too also had a large population of Spanish origin prior to 1609, but now their numbers increased measurably. The exiles not only flocked to the capital and the other cities on the coast, where prosperity depended largely on privateering. Thousands of them also settled in the countryside as well. They brought with them the irrigational skills and hydraulic technology developed through centuries of agricultural improvement in southern and eastern Spain and thus had a major impact on rural productivity in the area. Much the same could be said for the other Ottoman protectorate, Tunis. There too the moriscos helped improve local agriculture, in addition to contributing as skilled workers (especially in silk and other textiles) in the urban sphere.

Looked at in the long run, the expulsion that began in 1609 proved to be the most dramatic, though certainly not the last, episode of forced population transfer between the Iberian peninsula and northwestern Africa. Its most immediate precedents were the exodus of Granadan Muslims after 1492; in 1502 and 1526, that is, when orders were issued for the conversion of all remaining Muslims in the kingdom of Castile and the crown of Aragon; and following the defeat of the Granada revolt in 1570. It would be forcing matters to refer to the exile decreed in 1609 as an internal shift—especially intense, to be sure, and in a single direction—within a morisco-Muslim world that embraced both sides of the Mediterranean. As has been noted, a great many moriscos, especially those far removed from the main areas of settlement, Andalusia and Valencia, had lost effective contact with Islamic society to the south, not to mention the use of the Arabic language they were now forced to learn for the first time. But it is important to keep in mind that there had been constant passage between north and south all throughout the long "morisco century" from the fall of Granada to the expulsion. And this is surely the most important factor in accounting for the most striking long-term aspect of the morisco diaspora: the relative ease with which the New Christian population was eventually absorbed into northern African society and culture.

It is equally necessary to keep in mind that not all of Spain's moriscos were expelled in 1609. While the king strongly resisted the numerous petitions he received from nobles, city councils, and even prominent clerics to make individual exceptions to his edict, a considerable if unknown number wound up remaining in the Iberian peninsula. Some did so under official aegis, as was the case with those Valencian moriscos—originally six families out of every hundred—who were exempted from deportation because of their specialized knowledge of agricultural technology, especially sugar and silk production. This was also the case of moriscos who by hook or crook wound up with papers attesting to their Old Christian status, or who otherwise managed to slip through the net. Others did so illegally, such as the New Christian population of the small Manchegan town of Villarrubia de los Ojos northeast of Ciudad Real, who exhausted every form of petition and protest before finally being forced to leave the country in 1611. That later the same year they had managed to sneak back from French exile and reestablish themselves in their old homes owed much to the strong support they received not only from the local lord but also from the bulk of the Old Christian population. Finally, an unknown number of moriscos simply wound up returning to Spain after spending some time abroad. That the Inquisition could still be trying individuals for crypto-Islamic practices decades after the expulsion speaks a world for the ingenuity (or good luck) with which a stubborn minority was able to stay in place, or refuse to accept exile as a final fate.

Of this grand, tragic displacement of humanity we hear very few voices directly speaking to us within the historical record. There is little to compare with, say, the Jewish sage Isaac Abravanel's bitter corpus of writings on the exile of 1492 or with the autobiographical texts which rabbis and others wrote in the aftermath of the earlier expulsion. Still, two works from the seventeenth century shed some very interesting light on the experience both of the exiled New Christians and those who stayed behind. The first is the so-called "Treatise of Two Roads." In part an autobiographical account and in part a treatise on morisco history, this text was produced in the 1630s or 1640s in Spanish by an unknown morisco then living in Tunisia. Written in Spanish and in Latin characters, it constitutes an unusual sort of parallel to the aljamiado literature of earlier generations of moriscos. There can be no doubt of the author's allegiance to Islam. Indeed, he interprets the expulsion itself in providential terms as the liberation of a people in bondage, thanks (rather ironically) to the tyrannical decree of the Spanish pharaoh, Philip III. Still, there can be little doubt that the author found much to miss in Spain. His work is steeped in Spanish literary culture and peppered with (not explicitly acknowledged) borrowings from writers such as Garcilaso, Quevedo, and above all Lope de Vega. It also has been read as including veiled criticism of the society that received the moriscos, along with no little nostalgia for certain aspects of the culture its author left behind.

One final and quite revealing work hails from a later generation. Its author was not a morisco, but rather one Muhammad bin abd al-Wahab al-Ghassani, a Moroccan who was sent to Spain in 1690–91 as an envoy charged with negotiating the release of Moroccan captives and with obtaining the return of Arabic manuscripts then languishing in libraries in Seville, Cordoba, and Granada. His lengthy account of his diplomatic mission contains little in the way of personal details. Spain impressed him—at one point he refers to it as full of "wonders of wonders, things that stun the mind and dazzle the intellect"—even if he is predictably dismissive toward Christianity and the rule of the "despot" king Charles II. Interestingly enough, he notes that while the Christians are "deeply set in error," the common people do not fail to speak with him and his entourage and listen to what they have to say about Islam. For our purposes what is perhaps most striking is how he records that throughout his journey northward from Andalusia he repeatedly met individuals and families who eagerly claimed to be descendants of the "Moors." Thus, while passing through Andújar he came across numerous individuals who told him that they belonged to the Serraj family which had converted in the late fifteenth century. Interestingly, those who were among the lower social strata (and even a notary) were willing to identify themselves as moriscos; their relatives from a high social level, however, claimed to be *montañeses,* that is, from the collective gentry of northern Spain and thus the epitome of pure blood and noble background. Al-Ghassani was not sure what to make of these ex-coreligionists. He recognized them as "remnants of the Andalus, but they have been too long in the affluence of infidelity."[1] That is, they were both attached to and distanced from a Muslim past that, while slowly fading from memory, still retained some of its earlier presence. Not an unfitting epitaph for morisco Spain.

FROM JEWS TO CHRISTIANS

Just as Spain stood out in the medieval and early modern periods for its abundant Muslim and then ex-Muslim population, so too was it (and Portugal) distinctive for housing what was by far Europe's largest group of converts from Judaism. While their presence profoundly marked all aspects of early modern Iberian history, only recently have the former Jews and their descendants received the scholarly attention that their importance warrants. Historians have made both too much and too little of the conversos. Excessive claims have been made for often dubiously identified individuals as the near-exclusive fount of early modern Spanish economic or literary dynamism. Yet other scholars have downplayed or ignored the truly unique nature and consequences of the converso phenomenon within a Europe increasingly accustomed to practices of spiritual dissimulation and subterfuge. It is high time for a new and realistic look at an extraordinary and often puzzling experience—one that poses an unusual challenge to many of the standard conventions of historical analysis.

CHAPTER 9

CREATING *CONVERSOS,*
1391–1492

THE PUZZLE BEGINS with names. The term present-day historians usually prefer for this group, *conversos,* actually appears only rarely in early modern documents. Other designations were used much more frequently. These ranged from "New Christians"—a label ex-Jews and their descendants shared with the moriscos—to the more colloquial *tornadizos,* which not only referred to those who "had turned" Christian but also to "those who having received the water of Baptism, then returned to their original vomit," in the choice words of early modern Spain's leading lexicographer.[1] The most notorious usage, however, was *marrano,* an insulting term of uncertain origin. What all these contemporary definitions had in common was shared reference to Jews who had converted—or had been converted—to Christianity. The distinction was not insignificant, as the entire history of the conversos—once again, like that of the moriscos—rested on what was universally regarded as their questionable loyalty to a majority religion many had accepted against their will.

The transformation of Spain's Jews into Christians was a much more drawn-out affair than that of the moriscos, who lost their status as Muslims in a single generation spanning 1502 and 1526. In the case of Judaism one must look further back for the starting point, at least to 1391. In June of

69

that year violent riots against Jews began in various Andalusian cities and soon spread to much of the rest of the peninsula. The outcome included the murder of thousands of men, women, and children, the destruction of various *aljamas* or Jewish quarters, and the forced conversion of countless numbers of survivors. The extent of the disaster is suggested in the note Reuven, the son of the famed Rabbi Nissim of Girona, wrote in the margins of his father's Torah scroll:

> Wail, holy and glorious Torah, and put on black raiment, for the expounders of your lucid words perished in the flames. For three months the conflagration spread through the holy congregations of the exile of Israel in Sefarad [Spain]. The fate [of Sodom and Gomorrah] overtook the holy communities of Castile, Toledo, Seville, Mallorca, Cordoba, Valencia, Barcelona, Tàrrega, and Girona, and sixty neighbouring cities and villages. . . . The sword, slaughter, destruction, forced conversions, captivity and spoliation were the order of the day. Many were sold as slaves to the Ishmaelites; 140,000 were unable to resist those who so barbarously forced them and gave themselves up to impurity [i.e. converted].[2]

The pogroms seem to have been spontaneous, and they involved a wide cross-section of the Christian population. Especially visible participants were the urban lower classes and the clergy, although in a few cases churchmen stepped in to protect the Jews. On the whole, however, royal officials, aristocrats, and the ecclesiastical elites proved unable or unwilling to fulfill their traditional role of defenders of the Jewish minority.

Exactly why this explosion occurred at this particular moment is still a matter of debate. There were ample precedents for violence against the Jews, even if nothing on this scale had taken place before. Worsening economic conditions generated social tensions, as did the irruption of plague beginning in the 1340s. It was also a period of major political instability— including weakened monarchical authority—throughout the peninsular kingdoms. In all these respects Spain's experience differed little from that of the rest of Europe, which saw a precipitous decline in the safety and welfare of Jews during the later fourteenth century thanks above all to the recrudescence of specifically popular antisemitism. The Christian lower classes took advantage of a period of widespread disorder to punish the Jews for their traditional roles as governmental and seigneurial administrators and tax collectors. Then as in other periods the easiest way to settle accounts with their Christian exploiters was to attack the non-Christian population which served the king, nobles, or higher clergy and depended on them for protection. The Jews—far more than the subject Muslims—found themselves in the middle of what was in large measure a class conflict transfigured into confessional terms.

That the violence was so much more extensive in Iberia reflected Spain's role as the principal locus of Judaism in western Europe. By the central centuries of the Middle Ages Spanish Jews had reached positions of political and intellectual authority unheard of in most of the rest of Europe. And while this was generally truer of the Islamic south than of the Christian north, throughout the peninsula Jewish economic prosperity permitted the building of flourishing communities and centers of learning. It was hardly a coincidence that so many of the greatest figures of medieval Jewish literature and learning were of Iberian background. These included the philosopher and theologian Maimonides, the poets Samuel ha-Nagid, Solomon ibn Gabirol, Moses and Abraham ibn Ezra (the latter also a famous exegete), and Juda ha-Levi, as well as renowned rabbis such as Isaac Alfasi of Lucena, Meir ha-Levi Abulafia and Asher ben Jehiel from Toledo, or Nahmanides of Girona. This Golden Age had its dark side, though. The price of toleration was submission, material and symbolic. The former ranged from paying higher taxes to risking sporadic episodes of violence. The latter comprised a multitude of the same ritual humiliations that prevailed elsewhere, including the occasional requirement to wear separate dress and signs marking them as non-Christians. On the whole, however, the Jews of medieval Spain attained levels of wealth, political influence, and social preeminence without equal elsewhere, which doubtless made the 1391 onslaught against them all the more traumatic.

The outcome of the riots satisfied no one. Following centuries of trying to baptize the Jews, Christians confronted an unprecedented situation of apparent if incomplete success. After a period of initial uncertainty, different tactics came into play. Lay and clerical leaders stepped forward with a mixture of old and new measures designed to place a stranglehold on Jewish communities while avoiding further popular violence. The early fifteenth century saw renewed efforts to bring about the conversion of the survivors. Three instruments in particular were favored. The first was an

intense campaign of preaching. The outstanding figure here was the Valencian Dominican Vincent Ferrer, whose vivid sermons before large crowds
from 1411 to 1416 insistently pressed the need to force "infidels" to accept
baptism. Second, a widely publicized debate was held in the Catalan city of
Tortosa in 1413–14. This "Disputation"—the last in a series that began in Paris
in 1240—obliged rabbis to answer the challenges of Christian theologians
in a public forum designed to confirm the "errors" of Judaism. The very real
risks it posed for the Jewish participants, along with the all-too-predictable
ending, further demoralized the remnant of believers. The final and perhaps
most effective form of conversionary pressure was the bevy of discriminatory laws issued in both Castile and Aragon in 1412–15. The new decrees
stipulated that henceforth Jews could not hold public office, nor exercise the
trades of tailor, carpenter, or butcher. They could wear only coarse clothing,
not finery, and were not allowed to bear arms. More than anything else, the
new legislation sought to cut off daily interaction between Christians and
Jews. The latter were forbidden to hire Christians to work with them, or to
eat, drink, bathe, or even talk with Christians. In consonance with St. Vincent
Ferrer's opinion that "he will never be a good Christian who is neighbor to a
Jew," a new law compelled Jews to live apart, in segregated quarters of their
own. Much of this legislation was not enforced, and in fact, the Aragonese
laws were repealed only a few years later. Still, their impact was felt all the
same. That the learned astronomer Abraham Zacuto later referred to them
as "the greatest persecution that has ever occurred" despite their proximity
to the disaster of 1391 gives some sense of the deep impression they made.[3]

   A period of relative calm followed this flurry of activity. The major new
development was the slow but inexorable shift in the focus of Christian attention away from the Jews and toward the converts. There was virtually no
precedent for the existence of the latter, and the novelty proved unsettling
to Old Christians and Jews alike. Moreover, their ranks continued to grow,
especially when prominent figures such as Jerónimo de Santa Fe and Pablo
de Santa María converted around the time of the Disputation of Tortosa.
Their promotion to high positions near or in the Church—Santa Fe was
named a papal physician, while the latter became bishop of Burgos—adver-
tised far and wide the material and social gains former Jews could expect
to make after crossing over to the other side. In fact, the opposite problem
soon appeared. Many Christians suspected that the ex-Jews were becoming

far too successful. The first episode of backlash was recorded in 1449. In Toledo an Old Christian named Pero Sarmiento, who had been appointed governor of the Alcázar or royal castle there in 1446, raised a mob to protest a new tax levied by the royal favorite Alvaro de Luna, who had long been seen as too closely allied with the conversos. The rioters sacked the houses of several New Christians, including Alfonso Cota, the treasurer in charge of collecting the tax. Fourteen other New Christians were removed from municipal office. In itself the incident differed little from the countless other minor revolts of this turbulent period. However, two aspects would turn out to have major consequences for the future. First, the specific target of popular opprobrium had shifted from the Jews to the conversos, now seen as their surrogates. Second, Sarmiento and his allies sought to make the changes they had wrought permanent. To that end they had the city council approve in June 1449 a new law—the so-called "Sentence-Statute"—which not only excluded converts from office but also placed further restrictions on their public roles, including their testifying against Old Christians in courts. The immediate reaction of the papacy against this challenge to the validity of baptism had little effect. The monarchy intervened to suspend the excommunication of Sarmiento and in the end, after initially revoking the legislation, wound up approving it. The Toledo laws were widely debated and aroused strong passions among opponents and supporters alike. They are now seen as an ominous harbinger of future developments, in particular the laws of racial purity that decades later would be promulgated throughout Spain.

Toledo was not the only city to witness the emergence of a broad-based alliance among Old Christians opposed to New Christian professionals, merchants, and elites. Similar tensions could also be found in the nearby town of Guadalupe. There a friar in its famous monastery, Alonso de Oropesa, wrote a treatise attacking discrimination against conversos based on their ancestry, but could do little to stem the rising tide of hostility to their public prominence. Riots also took place, in Toledo (again) and Ciudad Real in 1467, and in several Andalusian cities in 1473. That the conversos had joined, and even largely replaced the Jews as objects of popular violence, and that this unrest transposed the same sort of class conflict as before was made unusually apparent by a serious revolt in 1475 in Villena, a town near Alicante bordering on Castile which belonged to the powerful grandee

D. Diego Pacheco. The scribe who replied to Philip II's topographical questionnaire of 1575 explained with evident pride how Villena had reverted
to royal jurisdiction thanks to an uprising of the Old Christian commons
against the "many conversos who, enjoying the favor of the Marquis, obtained local privileges and offices, not only in his household but also in civic
government and the administration of justice." Thus, he wrote, the

> Old Christians armed themselves and killed all the converts and Jews they
> could find, all except those who managed to escape and could not be found,
> and they killed and cut the throats of all the other men, women and children,
> and raising their voices for the crown of Castile they besieged and conquered
> the castle, which was in the hands of the Marquis, and which was commanded
> by a relative of his who had sheltered many of the Jews and converts.[4]

This background of widespread civic violence and overt hostility not only
between Old and New Christians but also between different factions of Old
Christians led to calls for an extralocal, national solution to the social and
political integration of conversos. The remedy would be the Inquisition.

Despite its sweeping authorization to investigate and extirpate all kinds
of heresy, in its early years the Inquisition was concerned with only one
form of deviance. This was the crime known as "judaizing," or continued observance of the Jewish faith among the conversos. The royal letter
requesting the establishment of the Holy Office in Castile specified as its
motive the inability of the bishops—traditionally charged with punishing
heresy—to control the spread of "Mosaic heresy." A papal bull of November
1478 allowed the monarchs to name three inquisitors in each city and/or
diocese to investigate heretical beliefs. This gave them a powerful weapon
with which to resolve the Jewish, and now converso, "problem."

The initial target was Seville. The largest and most prosperous city in the
south, and one of the main centers of converso settlement, it had long been
suspected of harboring a nucleus of judaizers. In their first weeks of activity the newly appointed inquisitors arrested hundreds of New Christians,
including members of the city's most prominent families. Many others fled,
either to lands under seigneurial jurisdiction or across the border to Portugal
and even to North Africa. Soon the Dominican monastery proved too small
to hold the prisoners, and the Holy Office was forced to take up new quarters
in the royal castle across the river in Triana. According to one contemporary

account, more than six hundred conversos were burned during the open-ing decade of the new tribunal's existence, while some eight thousand were "reconciled," that is, had to do penance for the crime of judaizing.

The inquisitors' attentions were not limited to Seville. Soon their focus shifted to other cities, especially after the creation in 1483 of a nationwide council known as the Suprema, which assured both broader action and the beginnings of coordination among the various local efforts. Recent estimates suggest that around twenty thousand individuals received mostly harsh punishments, including almost two thousand executions, for being judaizers from 1481 to 1530. Yet despite this frenetic activity the Holy Office was convinced that backsliding among the conversos would not be elimi-nated unless they could be completely isolated from the surviving nuclei of Jews, who, thanks to their status as non-Christians, were not under the Inquisition's jurisdiction. The sort of discriminatory legislation that had been essayed earlier in the fifteenth century had obviously turned out to be ineffective, despite occasional revivals, as in the 1480 Castilian law in which the Cortes or parliament ordered Jews and Muslims once again to reside in separate *juderías* and *morerías*. Soon influential figures both within and outside the tribunal began to look to another, more drastic remedy: the expulsion of all Jews from the Spanish kingdoms, regardless of their status or religious behavior.

Why expulsion? Spain was hardly the only country to order the removal of distinctive ethnic and/or religious groups during the early modern era. In fact, if anything it could now catch up with its neighbors. England and France, for instance, had long before expelled their Jewish subjects, in 1290 and 1394 respectively. Nor would the exodus of 1492 be the last such popu-lation transfer. Various religious minorities were expelled from different states of the Holy Roman Empire once the Reformation got underway. This policy culminated in the exiling of the Huguenots or Calvinists from France in 1685 and the expulsion of twenty thousand Protestant peasants from the Archbishopric of Salzburg in 1731–32 (the latter were given refuge by the same Prussian ruler who was busy ridding his kingdom of Mennonites for refusing military service). In fact, Spain itself was no stranger to such radical remedies. Jews in the recent past had been obliged to leave diverse municipal, diocesan, and regional jurisdictions. A string of expulsions was decreed in Andalusia from 1481 to 1484, and similar orders were issued (though not enforced) in Aragon in 1486. In the years preceding 1492 the Spanish kingdoms increasingly favored separating Jews from Christians, both new and old. While the recently created Inquisition was not the only interest to exert pressure in this direction—municipalities and some bishoprics were also involved—it clearly was taking on a growing role in shaping governmental policies that eventually led to a general expulsion.

Viewed in retrospect, at least two other events of the 1480s can be seen as crucial in preparing the ground for the decision of 1492. The first was the Guadalupe affair of 1485. Both the town and its Hieronymite monastery housed significant minorities of conversos. Factional fighting within the latter and between the friars and the townsmen led to calls for the Inquisition to intervene. After an initial grace period, the tribunal cracked down on the New Christian population and executed some seventy-one persons charged with judaizing, while exiling many others. The Guadalupe trials drew wide attention not only for the unprecedented harshness of the sentences. The relentless campaign of the inquisitors also exposed to broader view the existence of alleged judaizers within one of Spain's most prestigious pilgrim sites. This discovery severely damaged the position of moderates within the order, such as Oropesa and Hernando de Talavera, who were known to favor more lenient methods in dealing with conversos. One immediate effect was the Hieronymites' decision to approve a blood purity statute in 1486—the first ever for a religious order in Spain. Thus, while the town of Guadalupe itself had no Jewish population at the time, the trial brought to public attention the penetration by their descendants not only of secular institutions such as city councils but also of a monastic order with especially intimate ties to the Castilian crown.

The other and more immediate influence on the decision for expulsion was the case of the *Santo Niño* or "Holy Child" of La Guardia, the most famous case of blood libel in Spanish history. In June 1490 a converso named Benito García confessed under torture to crucifying a Christian child from the town of La Guardia east of Toledo. He named as his accomplices two other conversos and a Jewish shoemaker named Jusé Franco, along with his father and brother. Inquisitor General Tomás de Torquemada took over the case in person and had it transferred to Segovia and then to Avila. Despite the many contradictions in the accuseds' depositions, they were found guilty and executed in 1491. A shrine to the victim was set up in the cave outside the town where he allegedly met his end, and from time to time his story was dusted off by opponents of easing restrictions on the conversos, such as Lope de Vega, who wrote a play about the case around 1605. Luis de Páramo, an official of the Inquisition and one of its earliest historians, later referred to the La Guardia trial as one of the more important incidents which led to the expulsion. Its impact on public opinion was immense, as news of the ritual murder circulated throughout the peninsula and even beyond.

Ferdinand and Isabel signed the official orders expelling the Jews in Granada on March 31, 1492. As in the case of the expulsion of the moriscos, most of the historiographic debate surrounding their decision focuses on two issues: its causes and its consequences. While there is no firm consensus in regard to either of these questions, some of the more extreme claims—such as Jean Bodin's charge that the expulsion was really a pretext for seizing Jewish property—have pretty much fallen by the wayside. The expulsion clearly belongs to that category of events in which it is impossible to separate ideological from more narrowly political (or economic) considerations. Isabel had certainly long been known for her animus against Spain's religious minorities. A leading theme in the propaganda favoring her ascent to the throne in the turbulent final years of her brother Henry IV's reign—and eventually in the historical image her chroniclers promoted—was harsh criticism of the laxity of Henry and his allies toward Jews and Muslims. While Rabbi Isaac Abravanel blamed both monarchs for the decision, he distinguished between Isabel's deep hostility to the Jews and Ferdinand's "haughtiness" after the capture of Granada. The latter reference suggests that political opportunity was hardly absent from their mix of motives. Expelling the Jews from both Castile and Aragon so closely on the heels of the final defeat of the Muslims would signal not only inside Spain but also beyond it the power and determination of a joint monarchy of recent creation and still of a highly personal—and precarious—nature.

At the same time the decree promised to solve the converso problem in that—the wording was very explicit on this point—the presence of the Jews was credited with facilitating judaizing on the part of New Christians. The removal of the former would obviously make heretical activity on the part of the latter all the more difficult. Among the other factors seen as intervening in this measure was the Inquisition's lobbying at court in its favor. It would hardly come as a surprise to find the Holy Office taking a major role in pressuring for such a step. Finally, it is even possible that such pragmatic politicians as Isabel and Ferdinand might have found some inspiration in contemporary millenarian currents that looked to mass conversions as ushering in the much-awaited Day of Final Judgment. The Franciscan Jerónimo de Mendieta wrote from Mexico in the 1590s that the providential mission of the Catholic king and queen had opened the way for the "final conversion of all peoples to the brotherhood of the Church."[5] Who knows whether some of this enthusiasm might not have influenced their decision, which they made when Cardinal Cisneros—whose famed mysticism was more than a little tinged with millenarian leanings—was gaining power at court? In fact, the fateful year of 1492 was when he succeeded Hernando de Talavera—a converso and a renowned religious moderate—as Isabel's confessor.

As for the consequences, while the exact number of persons expelled will never be known, the emphasis as of late has been to tone down the higher estimates of the past—it had been asserted that as many as four hundred thousand Jews had left Spain—in favor of a substantially smaller contingent. The net figure of forty thousand to fifty thousand exiles in one recent revision may be too low. But the suggestion that the overall number of Jews had been seriously lessened by persistent conversions before, during, and even *after* the expulsion—that is, on the part of actual exiles who finally converted as a means of returning to Spain after 1492—is quite plausible. The economic consequences, indirect as well as direct, have also been overstated. The widespread belief that Spain expelled a nascent middle class—in more extreme versions, its *only* middle class—greatly exaggerates the impact of an undeniably drastic measure. It is telling that the Spanish economy suffered no visible downturn in the aftermath of the expulsion—testimony, perhaps, to the strength of the expansionary phase during which it took place. It has even been suggested that New Christian emigration beginning in the 1480s had wreaked an even greater economic loss, given the fact that the conversos were generally wealthier than the remaining Jews.

No, the deeper impact of the expulsion has to be sought elsewhere, in its spiritual and cultural consequences. In this regard, the events of 1492 were seen far and wide as marking a watershed. For the Jews the decree led to collective tragedy, a new and far from liberating exodus that in the eyes of many ranked with the exile from ancient Jerusalem. In the words of Rabbi Elijah Capsali of Padua, it brought "the golden age that had been Spain to an end."[6] Meanwhile, for Christians throughout Europe it represented a triumph, a decisive, even audacious, decision that merited emulation elsewhere. But as far as its main purpose—to bring Spanish Judaism to a definitive end—was concerned, the measure fell short of the mark, at least in terms of the immediate future. The reconstitution of Spanish-speaking communities throughout the Mediterranean went a long way in mitigating the loss of the center of the Sephardic world. What is more, the Judaic tradition survived in the peninsula itself among conversos who chose to maintain their ancestral faith. The fate of Judaism in Iberia now rested in the hands of the beleaguered minority of New Christians. Its survival or extinction depended on the risky choices they were now forced to make.

CHAPTER 10

VIGILANCE THROUGH
VIOLENCE

IT IS A common irony of history that the best information about a social group often comes from its bitterest enemies. That certainly is true of the conversos. By far the most voluminous record of their activities can be found among the trial papers of the Inquisition. These sources give a richly detailed, if consistently deformed, view of a category of Spaniards who otherwise left few documentary traces, at least relating to what most interested both their contemporaries and present-day readers: their alleged or real Judaism. More will be said about the possible distortions of these records below. For the moment, the task is to chart the contours of Inquisitorial attention to the New Christians, along with the long-term rhythms of vigilance on the part of the Holy Office.

There were four main stages in the prosecution of conversos suspected of judaizing:

1. The initial period comprised the first four decades of the Inquisition's history, beginning with the early mass trials in Seville in the 1480s. This was by far the most brutal period of persecution, in terms of the numbers of individuals investigated, the proportions judged guilty, and the harshness of sentences imposed. It was also almost exclusively centered in cities, where most conversos lived.

2. A perceptible decline in the prosecution of converts followed beginning in the
    third decade of the sixteenth century. This was in part thanks to the thorough-
    ness with which the Holy Office had made its destructive way through the New
    Christian strata of Spain's cities. But there was also another factor. New heresies
    were claiming the inquisitors' attention: Protestants and the *alumbrados,* that
    is, illuminist and often antinomian mystics. This second period, which lasted
    roughly to the end of the century, saw numerous episodes of Inquisitorial ac-
    tion. Its overall intensity did not, however, match that of the opening stage,
    which suggests that the tribunal was settling down to a routine that, as far
    as the conversos was concerned, was only occasionally interrupted by major
    spurts of activity. It was also becoming increasingly preoccupied with Old
    Christians, and this meant novel—indeed, unprecedented—attention to Spain's
    rural population.

3. What brought the issue of crypto-Judaism back to life—and the Holy Office
    back to the cities—was the growing influx of Portuguese New Christians into
    Castile and, also to a considerable extent, to the New World colonies. Some
    converso merchants and artisans had already immigrated prior to Philip II's
    absorption of Portugal in 1580. But after that date far greater numbers of Por-
    tuguese New Christians moved to Castile to take advantage of the ample eco-
    nomic opportunities that awaited them there. This gave rise to the third, and
    what might be called the "Portuguese period," of the Inquisition's pursuit of
    judaizers. It lasted roughly from the 1570s to the 1660s. What proved most
    distinctive here was not just the foreign birth of the conversos. It was also the
    fact that many of them were indeed genuine crypto-Jews who had been much
    more willing and/or successful than their Spanish brethren in remaining at-
    tached to their ancestral faith. The larger numbers and greater visibility of these
    potential suspects were offset in part by the growing economic difficulties the
    Inquisition faced on an operational level. Also, during the central decades of
    this period the more influential of these conversos enjoyed some degree of
    political protection, as the monarchy found them—for a while—quite useful
    as financiers and administrators of customs and other governmental functions.

4. The final stage of the Holy Office's struggle against New Christian "apostasy"
    covered the seventy or so years from the mid-seventeenth century to the 1720s.
    Diminishing intensity marked this period as a whole. Nevertheless, it did see
    a number of trials against alleged judaizers of Portuguese extraction in several
    cities. It in fact ended with a sweep of conversos in Madrid, Mallorca, Seville,
    and Granada during the 1720s. This unusual outburst—which featured over

one hundred executions—turned out to be the last significant campaign against crypto-Jews in Iberian history.

It is difficult to estimate the numbers of individuals involved. Minimally accurate records of Inquisitorial activity do not survive for the six decades prior to 1540—precisely the period of the greatest (and most lethal) persecution of conversos. From 1540 to 1700 a minimum of 4,400 judaizers were brought to trial, the vast majority in the crown of Castile. This represents one-tenth of the tribunal's total caseload of 44,674 trials. If one considers the relatively muted attention to judaizers during this century and a half, at least in comparison with the preceding period, one might surmise that the Spanish Inquisition tried between fifteen and twenty thousand conversos for judaizing during the nearly 450 years of its official existence. What can hardly be questioned is that from the beginning, stamping out judaizing was regarded as its overriding task. Moreover, it applied its harshest penalty—capital punishment—more consistently in the case of judaizers than of any other group, with the possible exceptions of the initial and much smaller nuclei of Protestants and the moriscos following the revolt of Granada of the later 1560s. Inquisitorial Spain of both legend and reality would be unthinkable without the conversos. The inverse was pretty much true as well.

CHAPTER II

NEW CHRISTIANS IN
A NEW SPAIN

W HO WERE THE conversos, and how did they differ from their Old Christian neighbors? One can begin to answer these questions by pointing out the main traits that characterized the New Christians as a group. Four were particularly prominent.

First, conversos were closely linked with specific trades. Not surprisingly, many of these economic and professional activities had long been associated with Jews. In an often-quoted passage Andrés Bernáldez, a late fifteenth-century cleric and a thorough antisemite, wrote of the Jews that

> they were merchants and salesmen and tax farmers . . . and artisans such as cloth shearers, tailors, shoemakers and tanners, weavers, spice merchants, wandering salesmen, silk-makers, blacksmiths, silversmiths and other such trades; none of them ploughed the earth or farmed or was a carpenter or mason, rather they all sought easy jobs, and ways of making money without working hard.[1]

One spots several traditional anti-Judaic clichés in this sentence, but on the whole converso settlement patterns do seem to have been much more urban than rural. Moreover, their work preferences centered on the finishing crafts and petty commerce. So much is suggested by the information on residence and occupations from the early trials of the Inquisition, which shows a clear preponderance of small-scale artisans, especially in the textile and leather sectors, as well as blacksmiths and silversmiths (the latter doubled as moneylenders). Other, outside documents paint the same picture. Thus, for example, a list of 218 conversos from the cities of Valencia and Xàtiva drawn up for tax purposes in 1488 shows the highest ranks held by merchants, followed by a few professionals and a large majority of artisans. To be sure, not all conversos were town dwellers. Inquisitorial sources from Extremadura document more than a few New Christians working in agriculture and with livestock. Yet what stands out even here is the strategic role of conversos as middlemen between town and country. Not a single convert was *only* a farmer. Rather, all combined rural work with commerce and other distributive activities.

Bernáldez's list was far from complete. Another way to look at the question of the socio-occupational profile of the conversos is to inquire which trades were most closely identified with them. One notices a few departures from the occupational patterns of their Jewish ancestors. The close though hardly exclusive linkage between late medieval Jews and leather work and bookbinding, for instance, was diluted in the early modern era, thanks to the expansion and transformation of these forms of fairly skilled labor. Other trades, however, passed from Jews to conversos without any fuss. Two examples are auctioneering and trading/processing coral. Perhaps the single trade most closely identified first with the Jews and later with the conversos was medicine. This was true above all of the higher ranks of medical practice. The conversos' public reputation as physicians did not extend to their fellow university-trained professionals, the lawyers. Instead, it was a direct inheritance from the medieval past, when Spanish Jews' exposure to the Greco-Arabic tradition of learned medicine led them to become the leading experts in Europe.

Perhaps the single greatest change in the occupational profile of the conversos took place with the Portuguese immigration beginning in the later sixteenth century. During this period a new category emerged, that of *hombres de negocios,* or businessmen who operated on a large and, in some cases, even international scale. These families had their origins in the more prosperous merchant houses of the main Portuguese port cities, especially Lisbon. Gradual penetration of the lucrative northern African, Mediterranean, and transatlantic trades allowed them to accumulate considerable amounts of capital. Instead of investing these proceeds in the traditional outlets of land, titles, and seigneurial rights, they turned instead in the direction of state finance, first in Portugal and then directly in Madrid. The royal favorite the count-duke of Olivares warmly welcomed them beginning in the 1620s as a cheaper and more submissive alternative to the Genoese bankers who had controlled royal finances since the time of Charles V. In return the Portuguese subscribed a series of *asientos* or contracts that guaranteed the state's schedule of payments both in Spain and throughout the empire. Their willingness to bankroll the Monarchy at a moment of crucial need allowed them to place family members and clients in key positions in the royal administration, especially as collectors of taxes. These included classic levies such as the *alcabala* or general sales tax, customs and shipping duties, and the wool export charge, as well as more recent expedients, such as the royal monopolies of salt, documents stamped for official use, and above all tobacco.

Seen in the long run, the conversos turn out to have formed an important, albeit hardly the only, sector of the urban middle classes. That they were town dwellers does not mean that they lacked ties with the rural world. On the contrary, it was precisely involvement in commerce which allowed many of them to act as middlemen providing the crucial links that facilitated the exchange of goods and services between city and country. At the same time, while the conversos numbered among their ranks a disproportionate share of the greater merchants of the realm, most were nevertheless artisans and shopkeepers possessing more modest wealth and social status. They occupied, in short, a middling position within contemporary hierarchies, and one that provided reasonable opportunities for upward social mobility.

Mobility was precisely the second feature of this group. A high degree of geographic mobility had long been associated with the Jews, and this trait appears to have characterized the conversos as well. Many of the latter left their places of origin to settle elsewhere, usually for the same reasons of economic betterment that accounted for the pronounced mobility characteristic of Iberian society as a whole. That the New Christians were credited with even higher levels of displacement was probably due to three factors. The first involved the more frequent travel and migration associated with urban occupations, especially those linked to commerce. Greater geographical mobility also derived in part from the desire to leave behind the cities where relatives had been tried by the Inquisition and thus to avoid the public infamy attached to families found guilty of judaizing. Hence the ease with which one finds examples of penanced conversos and their kin moving, in addition to changing their names, in the wake of a trial. There was also a third, powerful stimulus to geographic mobility. This was the tendency noted above of many conversos—and the seventeenth-century Portuguese migrants in particular—to constitute large-scale, family-based networks for trading and administrating state revenues. This occupational pattern required substantial dispersion of the kinsmen and clients who served as local agents, shopkeepers, and distributors of goods. Temporary movement was constant within these networks and went a long way in accounting for the conversos' contemporary reputation as a restless, unsettled group.

The other side of this coin was the ability of converso families to aspire to social mobility as well. While most of this promotion is hidden from the historical record, it is clear that over time numerous New Christians were able to convert their prosperity and professional expertise into higher social standing. In a few, truly spectacular cases, conversos were able to rise from humble beginnings to the top rungs of the social ladder. This was true of, for example, the Bernuys lineage. This family, which originally began as modest merchants operating in northern Castile, increased its scale of operations until it had branches operating in the rest of Europe, above all the Low Countries and France. In 1566 the main line was able to exchange sponsorship of a loan to the crown for a patent of nobility. Not long afterward it purchased the title of marquis of Alcalá del Valle, named for a village near Ronda. The family also acquired seigneuries and the concession of taxes in other parts of Andalusia, notably Benamejí, in the province of Cordoba. All this involved forging some genealogies while forgetting others, buying false certificates of blood purity, and otherwise covering up the mention of a family *sambenito*—the penitential garb that indicated prosecution by the Inquisition—that hung in the Dominican monastery of Santo Tomás in Avila. In short, the Bernuys ran the course from late medieval beginnings in the Jewish quarter of Avila to becoming nobles in the sixteenth century, marquises in the seventeenth, grandees of Spain in the eighteenth, and bankrupt in the nineteenth. Theirs was an exceptional case of patient, generation-by-generation movement up (and eventually down) the social scale. But they were not the only ones to follow the same route. Indeed, by the seventeenth century, and even earlier, many Spanish aristocrats possessed some Jewish ancestors, even if they had been generally successful in disguising these tracks.

A third collective characteristic marking conversos is what has been referred to as "endogamy." This is a misleading term, in that endogamy—normally defined as the limitation of marriage choice to persons within a specific group—is a standard, not exceptional, feature of social organization. Whether one social circle is more endogamous than another depends on whether one judges as large or small the size of the effective pool of marriage partners. It has not yet been proved that New Christians intermarried more than Old Christians, or that they restricted their search for spouses more than other social groups both above and beneath them on the social scale. Most significantly, there is little systematic evidence to show that conversos continued what were seen as typical marital practices among late medieval Jews. These included cross-cousin alliances or uncle-niece unions—both found frequently among Old Christians, by the way—and above all levirate marriages between a widow and her husband's brother.

What is clear is that contemporaries *believed* conversos to be a tight-knit group. And it is not at all difficult to find compelling reasons for conversos to marry among themselves. First, the stigma attached to New Christians discouraged many Old Christians from running the risk of becoming tainted themselves. Moreover, the relative socioeconomic homogeneity of the conversos as an urban middle and lower middle class meant that they did not have to look very far when searching for spouses from the same occupational and income background. Third, the crucial reliance on kinship for the functioning of the extended networks characteristic of trading "diasporas" similarly pressured their participants in the direction of tighter patterns of intermarriage. Finally, there was a strategic factor of special importance to judaizing conversos: the need for close family solidarity to avoid being discovered naturally encouraged marrying within the smallest pool possible. Once again, more research will be needed to turn these contemporary impressions into documented conclusions. But that there were cogent reasons for some conversos—once again, particularly judaizing conversos—deliberately to circumscribe their circles of intermarriage cannot be questioned. Neither should one doubt that those conversos who opted for assimilation would be tempted to adopt precisely the opposite strategy.

A final social characteristic of the New Christians involves their residential patterns. The frequent interurban mobility of the conversos has already been alluded to. But what of their settlement patterns within the cities they inhabited? Prior to 1492, the newly minted converts often continued to live in the same areas they did before. Indeed, it was precisely their proximity to their former coreligionists that the legislation of the fifteenth century, and ultimately the expulsion of the Jews, hoped to undo. An unusually thorough study of the city of Toledo—home to one of the most distinguished Jewish, and then converso, communities—shows that the New Christians' initial close identification with the Jews weakened with the passage of time. A list from 1495–97 of conversos whose penalties for judaizing had been commuted shows them distributed among all parishes in the city, yet favoring certain ones over others. These were Santo Tomé and San Martín in the southwest, along with San Román, Santa Leocadia, San Vicente, and San Nicolás toward the north. These coincided for the most part with late medieval Toledo's two *juderías,* the larger one centering on Santo Tomé and San Martín and the smaller one close to the cathedral in the center. Partial data from other cities reveal much the same pattern of persistent occupancy of former Jewish areas by fifteenth-century conversos. Thus notarial documents from Seville show local New Christians continuing to reside in the parishes of Santa Cruz and Santa María la Blanca, the latter having been a synagogue converted into a church in the later fifteenth century. Source problems obviously make it more difficult to trace conversos with the passage of time. Still, the data from the Toledan study uncover the conversos' lingering attachment to their loci of origin, even as their participation in parish and conventual life became more pronounced—one might say regular—thanks to their patronage of family tombs and chapels, the profession of sons and daughters in monasteries, and the like. The absorption of standard Catholic practices within older venues and social networks thus suggests some sort of balance between growing interaction with Old Christians and maintenance of an ethnic identity still removed from the mainstream. Significantly, while converso women could be found in every convent in Toledo, thanks to family-based patronage strategies there were a handful of new foundations whose members were *exclusively* conversas.

Such details merit pondering. Still, the overall drift was moving in the opposite direction. The deeper problem involved in summarizing the conversos as a group was that as time went by they became increasingly difficult to *see* as a group. Many historians have assumed either that the New Christians actively resisted assimilation or that Old Christian hostility denied them any possibility of it. Such views derive in large measure from relying on Inquisitorial records for reconstructing converso history. These sources highlight as a matter of course those converts and their descendants who were tried for judaizing. Their focus on conflict moreover winds up emphasizing the degree of mistrust between the two blocs of Christians. What they do not document all that readily is the absorption of conversos into Old Christian society, above all through intermarriage. This, the true key to assimilation, paradoxically becomes harder to detect as it becomes more frequent.

Another distortion originates in the modus operandi of the Inquisition itself. Its penchant for occasional macro-scale show trials, which generated widespread publicity for the Holy Office and allowed its officials to demonstrate their zeal and efficiency to society at large, seems to have been designed to frustrate converso aspirations to assimilation and upward mobility. While many of the autos da fé of the period featured New Christians, one is especially interesting in terms of what it reveals about the nature and extent of converso assimilation. The Kingdom of Murcia hosted a series of major trials for judaizing beginning in the early 1560s. From 1560 to 1571 some 345 conversos were tried in the city of Murcia alone. The victims included prominent members of the local oligarchy, and in particular aldermen and other municipal council members. Despite their New Christian background, many of these individuals had prospered and managed to enter the local ruling class through the purchase of patents of nobility, offices, and *ejecutorias* (certificates of blood purity), a matter that will be dealt with further below. It was in fact the very success of the conversos that triggered a reaction by their Old Christian rivals, who denounced them to the Inquisition on charges of judaizing. The Holy Office responded with shocking violence and executed 135 persons in Murcia, along with dozens of others in nearby towns, especially Lorca and Hellín. Matters got so out of hand—criticisms of the local inquisitors' brutality and corruption reached as high as the royal court and Rome—that the Suprema decided to send an official to investigate. This "visitor" read through the trial papers and uncovered numerous abuses, mistakes, and lapses of procedure, ranging from outright venality to acceptance of false testimony and the improper use of judicial torture.

In the end the Inquisition made amends and repaired the torn fabric of local society by consolidating the status of the surviving members of the decimated converso families by—irony of ironies—awarding them the status of familiars in the Holy Office.

What is most striking is what this episode reveals about the conversos themselves. Two points may be made in this regard. Such intensive persecution suggests, to be sure, that the converso elite met with firm limitations on its ability to integrate itself into local society. Evidently, to be a New Christian was to live in a condition of permanent risk of being denounced whenever a situation of rivalry or conflict might arise. Yet this conflagration also testifies to the very success—never definitive, and always in jeopardy, but success all the same—some of these families had achieved in their attempt to scale the heights of civic power. Had they not represented a significant challenge to existing power structures, the Old Christian faction(s) would not have bothered to take such dramatic steps to liquidate them. Needless to say, what went wrong in Murcia and Lorca went right in many other cities, where the upward mobility of the conversos did not provoke such a violent reaction. The other lesson this story teaches is that by the mid-sixteenth century, these clusters of conversos—and doubtless many others elsewhere—would be better referred to as a quasi-ethnic, not religious, group. The judaizing for which over one hundred persons were burned was the product of inquisitors who used patently false testimony and torture to force confessions to heretical practices which most likely had not taken place. Conversos in mid-sixteenth-century Castile could still be identified as such with relative ease. But that they were judaizing to the extent that their grandparents did is much more difficult to believe—a fact which provides yet another proof of their slow, if painful, assimilation into Christian society.

The history of this absorption was far from linear. For just as the conversos of Castile and Aragon began to drop out of sight, especially in larger and rapidly growing cities such as Madrid, the influx of Portuguese New Christians disrupted the process. Many of the latter, once again, were judaizers and actively strived to avoid absorption into the Catholic mainstream. While Lerma and Olivares were royal favorites they could count on a certain degree of protection, as both were willing to harness the Inquisition in exchange for bribes (Lerma) or active collaboration in royal finance (Olivares). After the latter fell in 1643, however, the persecution of conversos began anew, and the

following two decades saw the trials of some of the richest and most important New Christian families. All the same, Inquisitorial attention continued
to focus almost exclusively on the Portuguese. Spanish converso families
of long standing found themselves less subject to persecution as time went
by. By the early eighteenth century, following the final wave of trials against
Portuguese judaizers in the early 1720s, there was only one spot in Spain
where conversos stood out as such. This was Mallorca, where the local New
Christians known as *xuetes* (in Spanish *chuetas*) had been subject not only
to informal discrimination but also to legal segregation, including binding
residence apart from Old Christians in a neighborhood of their own. This
case, which involved the formal creation of a public category of outcast
lineages, was unique in many respects, not the least being its survival until
well into the twentieth century. Elsewhere in Spain, converso identity was
not institutionalized, with the partial exception of the variable effect of the
statutes of blood purity (more on this below). And in retrospect it seems
quite significant that despite many proposals to the effect, no general census
of New Christians was ever undertaken.

One can hardly deny the magnitude of the generational shift toward the
end of the sixteenth century, when Portuguese immigrants began to replace
native Spanish conversos as the leading suspects of judaizing. Yet one crucial
aspect of this history which apparently suffered very little change was the
public attitudes of the Old Christian majority first toward the Jews and then
toward the conversos. Nevertheless, even so straightforward a story has one
or two bends in its path.

CHAPTER 12

THE PERSISTENCE OF ANTISEMITISM

I F EARLY MODERN Spain succeeded in eliminating its Jews, the same could not be said of the memory of them. Even when Judaism no longer flourished in its midst, the figure of the Jew played a vital, if negative, role in defining the Catholic commonwealth. Antisemitism had long been an integral part of Christian identity, and all the classic elements of this tradition were found in depictions of Jews in early modern Spanish liturgy, literature, theater, and folklore. Hence the habitual litany of religious tropes—the original charge of deicide, along with ongoing rejection of the revealed truth of the New Law—combined with the age-old catalog of undesirable personal attributes (avarice, astuteness, blindness, vengefulness, and even sexual depredation) to produce a thoroughly pernicious image of the archetypical Other. What galvanized this familiar construct was fear, above all belief in the very real power of the Jews and in the existence of a secret conspiracy among them to destroy Christianity. The strong similarities between this notion and contemporary credence in sects of witches were not limited to the catalog of malign intentions and traits assigned to both groups. They also extended to the procedures used to expose and punish them, ranging from secret denunciations to death at the stake.

Iberia developed two intriguing—as well as ominous—variants in this seemingly timeless tale of never-ending Christian antisemitism. The first involved an unusual yet hardly unique paradox, that of a profoundly anti-Judaic culture within a society which lacked Jews. Spain had evolved from full participation in "classic" antisemitism as manifested in real social, economic, and political conflicts involving Jews to a context wherein fear was powered not by direct confrontations, but by memory and other shadows within the collective imagination. The accent thus shifted from a sense of immediate peril to a more diffuse emphasis on secrecy and dissimulation. One result was that many Spaniards genuinely feared that their society housed multitudes of hidden Jews and Muslims. The sporadic discovery and punishment of heretics by the Inquisition merely reinforced this notion.

Further heightening this suspicion was the sheer difficulty of identifying the enemy. The discourse of the period makes surprisingly little reference to the physical appearance of Jews. Some writers did evoke familiar stereotypes of physical difference; hence the evocation of "a man attached to a nose" in a famous poem by the arch-antisemite Francisco de Quevedo.[1] Yet a far greater anomaly is the absence of mention of characteristics which in other periods were looked on as reliable indicators of Jewishness. Especially noteworthy is the contrast with modern racism's unshakable confidence in its ability to spot Jews thanks to their hair color, smell, and other physical traits.

One faces here a different, less confident form of antisemitism, one in which the host society—so to speak—has little faith in its capacity to recognize the enemy in its midst. In this sense early modern Spain lived a moment of parenthesis between medieval and modern credence in the power of physical differences to mark the difference between Jews and the rest of the population. Contemporaries readily acknowledged the difficulty of detecting Jews. Thus the playwright Luis Quiñones de Benavente—another obsessive antisemite—confessed that "recognizing [a Jew] is difficult" and that one must look to "hidden body signs," which included a tail and male menstruation![2] What most bolstered this sense of uncertainty was the disappearance among conversos of the two traditional modes of marking Jews. The first was, of course, circumcision. This practice all but vanished after the initial period of Inquisitorial persecution and lived on only in a small number of more fervent judaizing families of Portuguese origin. The other was the distinctive signs or clothing Jews were obliged to wear during much of the Middle Ages, for example the ones legislated in the Castilian

law code known as the Siete Partidas. Old Christian bewilderment as to
how to recognize Jews when they became conversos was reflected in a
royal order of 1433 in Catalonia that regulated the worrisome interaction
between recent converts and Jews. The writ commanded the Jews to wear
the traditional signs of distinction: special hats, robes, and a "large yellow
or red circle . . . on the breast . . . which has long been the custom."[3] The
problem soon became a different and more difficult one: that of divining
Jewishness among those who were no longer officially regarded as Jews, that
is, the converts themselves.

That the situation changed dramatically when the Jews became conversos
and could now take advantage of new possibilities for deceit and dissimulation was widely recognized. So much so, in fact, that it frequently surfaced
as a cliché in foreigners' remarks about Spain. People in the rest of Europe
had long suspected that the Iberian peninsula was overrun with Jews and
Muslims. The new twist was the belief that these enemies now lived and
operated in secrecy. As a result, it was impossible to distinguish sincere
Christians—rumored to be very few—from Jews and Muslims who now
disguised themselves as Christians. From Erasmus to Voltaire, European
observers from afar equated Spanishness with Jewishness or referred to the
countless numbers of false Catholics. (Some of this was wishful thinking. Sir
Edwin Sandys, who affirmed that "Marrany, baptised Jewes and Moores"
outnumbered true Catholics in Spain, further wrote that "were it not for the
Inquisition, [the Spaniards] would . . . turne Protestants in short time"!)[4]
Spanish Old Christians must have been galled to find these foreign heretics
taunting them as stand-ins for their despised enemies. William of Orange's
depiction of the duke of Alba as a "new creature of Jewish unbelief" and
"Moorish tiger-beast" was merely one example of how Spain's domestic
experiments in conversion led to unexpected—and undesirable—consequences for its image beyond its borders.[5]

The other anomaly—actually, novelty—of early modern Iberian antisemitism was the way in which Jewish or Muslim identity gradually took
on a pronounced racial cast. As one expert has put it,

> Cryptojudaizing proved . . . to have rather shallow roots in Castile. A genera-
> tion or two after the Expulsion, it died out quite quickly. . . . Cryptojudaizing
> continued to live as a reality—with fateful consequences—mainly in the
> Spanish-Catholic imagination. As converso society changed in the period fol-

lowing the Expulsion, so too did Old Christian attitudes about conversos. . . .
By the mid-sixteenth century, there was increasing use of collective terms . . .
[which] reflected an emerging view which emphasized the conversos' pur-
ported ethnic or racial traits.[6]

While there is reason to suspect that this trend considerably antedated the
sixteenth century, there can be little doubt as to the significance of the shift
toward a new definition of Judaism. It would be overstating it to affirm
that what was formerly looked on as a religion was now seen as a race. But
something akin to this transition—with all its overtones of modern racial
antisemitism—was well underway. Spain differed little from the rest of
Europe in the catalog of characteristics—invariably depicted as vices—attributed to the Jews. And it was hardly the only corner of the continent to
believe that these traits were inherited by descendants of Jews despite their
having been baptized. But the intensity of this belief, and of the sense that
the Jews represented a biological danger to the racially defined Old Christian
community, had little counterpart outside the peninsula. This was thanks,
obviously enough, to the absence of the same sort of large-scale "converso
problem" elsewhere. But it seems also to have been nourished by what one
scholar has labeled the profound "genealogical mentality" of late medieval
Spain, which emerged within a specific context of confessional and social
conflict that "elevated genealogy to a primary form of communal memory"
for Christians as well as Jews.[7]

Indecision as to who really was or should be counted as a Jew and fear of
the consequences of this uncertainty for the integrity of the Christian community wound up intensifying the traditional antisemitism early modern
Spaniards inherited from their ancestors. Yet something also remained of
the earlier give-and-take among different religious confessions that had
proved so distinctive a feature of Iberian society during the Middle Ages.
This unusual—and for the majority surely unwanted—legacy from the past
helps explain the lingering expressions of sympathy, and on a few occasions
even admiration, for the Jews. Such assertions came few and far between, to
be sure. Still, there are enough traces in the historical record to serve as a bit
of counterweight to the suffocating antisemitism of the Catholic majority.

As one would expect, most expressions of what might be called philosemitism originated with conversos, and converso intellectuals in particular.

Perhaps the best-known exemplar of this current was the humanist Benito
Arias Montano. Arias was a distinguished scholar whose deep biblicism led
him to undertake a remarkable—and strongly sympathetic—ethnographic
reconstruction of Old Testament Judaism as part of his preparation of the
1571 Antwerp Polyglot edition of the Bible. Other antiquarians went beyond
his indirect approach and alluded not just to the Jewish past but also to the
coexistence of different faiths. The cleric Luis Hurtado de Toledo explicitly evoked medieval toleration in his 1576 description of Toledo when he
explained the etymology of the Bisagra Gate as being named for the *Via
Sacra,* thanks to its link with "the three foundations of the three laws that
were tolerated in Toledo, of Jews, Muslims, and Christians."[8] Both Arias
Montano and Hurtado de Toledo hailed, to be sure, from converso families.
But a similar interest in Jews, along with the odd manifestation of respect
for Judaism, can be detected in Old Christian circles as well. It accounts
for the impressive presence of Judaica in, to cite one instance, the library
of the great sixteenth-century bibliophile Diego Hurtado de Mendoza. It
also helps explain the occasional expressions of sympathy for Jews as fellow human beings found in Inquisitorial denunciations. Important veins
of "popular toleration" occasionally find expression in early modern trial
records. Depositions from rural Soria in the 1480s show not only frequent
interaction among Jews, Old Christians, and conversos in daily settings
of work and neighborly relations. They also depict average people—one
Gil Recio of the village of Agusejo, for example—posing questions such as
"who knows which of the three laws is the one God likes the most?" They
moreover find the same persons asking (as did Blasco Rodrigues, a public
scribe in Soria), "Why do you think there is much difference between our
law and theirs [Jewish law]?" and answering, "It's only that we [Catholics]
confess to a man and the Jews [pray] to a wall."[9]

Fascination with the forbidden, a certain independence of thought, even
grudging sympathy—these were merely a few of the attitudes that mixed
with set codes of condescension to generate what was in many respects the
oddest, and the most ambiguous, expression of Christian interest in Judaism:
what could for lack of a better term be called "Jewish humor." Early modern
Spanish literature was full of often subtle, and on occasion obsessive, references to Jews and conversos. Most of these were intended to be funny, and
elements of play were often involved. This was the case of the court jester

Francesillo de Zúñiga, who laced his self-styled "burlesque chronicle" with references to his own converso background and that—not always so cheerfully acknowledged—of others. Similar Jewish jokes, so to speak, were associated in particular with the picaresque novel, a genre light and humorous on the surface, but which could also house deeper meanings when it chose. Such references were typical of the very first exemplar of this tradition, the anonymous *Lazarillo de Tormes* of 1554, whose opening page is literally riddled with sly reminders of the protagonist's converso father (along with not so sly mention of his morisco stepfather). The shaky ethnic origins of the protagonist became a stock feature of the genre and figured especially prominently in, say, Mateo Alemán's *Guzmán de Alfarache* (1599–1604) or *La pícara Justina* (1605) of unknown authorship. And lest one suppose that this feature was somehow the invention of converso writers themselves, it should be kept in mind that the most blatant between-the-lines references to New Christians appear in the 1626 novel *El buscón* by the Old Christian (and hardened antisemite) Quevedo.

One senses that most such mentions partook of a pattern of verbal play that formed a standard part of early modern Spanish humor, and one that challenged readers to recognize a sort of authorial inventiveness in insult and innuendo. An invitation such as that of Alonso Núñez de Reinoso (another writer of converso origin) to divine his hidden meanings—"beneath [my] wittiness there are great secrets"—probably had more of a joking than a serious quality to it.[10] Still, it is striking how references to conversos were laden with irony. That a deliberate ambiguity enveloped many of these efforts at humor gives one the same reason to pause as the marquise of Villars' remark that while some Jews were being burned alive at the notorious Madrid auto da fé of 1680, "others are employed in finance, well-considered and respected and are nevertheless recognized as being from Jewish families."[11] If it is hard to know what to make of such contradictions, it is harder still to decipher the deeper message underlying codes of laughter lurking in places where one is frankly surprised to find it.

CHAPTER 13

REJECTION
AND ASSIMILATION
A POROUS PURITY

B Y FAR THE most infamous manifestation of the racial definition of
Jews was *limpieza de sangre,* or blood purity. Early modern Iberia
begat a unique legal and biological construct based on the supposi-
tion that religious difference "infected" the blood of the persons carrying
it. As a result, a propensity to heterodoxy could be inherited from one
generation to another. The royal confessor and Inquisitor General Antonio
de Sotomayor put it succinctly in a 1632 memorandum: "This nation [the
Jews] have this fault [heresy] so deeply buried in their entrails that some
people say that it is a real infection and disease of their blood and that it is
found in everyone touched by this blood, [and] that it is in a certain way
for them what original sin is for everyone else."[1] The inclusion of the cau-
tionary "some people say" suggests that there was room for disagreement
over aspects of this theory. Indeed, the distinction between pure and impure
blood was engulfed in controversy from the very beginning. Opposition to
this belief ran from start to finish of the early modern era and was often
expressed publicly. Far from being an unquestioned foundation of Spanish
culture, limpieza brought into the open unresolved tensions in theology
and scientific thought. Above all, it served as a means less of blocking the

absorption of conversos into Old Christian society than of functioning as a yardstick of measuring different levels of and paths to assimilation.

Before documenting these assertions, a word should be said about the problem of researching and analyzing blood purity. Despite the interest of this theme, relatively little work has been done on the question of limpieza. This can be attributed in part to an obvious epistemological difficulty: how to reconstruct a social process—in this case a combination of religious and racial assimilation—that by its very nature does its best not to leave any traces. In practical terms, limpieza worked by requiring candidates for certain privileges or offices to prove their "pure blood" by providing elaborate *ejecutorias*. These texts reconstructed family genealogies by supplying answers to a lengthy questionnaire concerning three or so generations of both consanguineal and affinal kinsmen. Such affidavits were assembled by delegates appointed by the institutions involved, whose expenses were paid by the candidates. The delegates often traveled considerable distances—or arranged for local representatives to carry out their duties—in search of information in the places where the candidate's families had resided. Their investigations relied more than anything else on collective memory and on the assumption that people would continue to remember the converso roots of individual families. Departing from normal practice in contemporary law courts, limpieza inquiries specifically accepted, and even privileged, the testimony of women as the persons most familiar with local gossip. They also encouraged testimony from the clergy, whose indirect knowledge of family secrets derived from the confessional. In the end, most of the surviving documentation involves successful candidates. The cases in which limpieza failed to be demonstrated left behind scant traces amid the mountains of paper produced.

It is not hard to see why historians have until recently been content to study the theory of blood purity, while leaving unattended the question of its real incidence in society. Another matter is the strong ideological valence of this strand of racialist thought. As is true of many of the more controversial aspects of early modern Spanish history—particularly those having to do with the Inquisition and its vision of religious orthodoxy—a spider's web of myth has been spun around the doctrine of limpieza. Finding one's way amid this confusion means not only separating theory from practice. It also obliges the historian to pay special attention to signs of dissonance instead of assuming the existence of a massive social consensus in favor of what sometimes turned out to be a disruptive public policy.

One of the principal qualifications to keep in mind is that the practice of blood purity was far from universal. Only certain institutions demanded demonstration of pure blood as a condition for membership. A rapid overview of the venues involved includes the following:

- Municipal governments. This is, of course, where blood purity first appeared, in the form of Toledo's Sentence-Statute of 1449. (This law did not stick, by the way. After its initial ratification by the monarchy, it soon lapsed and was not reinstated until 1566.) A number of city governments either drafted purity laws or solicited them from the crown. Just as important, however, were those which refused to do so. Such was the case, for example, of Granada. The preeminence there of both morisco and converso aldermen led the city to vote against a 1570 proposal in the Cortes to require "clean blood" of all such officials. Sixteenth-century protests by Old Christians who resented the presence of New Christians in municipal office differed little from the complaints that led Toledans to follow Pero Sarmiento in his protest in 1449. If anything they were more bitter, as well as more numerous. For sheer antisemitic invective, few earlier texts could compare with the so-called Laín Calvo-Nuño Rasura satire of 1570. This diatribe against what its anonymous author portrayed as a converso monopoly over the government of Burgos provides the clearest proof of the inability or unwillingness of local and royal authorities to make blood-purity standards a binding condition for holding civic office.

- Religious orders. The other major battleground of proponents and critics of limpieza in the second half of the fifteenth century was the regular clergy. Particularly affected were the Hieronymites, the most prominent native Spanish order, founded in 1373. Their widely acknowledged willingness to accept conversos left them especially vulnerable during their conflicts with rival orders. The Inquisition undertook violent campaigns in the 1480s against two of their leading monasteries, Guadalupe in Extremadura and La Sisla near Toledo, and executed well-known members of both houses. In 1493 the shaken survivors tried to repair the damage to the order's reputation by passing a law stipulating blood purity, the first such statute to be applied to a religious order in Spain. (The prohibition originally applied only to descendants of Jews, but in 1552 it was extended to include those of Muslims as well.) Virtually all the established religious orders were much slower to mandate limpieza. In fact, the more innovative foundations of the Counter-Reformation openly opposed blood-purity regulations. This was true above all of the Jesuits, whose founder Ignatius of Loyola publicly derided the concept, and whose early leaders included several notorious conversos, such as Diego Laínez, the company's second general. However, in the end the Jesuits bowed to reality, and beginning in 1593 they required pure blood for admission to the order in Spain. Much the same could be said of the Discalced Carmelites. Despite the fact that the founder of the female branch was the granddaughter of a Jewish merchant penanced by the Inquisition of Toledo in 1485, in 1597 Teresa of Avila's followers also wound up moving over to the other side.

• *Colegios mayores.* University colleges turned out to be one of the main bastions of blood-purity regulations. Since the more prominent among them saw their function as training future elites for state office, they devoted much time and effort to selecting candidates for the limited fellowships available. Applications included investigation of *vita et moribus*—literally the "life and habits"—of aspirants, and impurity did not take long to become formal grounds for disqualification. In fact, the first institution in Spain to decree a statute of exclusion on religious-racial grounds was the Colegio Mayor de San Bartolomé in Salamanca, around 1482. It was quickly followed in 1488 by the best-known Spanish college outside Spain, the Colegio de San Clemente, attached to the University of Bologna. There the original call for limpieza avowed that it was needed to end the conflicts between Old and New Christians that had led to the expulsion of some of the latter. However, conversos continued to enter this prestigious institution, and in 1492 the students even elected a converso rector, who was murdered the following year! Other colegios mayores followed suit, including the main colleges of the universities of Valladolid (Santa Cruz, in 1488) and Alcalá (San Ildefonso, 1519). But one must also remember that the failure of virtually all the lesser colleges to adopt blood-purity statutes meant that even in formal terms, university education in Spain was open in many cities to New Christian students wishing to follow this especially lucrative path to upward social mobility.

• Cathedral chapters. In the end, only a minority of Spanish cathedral chapters screened candidates for prebends and benefices for limpieza. And even among those which did, the statutes were not always enforced. Hence the numerous complaints throughout the sixteenth century regarding the many conversos who held canonries in, for instance, Seville. The cathedral of Badajoz appears to have been the first to insist on pure blood, in 1511. But by far the most famous case was that of Toledo. In 1546 Juan Martínez Silíceo was named archbishop of Toledo, one of the largest and wealthiest sees in Christendom. Silíceo was from Old Christian peasant background, and having tenaciously climbed to the top, he now planned to make the most of it. He wrote his former pupil, Prince Philip, and others to inform them of the scandalous state of the Church in Toledo. "Not only the majority but nearly all the parish priests of his Archdiocese with a care of souls . . . are descendants of Jews," he claimed and affirmed that the same could be said for many clerics holding higher offices in his see.[2] He thus pushed through a statute mandating limpieza in the cathedral chapter. This met with substantial opposition from the canons, Old Christian as well as New, who did not care for anyone tampering with their privileges. Philip was scarcely more enthusiastic, and a year later he suspended the measure. Silíceo won in the end, however, and Philip reluctantly ratified his law in 1556. Only a handful of other cathedrals followed Toledo's example, and by the end of the sixteenth century limpieza was an established principle, if not practice, in fewer than a dozen chapters.

• Military orders. The greatest resistance to the entry of descendants of Jews could be found among the various military orders of the peninsula. The habits and *encomiendas,* or perpetual grants of income, they awarded were perhaps the single most sought-after source of wealth and status in early modern Iberia. However, even here the strict application of limpieza rules was rather uneven, at least at the beginning. The orders of Alcántara and Calatrava were the first to dictate blood purity, both in 1483. The others eventually followed the precedent they set, and by 1555 the last holdout—oddly enough, the most prestigious order, that of Santiago—finally joined the rest.

• Confraternities and guilds. Only a small number of lay brotherhoods and guilds put into effect blood-purity statutes. Those which did tended to have more elite members. This was true of the lay confraternities in, say, the city of Zamora. There limpieza was required in noble and clerical brotherhoods, but not in the far more numerous popular ones. And even when elite corporations did adopt blood-purity restrictions, the concern about the presence of conversos often seems rather nominal. Such appears to have been the case of Madrid's College of Lawyers. Its imposition of a limpieza statute at the late date of 1684 suggests that it took the period's pronounced downturn in litigation to bring such a measure to the fore.

• Private corporations. A number of micro-corporations regulated by civil law also stipulated conditions of limpieza. This applied especially to entails, which by the seventeenth century systematically prevented New Christians from inheriting family property. Hence, a clause from an eighteenth-century Valencian testament listed among the sorts of persons excluded from future benefits anyone of "whichever bad race, a Jew, Moor, or converso, or any other sect."[3]

- Emigration. Limpieza was a prerequisite for eligibility for the most innovative form of geographic mobility in early modern Spain, passage to the Indies. After some initial back and forth, in 1522 Charles V forbade emigration to the New World by "anyone recently converted to our Catholic faith, either Moor or Jew, or his children," unless he had express license from the king. The dubious efficacy of administrative oversight, combined with the relatively late creation of Inquisitorial courts in the New World—the first, in Lima, was founded in 1570—pretty much rendered this law a dead letter. As the secretary of the Holy Office in Arequipa wrote the Suprema in 1570, "I assure Your Worship that in regard to the few Spaniards who reside in this land there are twice as many conversos here as there are in Spain."[4]

- Last but hardly least, the Inquisition. Ironically, the Holy Office was one of the slowest institutions formally to require limpieza of its members. Its statute dated to 1572.

In short, only certain types of groups adopted official rules to exclude participation by converts and their descendants. As a result, many of the basic forms of social organization in early modern Iberia were not subject to restrictions on family background. Much the same can be said of the geographic distribution of limpieza laws. Although a full comparative registry of legislation has yet to be assembled, it is clear that blood purity was far more of an issue in Castile than in the crown of Aragon. While various factors help explain the relative disinterest in limpieza outside Castile, doubtless the most important was the existence of different mechanisms for demonstrating membership in the nobility. In the crown of Aragon nobles were defined by convocation by the Noble Estate in parliament. Such bodies kept lists of members and duly registered new privileges of nobility. This degree of formality contrasted with the much more fluid situation in Castile, where nobility rested fundamentally on public reputation. This much more hazy—and flexible—criterion encouraged recourse to subsidiary checks on social mobility, such as limpieza. Moreover, blood purity was more closely identified with institutions which traditionally played a far greater role in Castile than elsewhere. This was especially true of the military orders, which flourished throughout the Monarchy, yet were far more privileged and well endowed in Castile.

There was another factor at work here: that of the influence of a diffuse but very real public opinion. It may well be that public discourse touching on limpieza was less favorable to it in the crown of Aragon. In any event, there seems to have been far less discussion of blood purity there as opposed to Castile, which reflects its far lesser incidence in local society. Serious efforts to implement limpieza generated discussion and even criticism. Indeed, as one historian has put it, the most "extensive premodern discussion about the relationship between biology and culture" emerged during the ongoing controversy over limpieza and converso exclusion in Spain from 1449 to 1550.[5] Nothing could be further from the truth than the cliché of early modern Iberian society united in a firm consensus favoring racialist exclusion.

Criticism of both the concept and practice of limpieza was widespread and forthright. Among the numerous objections raised, two were repeatedly stressed. The first involved theology. Many saw blood purity as contravening standard doctrines regarding the efficacy of baptism and the desirability of welcoming converts to the Church. It moreover meant tying the chances of salvation of individuals to the identity of their ancestors. It was in this vein that Francisco Ortiz, a Franciscan friar tried by the Inquisition in the 1530s, ridiculed the Holy Office's interest in his converso background by affirming that "in the hour of my death . . . only what I have done will matter; who my grandparents were will neither condemn nor save me."[6] This emphasis on theological principle found many defenders, particularly within the clergy. It was articulated early on, for example, in the manuscript treatise *Light for the Knowledge of Gentiles* (1464) the Hieronymite friar Alonso de Oropesa wrote in response to Pero Sarmiento's 1449 racialist Sentence-Statute in Toledo. Criticism along the same lines was later voiced by the Sevillian preacher Domingo de Valtanás, who wrote a tract against limpieza in 1557, and his fellow Andalusian Diego Pérez de Valdivia, one of the leading preachers of his time. Indeed, there was so much negative comment on the blood-purity laws that in 1572 the Inquisition ordered an end to all public debate of the matter.

This prohibition failed to stick, but it may have contributed to shifting the grounds of discussion in a more pragmatic direction. In the end most of the criticism focused on practical matters, especially the frequent contravention of the law through bribery, forgeries, and the like. This was the tactic adopted by the Dominican Agustín de Salucio, who, after preaching a sermon at court against limpieza, managed to print his text around 1600. Salucio was careful to focus on questions of legal procedure and limited his attacks to the way the statutes encouraged recourse to false documentation and perjured testimony. What is perhaps most striking is the sympathetic response Salucio received from powerful figures at court, such as the royal favorite Lerma. Even some of the members of the Council of the Inquisition conceded that the blood-purity statutes needed reform. It hardly comes as a surprise to find Miguel de Cervantes shortly thereafter overtly satirizing blood purity in his comic play "The Spectacle of Marvels" (published in 1615). In this Iberian variant of the folktale of the Emperor's New Clothes, a pair of tricksters fools the inhabitants of a village into admitting that they saw figures which would appear invisible to descendants of conversos or persons of illegitimate birth. It would be hard to imagine a more eloquent comment on the contemporary obsession with limpieza than this sharp but hardly unique exercise in the sort of "Jewish humor" alluded to above.

Clearly the time was ripe for some sort of reform, particularly since the reign of Philip III opened with a considerable relaxation of the atmosphere of religious war that had prevailed while his father reigned. The new king signed a truce with Protestant heretics—the English—in 1604, and in the same year he approved (in exchange for a substantial loan) a pardon for conversos who faced prosecution by the Portuguese Inquisition. Still, it was not until the end of his reign and the early years under his successor Philip IV that concrete proposals began to circulate and, what is more, were acted upon. Two of these reform projects were of unusual interest. The first was a lengthy memorandum written in 1619 by Martín González de Cellorigo. The author—an Old Christian and administrative official of the Holy Office—urged easing up on Inquisitorial prosecution of Portuguese conversos. He went on to criticize the blood-purity laws for failing to distinguish between sincere Christians and judaizers among the conversos and suggested in true *raison d'état* fashion that rigorous enforcement of such statutes led to more judaizing rather than less—an argument that would be taken up later by Spinoza. The other text went a step further. In a book published in 1622—that is, immediately after Philip IV's accession to the throne—the Portuguese merchant Duarte Gómez Solís not only advocated putting an end to the Inquisition's vigilance of the New Christians. He also unfolded a full-scale mercantilist program which proposed taking advantage of the Portuguese conversos' experience in overseas trade to solve the many problems facing the Monarchy, especially the crisis in state finance. Relaxation of blood-purity rules figured as one among the many measures favoring the New Christians in return for their collaboration and investment in this reform project.

The mercantilist cast of this and other proposals fit in well with the program for economic and political regeneration devised by the new favorite, the count-duke of Olivares. In 1623 the junta he convened for drafting reform legislation propounded important changes in limpieza procedures. These included lowering the level of proofs required for demonstrating blood purity and prohibiting relying on rumor as a disqualification. Olivares also ordered all *libros verdes*—anonymous manuscripts of genealogical information which documented past intermarriage between prominent aristocrats and converso families—collected and burned as libels. At no point was the all-powerful minister able to contemplate eliminating pure-blood legislation altogether, even if during his regime the idea was broached by Inquisitor-General Andrés Pacheco, who argued that the full assimilation of conversos showed that such laws were no longer needed. And while Olivares was able to protect many of the Portuguese converso financiers in Madrid, he was not able to prevent his enemies from mobilizing public opinion against his policy of leniency. After his fall in 1643 the Inquisition renewed its pressure on the conversos. A series of trials during the 1650s and 1660s in particular effectively put an end to the once-powerful "Portuguese lobby." The sensitive nature of this issue meant that blood-purity legislation lingered on vestigially until the end of the Old Regime. Long after all prosecutions of judaizing had ceased, limpieza was still demanded for a wide range of honors and offices. Thus when the enlightened cleric Juan Antonio Llorente was appointed as a commissary of the Inquisition in 1785, he had to prove his limpieza. He not only commented in his autobiography on the absurdity of this stipulation. He also calculated that demonstrating that he had not descended from Jews, Moors, or heretics over ten generations would involve investigating some 4,095 direct ancestors. What is more, "if the name of someone of [Jewish or Muslim affiliation] appears in the records of the Holy Office," he remarked, "there is no way to prove that that I do *not* descend from that person."[7] By this point it was more than obvious that blood purity had become a mere formality. However, it was a formality that no one dared abolish. Indeed, it was still required of candidates to the Spanish officer corps as late as the 1860s.

In the end, what were the consequences of these racial laws? Judging from the case of the city where it started, limpieza left less of a mark than was once thought. Toledo is an excellent place to assess the impact of such laws, for two reasons. First, enough conflict took place to force the adoption of blood-purity restrictions on several occasions, beginning with the Sentence-Statute of 1449 (reimposed in the 1560s) and followed by Archbishop Silíceo's famous 1547 mandate for the cathedral chapter. Second, Toledo had a large and, what is more, well-documented population of Jews and converts. By 1486—the year of a massive punishment of judaizers, which produced a detailed registry of local conversos—New Christians comprised some 15 to 20 percent of the city's population and were unusually well represented among artisans, notaries, and merchants. Recent studies have demonstrated the presence among officeholders in the mid-sixteenth century of descendants of the conversos penanced by the Inquisition. Moreover, by that point the upward mobility of these New Christians had been facilitated by substantial marriage outside converso families, which furthered their absorption into Old Christian society. The better-off grandchildren and other descendants of those penanced in 1486 had found it relatively easy to enter into the local oligarchy, thanks above all to the crown's sale of aldermanships and other municipal offices. In this case, one must conclude that while pure-blood statutes, like Inquisitorial action, expressed "constant hostility directed against the new converts from Judaism," neither of them "succeeded in permanently removing conversos from their posts."[8]

Most historians today no longer accept earlier interpretations that saw limpieza rules as condemning conversos to membership in a separate caste living on the margins of society. For one thing, it is simply too easy to document the presence of New Christians in every single institution that blood-purity legislation was designed to keep them out of. In fact, the inquisitors themselves constantly complained about the ease with which conversos obtained certificates of limpieza. Thanks to such lenience, ran the lament, they wind up holding "honorable offices, traveling to the Indies and becoming priests and friars."[9] All the same, one should not go to the other extreme and say that these laws had no effect. In the end limpieza worked as a check—the efficacy of which depended on circumstances and the specific parties involved—on the aspirations of a social category that in normal circumstances could have reasonably expected to enjoy a fair degree of upward mobility. The onerous requirements of pure blood merely added to the risk involved in social promotion. The extra wedge of unpredictability it introduced surely led many families to decline to press their advantages out of fear of the exposure that failure would bring. In this sense limpieza contributed to a net loss in dynamism in early modern society. It also imposed a heavy economic cost in terms of misspent scarce resources, in addition to an incalculable human cost in terms of the suffering it caused, especially on those occasions when survival itself was at stake.

The racialist thought behind limpieza de sangre was not unique to Spain. It was found throughout early modern Europe, in different forms and applied to diverse social and ethnic groups. What was unique to Spain was the visibility and intensity of this particular form of discrimination. That, and the way it in the end wound up focused on the Jews. For perhaps the oddest paradox of limpieza was the way in which the descendants of Muslims, while formally included in blood-purity legislation, were nevertheless often informally spared its application. This was not just because the statutes were written with conversos, not moriscos, in mind. It was also because early modern Spaniards thought of Muslims in ways fundamentally different from the way they construed the category of Jewishness. This was seen above all in the curious case of the remnants of Moorish nobility which remained in Granada following the conquest of 1492. In recognition of their potential usefulness in Christianizing the morisco masses, families such as the Granada Venegas or the Núñez Muley received substantial privileges and benefits. These marks of distinction not only included important tax exemptions and the right to sit on the city council. They also meant that they and their descendants would not be affected by standard restrictions regarding blood purity.

No such exceptions were made for the Judeo-conversos. For in the end the impure blood that Spanish Christians feared contact with was Jewish. The moriscos lived too much on their own and posed little real threat of contamination. The same could not be said of the conversos, however. They lived in the very midst of Christian society, and thanks to their baptism they could now aspire to achieve positions of power and influence over the lives of others. Limpieza de sangre thus functioned as a sort of populist recourse, a means of conferring a lesser yet universal nobility on all Old Christians. (A committee of the Cortes or parliament of Castile put it succinctly when it noted in 1600 that there were two types of nobility in Spain, "a greater, which is that of *hidalguía* [gentility], and a lesser, which is that of limpieza, whose members we call Old Christians.")[10] Hostile contemporaries perceived its effects as "preferring to learned and wise men rude peasants, clumsy villagers and ignorant shepherds."[11] That it for the most part failed in this aim was perhaps the best testimony to the effective assimilation of the conversos.

CHAPTER 14

JUDAIZING AND THE IMPOSSIBILITY OF ORTHODOXY

I T IS TIME now to turn to those conversos who consciously rejected the path of assimilation and who opted instead for some degree of allegiance to their ancestral creed. The real extent of what the Inquisition referred to as judaizing is the single most controversial issue in the ample and growing historiography of early modern Spanish Judaism. It is obvious that the exact numbers of these crypto-Jews, or even more generally the proportion they constituted within the overall body of conversos, will never be known. (This is not unusual in early modern history; who, for example, can say with certainty how many Englishmen and women practiced Catholicism under Elizabeth I?) Still, educated guesses can be made about many aspects of their history—and few would doubt that it is an interesting history indeed.

The difficulties of charting the contours of a secret religion are compounded by the sheer impossibility of knowing which inner convictions lay behind or beyond outer practice. This is especially true of individuals whose very intention was to dissemble, to simulate one set of beliefs in order better to serve another. Rather than spin wheels endlessly about matters that by their very nature cannot be known, it would be more useful to approach religious experience as a spectrum that ordered a wide range of possibilities. At one end one finds crypto-Judaism or even open adherence to Judaism of the sort that characterized the (admittedly miniscule) body of martyrs who refused to disguise their loyalty to the faith of their fathers. At the other extreme stood full and willing adherence to Catholicism, including a normative antisemitism. In between loomed numerous niches or positions for spiritual self-fashioning. Two qualifications need to be made concerning the factors which influenced location on this spectrum. First, fundamental choice was almost always made by individuals and their families. There were, to be sure, instances in which judaizers met and even worshiped together in larger communities. But in the long run, circumstances forced crypto-Judaism, and indeed any significant deviation from Catholic ortho-doxy, to reduce its scale of organization. To do otherwise inevitably meant detection. Second, high levels of instability often marked one's position on the spectrum. Not only could individuals shift from one stance to another (and back) during their lifetimes. The general tendency to judaize was also subject to important shifts, above all as a consequence of the mass migration of Portuguese conversos to Castile beginning in the mid-sixteenth century. The much higher proportion of judaizers among the Portuguese meant a sudden injection of crypto-Judaism, which now began to thrive in places where it had been dying out.

What can be said with a fair degree of assurance is that even if most conversos the Inquisition tried in its initial stage were judaizers—and this is a reasonable if unprovable assumption—crypto-Jews seem quickly to have become a minority by the end of this phase. A plausible reconstruc-tion of the long-term evolution of secret Judaism would place its high point during the first Inquisitorial generation of the 1480s. The visible slowdown in persecution beginning in the 1520s inaugurated a period of presumably steady decline which lasted until the arrival of Portuguese judaizers in the later sixteenth century. In the early seventeenth century the hitherto positive correlation between Inquisitorial activity and the extent of crypto-Judaism began to break down. Under Philip III and during the first half of the reign of Philip IV there were relatively few trials of judaizers, and this despite some evident signs of clandestine observance. The renewed persecution of the 1640s through the 1660s put an end to large-scale judaizing among the

Portuguese. By the time of the final mass trials of the 1720s, judaizing was on its last legs, at least in the major urban centers. Elsewhere it remained a vestigial activity at best.

In retrospect it thus appears that the circumstance that most affected the ups and downs of crypto-Judaism in early modern Spain was the influx of Portuguese conversos that began roughly a century after the Inquisition commenced operations. Three factors in particular accounted for the development of an especially resilient crypto-Judaism in Portugal. As noted above, most of the conversos in Portugal were descendants of Jews who were expelled from Spain in 1492—that is, persons who demonstrated a singularly strong commitment to Judaism by choosing exile over conversion. The mass baptisms of 1497 that turned them into New Christians were moreover the product of a much higher level of coercion; this time the Jews simply were not given a choice. To make this more palatable the Portuguese monarchy was willing to delay the introduction of an Inquisition on the Spanish model. The fact that such a tribunal was not created definitively until 1536—the second contributing factor—gave the Portuguese conversos enough breathing room to organize their modus operandi and networks of crypto-Jewish observance. Finally, the Portuguese New Christians, while well represented in the larger cities, also tended to live in small and often remote settlements. Many of these were clustered close to the Spanish border, especially in the northern half of the kingdom. That—and the fact that Portugal had a smaller urban population than Spain's—meant greater opportunities for seclusion and thus distance from watchful Old Christians. This different pattern of distribution in terms of both time and space permitted a much more deeply rooted adherence to Judaism and gave rise to a greater willingness to take risks to observe the faith. The upswing was that while at first Spanish Old Christians proved ready and willing to believe that most conversos were secret Jews—the priest-chronicler Andrés Bernáldez wrote that they awaited liberation like the ancient Hebrews in Pharaoh's Egypt—by the end of the sixteenth century this suspicion had changed direction and now attached itself to the Portuguese immigrants. That judaizing was increasingly seen as a crime committed by foreigners fit snugly into the overall patterns of Inquisitorial prosecution, which associated the threat of heresy with outsiders and disciplined native Old Christians almost exclusively for minor offenses such as blasphemy and superstition.

As for the contents of early modern Iberian crypto-Judaism, the most valuable information is found in the voluminous documentation of the Inquisition. Obviously such sources must be used with caution. Several of the normal procedures of the Holy Office worked to undermine confidence in the literal truth of many of the accusations it leveled against those it charged with heresy. First, its strict code of secrecy made it uniquely vulnerable to false testimony on the part of hostile witnesses. The Inquisition itself was acutely aware of this problem. It did its best to obtain testimony from as broad a range of sources possible and even proved willing to exclude patently hostile testimony on grounds of bias. Second, many prisoners confessed all too readily to the lists of Jewish practices assembled from the depositions. The reason for this was simple: it was standard practice for the Inquisition to show lenience for first-time offenses. If a prisoner readily confessed and showed signs of repentance, he or she could expect to receive a light sentence. Punishment usually included, along with the confiscation of property, an act of public penance, the obligation to wear the penitential garment known as the *sambenito,* and perhaps a short period of imprisonment or exile from one's place of residence. It was a rare judaizer indeed who did not accept such terms, especially as the tribunal read stubborn defense of one's innocence as a refusal to cooperate. Recidivism was a different matter. The court understood being caught committing the same offense twice as a mockery of its authority, as well as a refusal of the pardon offered the first time. Even genuinely penitent *relapsos* could expect to receive the death penalty, and many did. Thus if during the first encounter with the Holy Office the suspect was all too willing to confess, in the second round he or she proved much more reluctant to do so. Confessions of guilt at this stage often required the use of torture—in itself not the most reliable means of establishing the truth. The net effect was to render problematic confessions obtained in all stages of the judicial process.

Still, there is reason to believe that the doubt such procedures raise applies more to the guilt of the specific individuals involved than to the content of the crimes under consideration. Some scholars have read the stereotyped, repetitive nature of testimony against conversos as evidence of their fabrication by the court trying them. But it is just as easy to believe the opposite: that these charges reflect a sort of basic minimum of crypto-Judaism, a central core of practices by which the judaizer could demonstrate adherence to the

Law of Moses. Favoring the latter interpretation is the fact that the same practices show up not only in the testimony of judaizers who took advantage of the Edicts of Grace, or semi-amnesties that the Inquisition occasionally offered to those willing to confess their faults. They also were present in the depositions of the *espontáneos*. These were those individuals who, lacking the benefit of the Edict, nevertheless appeared before the inquisitors of their own volition—or more likely at the behest of their confessors—to be penanced. The congruence between the conduct all these judaizers admitted to and that allegedly found among their less cooperative peers is simply too close to lead one to accept that their crimes had been entirely invented by the judges.

That said, one wonders how judaizing conversos actually learned about Judaism. Of course, in the early years they could rely on their own personal experience as Jews. And at least during the first or second generations, they could turn to older family members for advice and knowledge. Still, after a certain point they were left to their own devices. Lacking rabbis and the liturgy of the synagogue, deprived of access to the sacred texts and to education in Hebrew that would make them intelligible, and no longer able to rely on communal institutions and services such as the ritual slaughtering of animals for food, the conversos were cut adrift from virtually all aspects of the normative Judaism of their ancestors. Even the apparently simple matter of calculating the dates of the holidays posed an enormous challenge. Within this vacuum of religious knowledge they had to shift for themselves and come up with their own solutions to the daunting challenges at hand.

Here the interrogations of the Holy Office provide some interesting clues. The inquisitors understood their most pressing task to be a social one: to reconstruct the complete circle of heretics, that is, the network of shared identity and mutual support that made secret observance possible. Yet they were also eager to single out those judaizers whose greater or more exact knowledge allowed them to instruct others in the mysteries of the faith. These religious specialists—referred to in administrative jargon as "dogmatizers"—merited the tribunal's undivided attention, as did the question of exactly how and from whom they obtained their experience and information.

What the judges found was a mixture of traditional lore handed down in family circles, along with some patchwork reconstruction of Judaic tenets and ritual cobbled together from a wide range of often unpredictable sources. In terms of the latter, scholars and even university-trained professionals had numerous texts in Latin from which to piece together their knowledge of Judaism. Thus the Castilian crypto-Jew Luis de Carvajal, whom the Mexican Inquisition executed in 1596, wound up memorizing Maimonides' Thirteen Principles—the leading statement of Jewish doctrine from the Middle Ages—after locating it in a biblical commentary in the library of a local monastery. But even less well-educated commoners were able to amass an impressive amount of information about Jewish beliefs and practices from vernacular sources. The principal fount of knowledge was, of course, the Christian Old Testament. And while Catholics were not allowed directly to read the Bible in Spanish during this period, enough of it was available in translation in books of hours, devotional tracts, and religious poetry (such as the works of Luis de León) to furnish them a broad understanding of ancient Judaism as it was depicted in both testaments.

Despite the undoubted centrality of the Bible in the task of constructing Judaism anew, other texts made important contributions to this task. Among works from the classical period, the most frequently read by far were the histories of Flavius Josephus. Both his moving chronicle of the revolt against the Romans that led to the definitive destruction of the Temple and his detailed examination of the "antiquities" and customs of the Jewish people found numerous readers during the early modern era. Patristic literature also had much to say about (and against) Judaism, as did contemporary devotional guides. For example, Luis de Granada's best-selling *Símbolo de la Fe* (*Symbol of Faith*, 1583) contained numerous lengthy citations from and commentaries on the Old Testament. Works whose aim was to shore up the Christianity of conversos often wound up backfiring. The converso physician Isaac Cardoso, who in 1648 abandoned a prominent practice in Madrid to take up a new life as a publicly practicing Jew in Venice, acknowledged that one of his early means of instruction in Judaism had been João Baptista d'Este's 1621 dialogue designed to convert marranos. In fact, even harsher polemics could wind up providing some of the best information on Judaic beliefs. This was certainly the case of Alonso de Espina's fifteenth-century *Fortress of Faith*, a rabid exercise in antisemitism which nevertheless listed in exhaustive detail a lengthy catalog of Jewish "superstitions." In short: if the Jews as the "people of the book" had been deprived of their basic text, some of their converso successors found means of compensating for this loss. Reading against the grain of intention, they gathered a surprising amount of valuable information about a creed that lived on in the writings of its enemies.

Comparing Inquisitorial testimony regarding practices from different periods shows how crypto-Judaism evolved. As one might expect, the first generation of judaizers was able to stay fairly close to traditional practice. Testimony from Guadalupe in 1485 and from Ciudad Real, Toledo, and other areas of New Castile during the first two decades of Inquisitorial activity—that is, both before and after the expulsion of 1492—shows pretty much the same thing. One finds ample evidence of sabbath observance, beginning with lighting of lamps and the cooking of food ahead of time, accompanied by bathing, cleaning the house, changing clothes, and the avoidance of work. Prayer books were used, and even in some instances shawls were worn, although most prayers were said in Spanish. Efforts were made to respect dietary rules, including the proper slaughtering of meat and poultry, abstention from forbidden foods, separation of kosher and nonkosher dishes (although apparently not of meat and milk services), and even the Talmudic custom of *challah* or tossing a small offering of bread into the fire. Most of the major holidays were observed, especially through fasts. Life-cycle feasts touching on birth and marriage seem to have differed little from local Christian behavior, although judaizers were credited with mourning practices that bore some resemblance to traditional *shiva* rites. Obviously, significant changes had taken place. Collective worship in synagogues had been eliminated, use of the Hebrew language had been considerably reduced, and converts had to participate in a wide range of Catholic sacraments. Yet not far beneath this new veneer of Christian practice, many of the rhythms of the daily and festive life of observant Jews continued unabated. With some effort, and depending on the intensity of outside curiosity, this continuity could moreover be effectively disguised.

If one compares this situation with that revealed by a detailed study of converso behavior in seventeenth-century Ciudad Rodrigo, a town in Extremadura which had received numerous immigrants from Portugal in the later sixteenth century, several contrasts with earlier patterns of judaizing appear immediately. Sabbath was still celebrated, so much so, in fact, that almost all accusations of judaizing were related to its observance. Prominent in this regard was the lighting of candles, donning clean clothes, and forsaking labor on Saturdays. However, only three of the main holidays were celebrated: Purim ("the day of St. Esther"), Passover, and Yom Kippur (called the "great day"). Moreover, neither Purim—traditionally a joyous occasion, so much so that it was known as the "Jewish Carnival"—nor Passover was treated as festive. Instead, all three holidays were observed by fasting, especially since the unleavened bread of the latter proved hard to obtain. (The new Purim fast was also lengthened from one to three days—yet another departure from tradition and its emphasis on celebration.) Just as predictably, Rosh Hashanah and Sukkoth—the new-year and harvest festivals which involved noise making and outdoor activities—had proved too indiscreet to survive. Ritual slaughter was also far less frequent and was usually resorted to only in the case of chickens, whose blood could be removed without much fuss. As for life-cycle events, circumcision had disappeared altogether. Neither was there any formal initiation of boys into manhood within the faith. While some mortuary customs remained intact, they too tended to be the ones that attracted the least attention, such as washing the body of the dead and fasting as a sign of mourning. And in terms of prayers, Hebrew was no longer used, with the sole exception of the name *Adonai* to refer to God. In fact, a frequent form of prayer was to recite the Christian version of the Psalms and then deliberately omit the *gloria patri* at the end.

In short, extensive changes had taken place in crypto-Jewish practice during the century and a half since the beginning of Inquisitorial vigilance. First and foremost, the need for secrecy had increased markedly. This in turn further reduced judaizing to its essentials. Many external markers of observance simply disappeared. These included circumcision, women's ritual bathing, ritual slaughtering and dietary laws, traditional dress and paraphernalia (shawls, phylacteries, and the like), and use of the Hebrew language. Holidays were also much transformed. Above all, they lost both their collective and festive nature. Fasts had emerged in the vacuum as the most important type of ritual behavior. While attracting less outside attention, they also helped assure avoidance of prohibited foods that formed part of the daily diet of Christians. Yet another reason for the way fasting replaced feasting was its penitential character. Most judaizers seem to have adopted a pragmatic attitude toward the need to assume the outward guise of Christianity. As one converso was overheard remarking to another during a dinner conversation, going to mass or taking communion mattered little, if one did it "in order to convince others."[1] Others, however, felt deeper sorrow over complying with the precepts of the persecutors. Luis de Carvajal, for example, explicitly confessed that he undertook his frequent penances and fasts as mortification for his outward conformity to Catholicism. As this and other cases suggest, much of the preference for fasting derived not just from its tactical advantages. It also served to express contrition for the inevitable but still lamentable deceits required by living as Christians.

A second condition forcing change was the loss of contact with formal Judaism. As noted above, Inquisitorial persecution swept before it synagogues, the rabbinate, formal training in Scripture and the post-biblical rabbinical literature (including the body of commentary known as Talmud), ritual baths and butcher shops—in short, all the institutions and figures of "normal" Jewish life in the Middle Ages. The sudden lack of religious professionals created a situation akin to the Protestant ideal of the "priesthood of all believers." As was the case with the moriscos, the laity stepped in to fill this vacuum. Women in particular took on new roles and responsibilities—so much so, that the inquisitors were soon convinced that they showed greater willingness to judaize than did men, whom they saw as assuming a more passive role while women took the initiative in observing ceremonial and other religious rules. Crucial to this reversal of traditional roles was a shift in the space of religious observance. The elimination of male-dominated institutions such as the synagogue, and the accompanying devaluation of sacred texts and commentaries, led to a new stress on the home as locus of faith. It also brought a novel focus on the sort of ritual behavior open to all as opposed to the book-centered learning that had served as the central foundation of rabbinical authority. The result was what one would label only slightly anachronistically as a radically privatized and personalized religion: a simplified, vernacular, and domestically centered Judaism that identified testimony of religious loyalty with prayers and other modest ritual gestures within the reduced—and hopefully discreet—sphere of the household.

The divorce from the normative structures of rabbinical learning and guidance not only had obvious implications for *halakhah,* or legally appropriate conduct. It also intruded into the sphere of dogma. Judaizers were forced to fend for themselves when making decisions not only about what to believe but also about how to behave. As noted above, the more enterprising (and better educated) among them could find enough sources with which to piece together a fairly coherent picture of their ancestral creed. But informing themselves as to how to determine *normal* Jewish doctrine, that is, doctrine that would pass for such outside the Iberian peninsula, in regard to typical daily-life situations—this was too much to ask. The factor of separation from orthodoxy, plus the weight of generations of Christian education, helped introduce numerous extraneous elements into a tradition that took pride in its capacity for resistance to assimilation. Elements of syncretism ranged from ever more frequent evocations of Catholic notions of sanctity—note the penchant for prayers to "St. Esther"—to the equally curious absorption of Christian (including specifically Protestant) attitudes toward martyrdom. The same could also be said of refraining from eating meat in particular during fasts, which was unrelated to any Jewish restrictions. Finally, some new adaptations appeared without any referents in either Judaic or Catholic tradition. This was apparently true of the converso custom of touching salt to one's lips that some seventeenth-century Inquisitorial documents mentioned. A traditional protection against the evil eye, it lacked any biblical base and came much closer to the shared Jewish-Christian notion of "superstition."

Whether such hybrid adaptations constituted a sort of "marrano religion" —a third way uncomfortably perched between Christian and Jewish orthodoxies—is still a hotly debated question. Some scholars see converso spirituality as a gradual process of simplification. Departing from mainstream foundations, it eventually evolved into a sort of free-form ensemble of vernacular tenets and practices. Others prefer to frame it as a variant of Jewish popular culture, distinctive though far from unique in its distance not only from Christianity but also from the formal, rabbinically based knowledge and practice of Jews elsewhere. One tendency within this latter approach has been to warn against portraying judaizing New Christians as radically isolated from mainstream Judaism. Conversos of Portuguese origin had more possibilities than one might imagine of maintaining contacts with practicing Jews elsewhere, especially following the establishment in the early seventeenth century of a large and influential Portuguese-speaking community in Amsterdam. The far-flung nature of this converso diaspora facilitated frequent travel to and from the Iberian peninsula. Human traffic of this sort allowed familial and other connections between public and secret Jews to prosper. Still, when all is said and done, it is hard to avoid the impression that even among the minority of conversos who were judaizers, those who were able and willing to cling to more than a minimal semblance of their ancestral faith were a privileged remnant indeed. Most of them had little choice but to make do with the spiritual resources at hand—such as they were.

Many contemporaries seem to have been aware of how New Christians loosened from their past theological moorings might evolve in ways unsatisfactory to either Judaism or Christianity. Hence the hoary cliché that conversos were neither Jews nor Christians. Instead, they were seen as forming a hybrid species, caught between two religions and true to neither. A wide range of observers already voiced this line of criticism by the end of the fifteenth century. Thus the prominent historian Hernando del Pulgar wrote that his fellow conversos were persons who "observed neither one law nor the other," halfway Christians and halfway Jews.[2] In a similar vein, Isaac Abravanel—the famed scholar who chose exile in Italy over conversion in 1492—warned his compatriots who stayed behind that they would not fully enter into either religion and would be distrusted by both. Perhaps the most curious articulation of this position was an anonymous satire written in the 1480s, known as the "Book of the *Alboraique.*" Its strange name derives from the reference in the Koran to *al-burakh,* the combination of wolf, horse, man, and other animals on which Muhammad was reported to have ascended to heaven from Jerusalem. The satire's unknown author took pains to distinguish sincere Christians from judaizers among the converts. He then went on to associate the latter with the qualities of this unusual beast: arrogance, greed, malevolence, and above all, insincerity and hypocrisy. In short, the *alboraique,* like the converso, was neither fish nor fowl, and its lack of clear definition made it an object of suspicion and mistrust.

That some Christian observers continued to regard conversos as not just Jews, but more specifically *defective* or incomplete Jews, sheds interesting light on the broader issue of how persecution and secrecy contributed to the evolution—some would call it dilution—of crypto-Judaism. Testimony in a case from the 1580s referred to the inhabitants of the village of Arroyuelos (Extremadura) as

observers of the Law of Moses, but who observe it just as badly as they observe the Law of Christ, for they know neither the rites nor the ceremonies, as there is no Jewish priest [sic]. They live only with the consciousness that they are Jews, and they do no more than declare themselves to be adherents of the Jewish religion and pray to Moses with the prayers of Our Holy Mother, which they direct to him, for they say that he is another God to whose care they commend themselves.[3]

To add insult to injury—and such was surely the purpose—the preacher of the sermon at an auto-da-fé held in Lisbon in 1705 ridiculed the conversos being penanced as being detested not only by Christians but even by Jews, thanks to their ignorance of proper Jewish observance.

Despite their intentions, even convinced, deliberate judaizers often found themselves far from normative Judaism. But was it true that they and conversos as a whole were rejected by Jews elsewhere? Most revealing here is the diversity of opinions *outside* the peninsula regarding the Jewishness of the Spanish converts. There is abundant evidence of their being condemned as spiritual traitors, who preferred the comforts of life to the rigors of witness to the faith through martyrdom. Yet from early on one also finds expressions of sympathy for their plight, along with recognition that "they serve[d] other gods against their will" and thus still merited consideration as members of the Chosen People.[4] Many commentators—rabbis among them—separated *anusim,* or forced converts, from *meshumadim,* or voluntary apostates. The former could turn to weighty authorities to justify their decision to become Christians. These included biblical examples, such as Esther, who kept her Jewish origins hidden until the moment came to save her people. They also comprised treatises such as Maimonides' *Epistle on Martyrdom,* a well-known text which could be read as justifying dissimulation if survival was at stake. In the end, Jews living outside Iberia were of a mixed mind when judging the conversos. Some looked on them as unfortunate brethren who could still strive for redemption. Others simply saw them as having left the common fold for good.

What, then, of the charge that the effects of clandestine dissembling led the heresy of judaizing to evolve toward new patterns of belief that were heterodox in terms of Judaic as well as Christian dogma? Despite the obvious difficulties in defining heresy within a confession that lacked both a firm doctrinal center and the institutional means of enforcing its creed, there clearly were ways in which the conversos' departures from rabbinical orthodoxy moved far beyond the bounds of the acceptable. The no-man's-land between Judaism and Christianity the conversos inhabited turned out to be a fertile ground for cultural innovation. Weakened attachment to tradition gave rise to a diffuse and inchoate body of literary and spiritual expression whose enigmatic content continues to pose a major challenge to the deciphering of early modern Spanish culture as a whole.

CHAPTER 15

IDENTITY
AND CREATIVITY

I T IS DIFFICULT, if not impossible, to speak of a converso identity in collective terms. This is not to say that New Christians altogether lacked a sense of belonging to a social category of their own, much less that they failed to recognize other members of the same group. Crypto-Jews in particular resolved the dilemma caused by the incompatible needs for secrecy and communal religious activity by inventing strategies for the identification of fellow judaizers. These included the use of coded language with which to test unknown persons. The *xuetes* of Mallorca, for example, referred to themselves as "servants of God" and waited for outsiders to catch the hint. And when an Extremaduran converso went to live in Madrid, his aunt there asked him "if he had his eyes open," which he later acknowledged was a means of "declaring oneself" a secret Jew.[1] But developing code words for recognition was a far cry from forging a collective identity understood in the usual sense of belonging to a stable community whose members were united by shared religious beliefs and practices, interlinked family ties, and close neighborly and economic relations. As noted above, such patterns quickly became rare following the initial crackdown by the Inquisition. By the seventeenth century the successful assimilation of the vast majority of Spanish conversos meant that most of the comparatively few New Christians who fit this bill were Portuguese. By increasing their visibility, their foreign origins did much to hamper their ability to follow the same route.

A sense of converso identity on an individual or family level is a different matter, though. What needs stressing is how outside pressure shaped the range of choices open to New Christians. Converts and their descendants had no alternative: even the most convinced judaizers opted to profess Catholic beliefs and practices in public, while remaining loyal to Judaism in their heart of hearts. But what started as an either/or choice soon gave way to a wider range of possibilities. As one scholar has put it, there were four types of conversos: those who wanted to be Christian and have nothing to do with Judaism, those who wanted to be Jewish and have nothing to do with Christianity, those who wanted to be both, and those who wanted to be neither.[2] The mere fact of having to face such choices forced many conversos to confront an existential dilemma of self-knowledge. One of the many paradoxes of the history of the conversos is that amid such harsh constraints some of them nevertheless took advantage of the situation to fashion themselves anew, both when converting to Catholicism and when "returning" to Judaism. Making such crucial decisions about one's inner allegiances and loyalties meant posing fundamental questions to and about oneself. How was the converso to deal with his or her personal and family past? Was there no alternative to accepting that one's ancestors were damned forever? Or could genuine conversion serve as the first step in the search for a retrospective redemption from which they might hope to benefit? Even closer to home, how should one deal with living relatives and friends, both those who clung to the former faith and those who moved on to a new one? How could one be sure that they would not let their own spiritual commitments override more earthly expectations of trust?

As cruel as these psychological dilemmas could be, they issued from the existence of very real and pressing options within a context of violent constraint and all-too-evident jeopardy. Occasionally, a document appears which allows the historian to glimpse something of these choices and the reasons why they were made. One such text is the diary written from 1520 to 1559 by the Valencian merchant Jeroni Soria. At no point does Soria admit to being a converso, although his recording that the Inquisition had condemned a close relation for judaizing is suggestive enough. Much more interesting—remarkable, in fact—is the brief sentence wherein he notes that as a child his father sent him to Genoa "so he could see if he was a Jew or where he came from."[3] The cryptic nature of this reference makes it impossible to know in which direction (if any) his father may have tried to influence his choice. Nevertheless, that some sort of decision between Christianity and Judaism existed—indeed, was required of him—can hardly be doubted.

A second episode involves a 1628 Inquisition report about two Jews—one from Pisa, the other from Turkey (and originally born in Fez)—who had had several conversations in the patio of the Alcázar palace in Madrid with one Pedro Gómez, a servant, who eventually denounced them.[4] The two Jews took for granted that Gómez was a converso, given his Portuguese origins. As one of them put it in his convoluted fashion, "No Portuguese could fail to have a bit of [Jewish] 'race' because so many of them [are Jews] and no one can deny this and you [the servant] have to have a bit of race [*alguna razita*] because all of us from there have some." Gómez played along and was even allowed to address them familiarly because, as the Pisan put it, "those of us who belong to the 'nation' treat each other thus." The latter went on to praise Jewish customs and contrasted the willingness of Jews to undertake manual labor with the Spaniards' noted aversion to work. He also criticized the Inquisition as a cruel and corrupt institution and warned Pedro that if he were caught, the best thing to do was to ask for mercy: that way "you will lose your property but you will save your life." He talked freely about circumcision, burials, and other Jewish rites, while his companion mocked the Catholic liturgy, boasting that during mass he recited to himself "bread and wine I see, in the Law of Moses I believe." Both of them confessed their outward adherence to Christianity and admitted to going to church in order to fool the "rabble." Yet the most significant aspect of their rich testimony is the noncoerced and spontaneous way in which they recounted to a supposed sympathizer how they maintained their Jewish practices and beliefs under the cover of dissimulation. Clearly, they too had made their choices, not only in favor of Judaism but also when they took additional risks to bring presumed coreligionists closer to proper observance.

Also worth stressing is the radically new situation in which judaizing conversos found themselves in terms of Judaism's own traditional markers of belonging. A number of well-defined means established identity for biblical and postbiblical Jews. Outward signs included respect for the rules and rites of purification (including food rituals) and, for men, circumcision. In principle Christianity introduced a radically new insistence on interiority and subjective adherence to faith, and while it soon developed a rich panoply of rituals of its own, these nevertheless downplayed the physical signs typical of the religion it claimed to supersede. For this reason Christians lumped Jews and Muslims together, caricaturing them as obsessively committed to now-defunct Old Testament prescriptions that required circumcision and the avoidance of bodily contamination. As noted above, the forced conversion of both groups to Catholicism ironically led to a new context in which the sudden elimination of the traditional means of signaling individuals as Christians or non-Christians left everyone involved without reliable criteria of classification. This failure of identification had its impact on identity as well. The unprecedented absence of readable criteria led to a fluid and unpredictable situation which conferred on individuals greater responsibility for shaping their own spiritual lives. And from within this void there emerged a host of idiosyncratic solutions to the spiritual challenges of the times.

These identity struggles would seem to be a rather recondite, even impenetrable problem were it not for the fact that much of the literary and cultural production of Golden Age Spain has been characterized as issuing from the unique existential drama of the conversos. It should be made clear at the beginning: wild claims have been made for the cultural impact of the converted Jews, especially during the 1960s and 1970s, which witnessed a "converso hunt" that threatened to reduce interpretation of literary works to a search for the genealogies of their authors. However, a more imaginative and less mechanical approach to this complex question has much to recommend it. One certainly cannot doubt the presence, indeed prominence, of conversos in many spheres of early modern Spanish culture. It is far less difficult to accept the suggestion that their condition as New Christians had something to do with this prominence, and that their family background often gave rise to singular responses, than to posit that they were united by a concrete way of viewing and interpreting religion, society, and politics. Thus, with greater caution in hand, one can begin to explore the role of conversos in the more public sphere of early modern Iberian culture.

On balance there were three areas of creativity in which conversos stood out as unusually visible protagonists. The first was religion, and more specifically, religious reform. New Christians loomed large among the many advocates of more interiorist and individualistic approaches to Christian faith in the numerous and diverse movements of spiritual renewal that characterized sixteenth-century Spain. Broad emphasis on intensely personal piety, and even direct mystical communion with the divine, was often accompanied by indifference to and even rejection of more collective religious practices. This personalist leaning was also reflected in a predilection for mental over oral prayer, frequent reading of devotional texts, and lay as well as clerical activism regarding pastoral and social concerns. Within this context it hardly comes as a surprise to find a marked enthusiasm among conversos for the new and humanistically informed spiritual program of Erasmus, as well as the more radical rejection of "externalist" religious practices associated with the nonconformist illuminists known as *alumbrados*. Well-known protagonists of Jewish origin of this rigorist "Pauline" Christianity included Alfonso and Juan de Valdés, the former a secretary to Charles V and author of a notoriously pungent satire of the papacy, the latter a widely read writer who from his exile in Naples led a movement for religious reform that many in the Church judged as perilously close to Protestantism. Another leader was Juan de Avila, an itinerant and highly charismatic figure who preached a rigorous program of moral and doctrinal renewal. He attracted many fellow conversos as followers, among them Diego Pérez de Valdivia, known for his preaching as well as his initiatives of social and moral improvement such as the founding in 1581 of Barcelona's charity hospice. An even bolder spirit was Luis de León, an Augustinian friar and one of Spain's greatest poets, whose intensely personal spirituality and belligerent defense of the Hebrew language and the Jewish intellectual tradition won him a spell in an Inquisitorial prison. The best-known spiritual leader of Jewish origin was, however, the most famous religious figure in Spanish history. That St. Teresa of Avila, the great mystic author and promoter of reform first within the Carmelite order and more generally in the whole of Spanish society, was the granddaughter of a judaizing cloth merchant gives some idea of the possible connections between individuals of Jewish ancestry and the many broadly based attempts at Catholic renewal in early modern Spain.

A second field in which conversos played a prominent role was in higher learning, including philosophy and the sciences, along with the learned professions, especially medicine. Representative figures include the humanist physician Andrés Laguna, who won a European-wide reputation for his

scientific studies, as well as for his translation into Spanish of Dioscorides'
classic treatise *On Materia Medica*. Other early modern medical specialists
of converso background included Francisco López de Villalobos, physician
to Ferdinand the Catholic and Charles V and author of one of the earliest
treatises on syphilis; Alonso de Santa Cruz, a cosmographer, mathematician, and astronomer also linked to the imperial court; Cristóbal Acosta,
who published one of the most frequently cited sixteenth-century treatises
on medical botany; Henrique Jorge Henriques, a Portuguese-born physician who issued in 1595 a series of dialogues under the title *Portrait of the
Perfect Doctor;* Cristóbal Pérez de Herrera, Philip II's personal doctor and
renowned for his many proposals for social and political reform; and Diego
Mateo Zapata, also a court physician, who successfully weathered not one
but two trials at the hands of the Inquisition.

A final area in which individuals of Jewish lineage distinguished themselves was in literature. The list of early modern New Christian writers
was a long one and included devotees of virtually all genres. While some
attributions of converso origins are fairly speculative, others leave little
room for doubt. One can hardly contest the Jewish roots of Fernando de
Rojas, the author of the first great masterpiece of the Spanish Renaissance,
the dialogue-play known as the *Celestina,* published in its definitive version
in 1502. Not only had Rojas's father-in-law been penanced for judaizing,
but the Inquisition exhumed and burned his own parents' bones, which
strongly suggests that they too had been convicted of the same crime. Other
prominent writers from convert families include Jorge de Montemayor, an
accomplished poet known above all for his best-selling pastoral novel *La
Diana* (1559); Mateo Alemán, the author of the picaresque novel *Guzmán de
Alfarache;* the playwrights Diego Jiménez de Enciso, Felipe Godínez, Juan
Pérez de Montalbán, and Luis Vélez de Guevara (the latter the best-known
of the group, and a loyal protégé of Olivares); and several poets, including
the Sevillians Juan de Jáuregui and Baltasar Alcázar, both friends of the
much more famous Luis de Góngora who, if he was not a converso, was
never able to squelch the rumor to that effect.

Bare lists of names, no matter their numbers or fame, do little to respond
to the thorny question of the likely effects of converso background on authors and their creations. It would be far more illuminating to examine
specific cases in which New Christian status or identity did or did not

manifest itself in the literary output of these writers. Take Juan Luis Vives, for example. The numerous published works of early modern Spain's leading humanist contain virtually no reference to his Jewish ancestry, much less to its deeply tragic quality. His father, Lluís Vives Valeriola, was a well-off cloth merchant of Valencia who traded with the Low Countries and Italy, while his mother, Blanquina March Maçana, hailed from a prosperous family of lawyers and notaries. Their undoing began in 1500, when the Valencian Inquisition discovered a clandestine synagogue in the house of his aunt Castellana Guioret, the widow of his father's brother Salvador Vives. She and her son were burned at the stake. Vives's father was similarly executed for judaizing in 1524, and in 1528 the body of his mother, who had died of plague in 1508, was, like those of Fernando de Rojas's parents, exhumed and burned in effigy. Vives himself had left Spain in 1509 and never returned to his homeland. Veiled criticism of the excessive power of the Inquisition and the fears and sufferings of exiles surface in some of his treatises, such as his commentary on Augustine's *City of God* (1522) and *On Making Peace* (1529). However, at no point in his work does he manifest any attachment to Judaism. Indeed, he devoted his final book, *De veritate fidei christiana* ("On the Truth of the Christian Faith," published posthumously in Basel in 1543), to demonstrating the superiority of Christianity to both Judaism and Islam. Vives drew heavily from earlier polemics, especially the well-known twelfth-century *Dialogue against the Jews* by Pedro Alfonso. Yet it is impossible to overlook how portions of this tradition fit in snugly with the contemporary message of Erasmian reform. This is true of his insistence on the superiority of the New Testament God of mercy over the Old Testament God of vengeful justice, and the call for demonstration of Christian truth through reason as opposed to "Jewish" literalism and reliance on argument by authorities. Equally Erasmian was Vives's studied avoidance of the Trinity (note that Pedro Alfonso had devoted a chapter to it). In short, Vives was a writer of undeniably Jewish lineage who, while not eschewing references to Judaism in his work, seems nevertheless to have handled the theme with circumspection. Above all, his references can be seen as forming part of a Pauline Christianity found among many other converts, who stressed the contrasts between the old and new dispensations in order to promote a more interior (and in some cases more intellectual) approach to matters of faith. Having moved on themselves from their ancestral point of departure, they looked to a more personalistic sort of religion to accommodate their individual choices along the road leading from Damascus.

Teresa of Avila resembled Vives in several key respects. While she had next to nothing to say about Judaism in general, like him she never referred directly to her own lineage in her voluminous letters, devotional treatises, and autobiographical texts. However, in at least one major departure, conversos appear as a theme in her experience and writing. In her home city of Avila, and elsewhere as well, Teresa depended on New Christians for vital support for her reform. Her references are elliptic, but the message is clear: she has no patience with distracting social concerns that stand in the way of her mission. These included prejudice against New Christians. Thus, when writing in her first-person account of the founding of the new Carmelite convent in Toledo, she dismissed local criticism of her patrons as insufficiently noble—probably code words for converso status—with a brisk "I have always esteemed virtue more than lineage."[5] Not surprisingly, Teresa repeatedly mocked blood purity in her private correspondence as well. It would not be pressing the point too far to link her undisguisable indifference to worldly notions of "honor" with her own family background as a New Christian. Her notorious combativeness and willingness to innovate, along with her fundamental insistence on the rock-bottom quality of interior faith, may well have owed some of their origins to the same roots.

The case of Luis de León was a different matter altogether. One does not have to strain to find Judaism in his work; it is present everywhere. The poet-professor assumed and admitted his converso background and went on from there to grapple with his Jewish heritage from a Christian perspective. What is more, he aggressively challenged the Inquisition during his imprisonment from 1572 to 1576, repeatedly asserting his scholarly and spiritual right as a Christian Hebraist to draw upon the Jewish interpretative tradition in his studies of—and vernacular translations from—the Old Testament. His forthright defense of *veritas hebraica*—the belief of humanists in the fundamental compatibility of the two Testaments and the ability of rigorous comparative philology to bring back to life the true meaning of the "ancient theology" of the primitive Church—provoked the ire of a trio of academic conservatives, antisemites, and their allies in the Holy Office. Many among his contemporaries considered him lucky to have been released from prison and reinstated to his chair at the University of Salamanca. After all, many conversos who were far more circumspect had fared much worse. One suspects that the friar had some powerful protectors, in addition to not a few sympathizers.

A final example reaches toward the other end of the New Christian spectrum. This was inhabited by conversos who not only acknowledged themselves as such and even drew some inspiration, so to speak, from their condition but who also went on to defend Judaism as a religion in preference to the Christianity they and their forerunners had been forced to accept. One especially eloquent instance of this admittedly unusual category was João Pinto Delgado. Born in the mid-1580s in Portugal, he and his parents eventually resettled in the Spanish Netherlands and then in Rouen. He published his first book there in 1627, a collection of poems on biblical figures written in Spanish. After a stay in Antwerp, Pinto and his family finally moved to Amsterdam, where he changed his name to Mosseh León and became a professing Jew until his death in 1653.

A glance at the content of some of his work shows a writer firmly committed to the defense of Judaism even while still nominally a Catholic. In his "Poem of Queen Esther," he recounts the biblical story in which the heroine, aided by the good counsel and righteousness of her father, Mordecai, saves her people from destruction at the hands of their enemy Haman, momentarily empowered by the arbitrary but absolute authority of a feckless and sybaritic king. And in "In Praise of the Lord" the poet exposes an impressively broad range of emotions: the shame produced by one's own weakness and constant moral failure; fear, of the sort that leads to falseness, sin, and neglect of duty; contrition for worshiping idols ("vain appearances") and for obeying a tyrant pope; hope for restoration of the Temple, the locus of both "holocaust" and "glory"; and a frank desire for vengeance, to make the Christians feel the "sharp blow" and "burning fury" of a just God.[6] It is hard to imagine a more powerful and direct evocation of the experience—and longings—of a judaizing converso. Still, he was not alone in his stance. Not only did other New Christians, such as the poet and playwright Miguel de Barrios, join him in celebrating in printed verse their return to Judaism. In one of the more singular cases of double identity of the period, the converso Antonio Enríquez Gómez wrote over two dozen plays and other acceptably Catholic works under the pseudonym of Fernando de Zárate. Then in 1656, after disappearing from view, he published several works celebrating the Jews and criticizing the Inquisition, especially for its execution in 1644 of the martyr Lope de Vera, an Old Christian convert to Judaism. After returning to Spain he was arrested and eventually died in prison in Seville in 1663. His was perhaps the best-known case of a "divided soul," caught between conforming publicly to one religion and committing oneself in secret to another, and most likely beset with doubts and hesitations regarding both.

Even so hurried an excursus should suffice to suggest something of the breadth of converso attitudes and of the endless possibilities for variation, mixture, and shifts of position along a spectrum that ranged from denial to defense of either faith. Above all, it urges the need for caution in the face of blanket generalizations and simplistic, a priori assumptions, such as the naive belief that identifying someone as a converso will lead to the discovery of some sort of "Jewish" attributes or that certain types of experience inevitably give rise to certain forms and themes of literary expression. In fact, precisely the opposite needs stressing: how hard it is to generalize about a shared converso identity or point of view in the face of the obvious diversity of opinion among New Christians themselves. That said, there is no reason to reject the notion that specific literary works did indeed reflect and address the predicament posed by the converso background of their authors and that other New Christians could have read such works with a special grain of recognition and sympathy. Such may have the case of the *Celestina*. Strong arguments have been made that this text expressed, however obliquely, the experience and worldview of a converso author. Its content, symbolic language and allusions, and formal devices have all been seen as mobilized in favor of a marrano message. These facets included covert references to Judaism, the Inquisition, and the need for (and ease of) dissimulation in religious matters, along with the use of equivocal language to convey a metaphysics that fundamentally was neither Christian nor Jewish. Particular emphasis has been placed on the final speech, the lament of Pleberio following the suicide of his daughter Melibea. Utterly bereft of any expression of standard Christian (or Jewish) hope in the afterlife, yet also removed from stoic confidence in the bedrock order of the universe, Pleberio closes the play as a figure forsaken within a vale of tears, condemning his world as a labyrinth of errors and a harbor of vain hopes. In so doing did he speak for all, or even most conversos? Surely not. Did he speak for some? Probably yes.

CHAPTER 16

DIASPORA WITHIN
THE DIASPORA

V IEWED IN THE long run, perhaps the most unusual feature, as
well as the one with the most far-ranging consequences, of the
history of early modern Spanish Jews and conversos was the way
in which the experience of exile led to change and renewal outside the
peninsula. The year 1492, far from bringing history to an end, inaugurated
a new era in Judaism, one in which *sephardim* or Iberian Jews played a
leading role, albeit on a stage that was considerably altered as it extended
outward. For an embattled remnant among the Jews who remained in Spain
and Portugal after converting to Christianity, this new diaspora wound up
facilitating their eventual return to Judaism. The transformation of New
Christians into New Jews through the emigration of thousands of Iberian
converts was doubtless the least anticipated end product of the expulsion.
But before examining this intriguing paradox more closely, one must chart
the main points of transfer and settlement that marked the boundaries of
the Iberian Jewish and converso world.

"World" is the appropriate term here. The Hispanic Jewish and New
Christian diasporas—as will be seen, the two were largely one and the
same, even if they did not coincide exactly—constituted one of the most
geographically dispersed and culturally cosmopolitan networks of the early

modern era. It expanded outward from its historical center in the Iberian peninsula to include both halves of the Mediterranean and much of northern Europe, as well as beyond, to embrace the transatlantic world and even the Indian subcontinent. And just as the center of gravity of the European economy as a whole shifted during the sixteenth and seventeenth centuries from the Mediterranean toward the Atlantic, the center of dynamism within the Sephardic diaspora similarly migrated from the Ottoman Empire, north-central Italy, and northern Africa to the Low Countries, the west coast of France, northern Germany, and finally England.

What set all this in motion was the expulsion of 1492, or more precisely, the exiling of Jews from Spain in 1492 and then the escape of some of those who had fled to Portugal and Navarre from forced conversions there in 1497–98. In retrospect, it is better to view these measures not as discrete historical events, but rather as the beginning of a lengthy chain of population transfers that provoked a series of profound changes. The sephardim dispersed in all directions; in fact, one group actually wound up in Zamość, in eastern Poland. Yet four major foci anchored their settlement during Judaism's long sixteenth century from 1492 to 1648, when the Chmielnicki massacres led to an exodus of Polish Jews toward western Europe.

The first was Italy. Ironically, the expelled Jews received the warmest welcome in Alexander VI's Rome. It did not take long for the Spaniards—joined by their Sicilian brethren, who were also exiled at Ferdinand's behest in 1492—to become one of the larger of the many *edoth* or "nations" comprising the unusually cosmopolitan Jewish community of Rome. In fact, the Spanish Jews were so numerous that they were able to create separate synagogues for Castilians and "Catalans" (that is, Jews from throughout the crown of Aragon)—a tendency similar to the different national churches Spanish Catholics founded in the same city. Papal policy in the long run oscillated between protection and sudden displays of hostility, the most memorable among the latter being the order officially to enclose all Jews in a single neighborhood in 1555. Still, the Spanish Jews were an important (and permanent) presence in Rome throughout the early modern period, and they maintained their ethnic identity in the face of Ashkenazic predominance within the board of governors and other communal institutions.

Other centers of migration of Iberian Jews in Italy included Naples, although they were expelled from this kingdom first in 1510 and definitively in 1541. Ancona, the Adriatic port of the Papal States, also housed a fair number of exiles. However, a dramatic crackdown on conversos by the Inquisition in the 1550s substantially reduced Ancona's role as a haven. Ferrara, which the independent Este dynasty ruled at this time, similarly received migrants from Spain. Particularly noteworthy was the establishment there of a press for printing Judaic works by and for sephardim, most notably the famous Ferrara Bible, a Spanish translation of the Torah published in 1553. Some exiles made their way even further north, to Lombardy, from whence they were expelled again by Spanish officials in 1597. Few Spanish Jews chose to reside in Tuscany at first, but by the late sixteenth century they found a warm welcome in its maritime centers of Pisa and especially Livorno. The latter soon became the most thriving trading center for Iberian and other Jews (and conversos) in the western Mediterranean. But it was Venice which won the most renown for sheltering Hispanic Jews. This was due not only to the visibility of its Jewish population as a whole following the creation of the *ghetto*—the first in Europe—in 1516. It also owed much to the fact that of the three nations into which Venetian Jews were organized, two—the Ponentines (Spanish and Portuguese exiles) and the Levantines (hailing from the Ottoman empire)—were of Iberian origin. While the third nation—the Germans, or *ashkenazim*—comprised the most numerous group, the other two were wealthier and included among their numbers many of the more distinguished members of the community. In the end, however, Venice and, indeed, Italy as a whole managed to retain only a portion of its Sephardic population. The papal campaign to force all Jews either to convert or to live in ghettos beginning in the 1550s, followed by a decline in economic opportunities during the seventeenth-century contraction of the urban economy, lessened Italy's appeal considerably. With the exception of Livorno, by the early 1600s the center of dynamism in the Sephardic world was moving elsewhere.

Before turning to the growing presence of Spanish and Portuguese Jews and conversos in northern Europe, however, one must recall that from the very beginning a significant proportion of the Iberian exiles elected to reside in the Islamic half of the Mediterranean. North Africa from Morocco in the west to the Mamluk sultanate of Egypt in the east, along with the Ottoman empire, accepted large numbers of Jewish migrants. This welcome merely continued medieval traditions of tolerance of Jews as *dhimmi,* that is, a protected if subordinated (and heavily taxed) minority. The exiles' reinforcement of existing communities soon led to concentrations of sephardim which dwarfed in size any of their centers within the Christian world. The Jewish quarter of Fez—the oldest in North Africa—housed some ten thousand inhabitants by the sixteenth century and boasted not only an impressive rabbinical establishment but also a printing press. And even though the Jewish community there declined in the seventeenth century, Sephardic Jews continued to play important roles in local politics and the economy, acting as diplomats and advisers, financiers, wholesale importers, and purveyors of supplies to the sultan's army.

Further east, Jewish traders, artisans, and even professionals could be found in large coastal cities such as Algiers or Tunis, and especially in Alexandria. Meanwhile, the Ottoman empire housed three main concentrations of sephardim. The capital, Istanbul, had over eight thousand Jewish families by 1535. Salonica came next. It was a manufacturing city whose numerous sephardim were divided into five Spanish and three Portuguese congregations, and whose members "speak as fine Spanish as they do in Toledo," in the words of an Old Christian who visited the city in the 1590s.[1] Finally Safed, in Galilee, became the center not only of a briefly flourishing textile industry but also of a major movement of renewal of kabbalistic and legal thought thanks to the efforts of famous resident scholars such as Joseph Karo (1488–1575), the half-Sephardic Isaac Luria (1534–72), and Moses Cordovero (1522–70). Other loci of settlement included Smyrna, or Izmir, the leading port on the western coast of Turkey, and Edirne (formerly known as Adrianopolis), a trade center on the highway from Sofia to the Bosphorus. Sephardim played key roles in urban and regional economies, but above all they served as crucial links in long-distance, pan-Mediterranean trade. Their connections with Venice proved particularly important in this regard and even more so after 1589, when the merchant Daniel Rodríguez established a free port in Split (Spalato) on the Adriatic coast of Croatia. That Iberian Jews enjoyed ample opportunities to prosper under the Ottomans was graphically demonstrated by the rise to fame and political influence of Joseph Nasi. Little is known of his early life, save that he was born in Portugal and raised officially as a New Christian. After passing through the Low Countries, France, and Venice, where he was involved in some sort of amorous intrigue that included his eloping with one of his cousins, he showed up in Turkey in 1554. There he openly reverted to Judaism and won fame as a political and financial adviser to the future sultan, Selim II, who named him duke of Naxos in 1566. In the end his notable good fortune as one of the first early modern "court Jews" turned against him, but while he was active at the Ottoman court he was arguably one of the more powerful figures in European politics.

During the century following the expulsion the Sephardic world continued to be resolutely focused on the Mediterranean. The emergence of an Iberian Jewish presence in northwestern Europe involved a second diaspora, and one which comprised not just publicly professing Jews, as in 1492, but also conversos. The latter were in fact a motley group. Some among them were trying to return to normative Judaism, while others were more or less conforming Christians who were drawn by kin and other ties to the expanding opportunities of the Atlantic economy. Their trek began in Antwerp. In 1537 Charles V permitted a group of conversos to settle there, although in 1549 he changed his mind and ordered the expulsion of all New Christians who had arrived after 1543. By the 1570s, the city housed around eighty converso families, comprising some four to five hundred members. Their ranks thinned toward the close of the century, as the Dutch blockade which increasingly hindered Antwerp's access to overseas markets encouraged some of the merchants to move elsewhere. Still, a remnant held on, attracted by being able to operate from a Catholic base that lacked an Inquisition. By the mid-seventeenth century they were joined by a small but significant stream of immigrants from Portuguese Jewish communities elsewhere in northern Europe. By the 1650s Antwerp's crypto-Jews held services in a clandestine synagogue, in addition to continuing to meet on a smaller scale in private homes, as in the past.

It did not take long for the conversos—some of whom were judaizers, and some not—to begin to look for other niches in northwestern Europe in which to settle. Despite the disruptions of its religious wars, France proved highly attractive. This was thanks to its more tolerant form of Catholicism, at least as far as Judaism was concerned, and above all to the ideal location of its western maritime cities, which provided convenient havens for both legal and illegal trade between the Iberian peninsula and the commercial centers of the north. To be sure, not all the Iberian New Christians congregated on the coast. When the future Basel physician Felix Platter studied medicine in Languedoc in the 1550s, he marveled at the huge number of marranos in Béziers, Narbonne, and Montpellier. In the latter city he roomed with one, Jacques Catalan, a well-known apothecary who laughed at the priests and spoke well of the Protestants as he gave him private lessons in the Old— not New—Testament. Still, the vast majority of conversos could be found along the Atlantic seaboard, whose ports they used both for transatlantic traffic and for shipments to and from the Iberian peninsula. Rouen, with its vibrant cloth trade, and Nantes were principal destinations. Bordeaux was another. Closer to the Spanish border was St. Jean de Luz, which served as a base from which to introduce goods (usually illegally) into Spain. Other entrepôts with converso populations included Labastide-Clairence and Peyrehorade, both villages inland from Biarritz, and Dax, a town nearer to the sea. Perhaps the largest and most active community was that of Bayonne. There the New Christians were confined to a district of their own, across the river from the old town. Known as Saint Esprit, this district was synonymous with Judaism. In all these places, royal protection permitted the conversos to weather occasional outbreaks of local hostility, which included public investigations by zealous clergy regarding the depth of their allegiance to Catholicism. By the 1680s, under Colbert—ever the mercantilist, he clearly valued the conversos' contribution to the French economy—the New Christians shed their earlier pretense and declared their Judaism by ceasing to have their children baptized. Along with Alsace and other border regions, the southwest continued to function as a center—albeit a minor one—of French Judaism well into the modern era.

Another area to which sephardim migrated was the Baltic, northern Germany in particular. The two main areas of settlement there were Hamburg and nearby Glückstadt, a city then under Danish control. The first Spanish and Portuguese émigrés arrived in the 1580s. They slowly made headway against considerable local opposition, especially from the Lutheran clergy, who intermittently campaigned to have them expelled. Once again, the sephardim carved a niche for themselves in finance—they founded Europe's first giro or exchange bank in Hamburg in 1619—and in trade in colonial and luxury products. The Spanish embargo of Dutch ports brought new prosperity to both cities, and the Iberians proved well placed to take advantage of the new commercial opportunities. All this won them grudging acceptance from the civic authorities, who finally permitted them to open a cemetery (in Altona) in 1612 and in the 1620s to build two synagogues. By the middle of the seventeenth century Hamburg had become famous for its small contingent of wealthy Jewish merchants, such as the Curiels and the Teixeiras, whose ever more visible role in long-distance trade allowed them to venture further into international finance and contracting for military and other supplies for a variety of states.

Important as Antwerp, Rouen, Bayonne, and Hamburg were, they all were eclipsed by what eventually became the northern capital of the Sephardic diaspora, Amsterdam. New Christians wishing to start new lives as public Jews first appeared there around 1595. Most came from Portugal, or indirectly from Antwerp, Hamburg, Emden, and other colonies of Portuguese converso merchants. Their choice of Amsterdam was a logical one. It was a uniquely open city, which welcomed all sorts of useful immigrants and others who wished to turn geographic mobility into social and economic advancement. The Portuguese Jews constituted one minority among many in this polyglot metropolis and numbered at their height some three thousand individuals—a very sizable concentration for Sephardic Jews, yet less than 2 percent of the city's population.

In the first years following their arrival the conversos played it safe and did not publicly advertise their Jewish background. As one recently imported rabbi wrote in 1616, the freedom they found in Amsterdam was one in which "each may follow his own belief, but may not openly show that he is of a different faith from the inhabitants of the city."[2] At the beginning they held services in private houses. Soon different congregations emerged. The first was Bet Jacob ("House of Jacob"), named for the merchant Jacob Tirado, in whose home it met starting in 1602 under the leadership of the Ashkenazi Uri Halevi. He was joined by a second rabbi, Joseph Pardo of Venice, in 1608. Neve Shalom ("Oasis of Peace") was founded the same year by a group of merchants headed by the Pallache brothers, who were not conversos but rather Moroccan Jews born and raised in Fez. A dispute between these two bodies gave rise around 1619 to a third and markedly more strict congregation, Ets Haim ("Tree of Life," later known as Beth Israel), whose rabbi was Saul Levi Mortera. Meanwhile, the growing community created other institutions to cater to its needs. These included a common cemetery, land for which was purchased in 1614 in the village of Ouderkerk outside the city limits; a charity fund, which included (among other provisions) subsidies designed to encourage poorer brethren to move elsewhere; and in 1615, a *dotar* or confraternity charged with providing dowries for girls of marriageable age both in Amsterdam and elsewhere in the diaspora. Another major step forward was the establishment in 1622 of a communal board comprising two adult males from each of the three congregations. In this as in many other aspects, the Amsterdam Jews followed the lead of their coreligionists in Venice, where self-governance rested firmly in the hands of the more prominent laymen and not those of the rabbinate.

Several factors led to the unification in 1638–39 of these separate and often quarreling bodies into a single, consolidated congregation, which soon received permission to hold its services in a building of its own. Prominent among them were growing numbers of newly arriving ashkenazim. In response, the new fellowship known as Talmud Torah limited membership to Jews of Sephardic ancestry, whose ranks were also expanding. (By 1620 the returnees from Spain and Portugal numbered some one thousand members, and the community continued to grow in the decades that followed.) Talmud Torah boasted four rabbis and a collective leadership of seven *mahamad* or lay leaders. This synagogue functioned in rather makeshift premises until 1675, when lavish celebrations were held to inaugurate the building in the Vlooienburg-Breestraat quarter known today as the Portuguese Synagogue.

This impressive landmark merely confirmed that Amsterdam had eclipsed Venice and all other rivals for the role of spiritual and material capital of the Portuguese diaspora. It was in fact the largest and most prosperous concentration of Sephardic Jews in northern Europe. The city's central role was reflected in other ways as well. As one might expect, it housed a wide range of cultural activities, in addition to serving as an active node of communication. Crucial to both functions was the printing industry. The Amsterdam sephardim published a minimum of four hundred books and pamphlets in Spanish and Portuguese during the seventeenth century. These titles covered an ample range of topics. They not only included medieval and recent classics, such as the works of Judah ha-Levi and Maimonides, or Joseph Karo's sixteenth-century guide to Jewish law, the *Shulhan Arukh*. Amsterdam also produced imprints of a more ephemeral nature, such as sermons, which were issued in abundance after worship commenced in the new synagogue in 1675. It even hosted the first major Jewish newspaper, the *Gazeta,* which was printed in Spanish from 1675 to 1690. Finally, local production also included secular works by Jewish writers, above all the plays of Miguel de Barrios, famed for their Calderonesque language and intrigue.

What made all this possible was, of course, the willingness of the Dutch Protestant authorities to countenance and even encourage a flourishing Jewish community within their midst. Several factors account for such toleration. First, ideology and sentiment favored the Iberian Jews. The Dutch looked upon them as fellow resisters against Spanish imperialism and its institutions, especially the widely hated Inquisition. Shared hostility to Spain was indeed the main theme of the sermon the distinguished rabbi Menasseh ben Israel preached on the occasion of the formal visit in 1642 to the Sephardic synagogue of Stadhouder Frederick Hendrik of Nassau and his son and daughter-in-law, parents of the future William and Mary of England. One should also keep in mind the influence of a philosemitic strain in the official religion of the Republic. Many Calvinists looked on Jews as fellow people of the book, that is, like themselves intense readers of Scripture. They were also seen as reliable anti-Catholics, not just politically but doctrinally as well, given their shared hostility to images and other instances of "papist" idolatry. Other, more pragmatic motives also played a role. The Portuguese Jews found acceptance because they either did not or were not allowed to compete with local economic interests. Their trading networks specialized in novel overseas goods such as diamonds, cinnamon, or coral and thus did not make inroads on existing Dutch activities. (Municipal legislation took care to nip any such challenge in the bud; hence the sephardim were not allowed to practice retail trade or to join most of the city guilds.) In other words, the civic elite looked upon the Portuguese Jews as a particularly useful category of foreigners. Indeed, they did not cease to be regarded legally as such until 1657, when they obtained the right to citizenship, although they continued to be barred from holding municipal office.

On balance, the famed toleration of Amsterdam was hedged with many such limitations. The Dutch looked away more than anything else, and they expected in return substantial discretion from the Jews. That the latter knew better than to call too much attention to themselves is suggested by their communal regulations which forbad loud celebrations, such as Purim parties, and expressly prohibited either oral or written discussion of religious matters with gentiles. The breathing space of the sephardim expanded only slowly and met with several setbacks along the long road to the acceptance they finally achieved. But tolerated they were. They were moreover not subject to any special taxation. And most unusually, they encountered remarkably little of the direct antisemitism that they were forced to put up with in the rest of Protestant as well as Catholic Europe. It has long been noted that Dutch Golden Age art shows little of the demonization of the Jews that was common coin elsewhere. If anything, it features neutral, even positive depictions of Jews. These include not just Rembrandt's famous portraits of individual sephardim, many of whom were his neighbors in the Vlooienburg quarter. Other contemporary Dutch painters also depicted Jews in their homes and in the new synagogue. The latter was the subject of at least two series of representations, Romeyn de Hooghe's 1675 prints focusing on the dedication ceremonies and Emanuel de Witte's three oil paintings of its interior. All these works, along with the young van Ruysdael's eerie sketches and two paintings of the Ouderkerk cemetery, not only broke with the conventional negative and caricatured iconography of Jews. As one scholar has put it, "for the first time in the history of European art, after centuries of artistic vilification, the Jews and their ways were the subject of naturalistic, even idealistic representation."[3]

If there was one matter more unprecedented than the toleration and philosemitism which developed in seventeenth-century Holland, it was the other, more private side of this story: the struggle of New Christians to become "new Jews." The history of Judaism had been marked by few occasions in which converts to Christianity, much less their descendants, were able to return to their ancestral religion. Seventeenth-century Amsterdam provided just such an opportunity. There, in new conditions of ample if not limitless freedom, the Iberian conversos could shed their outer garb of dissimulation and don the robes of public Jews, practicing as such.

The point of departure was not a promising one. Most of the conversos who arrived in Amsterdam could be said to be Jews by intention, but not in terms of knowledge or practice. Many of them were familiar with only a residual form of Judaism far removed from traditional rabbinical observance. The meager positive content of their faith was often overshadowed by vehement if private rejection of Catholic doctrine and rituals, particularly those most offensive to their sense of Judaism, such as the Trinity or the cult of images. The path leading to their new life was anything but easy. First, there was (for the men at least) the matter of learning Hebrew, not just enough to mumble their way through a few prayers but also to be able to educate themselves and their sons in the complex tasks involved in participating in a full-fledged congregation. Then there were rules to be absorbed, the hundreds of prescriptions and prohibitions that made up the thorough regulation of daily life known as *halakhah.* Not the least among the tasks pending was circumcision as adults. Many of the newcomers invested this act with a significance far outstripping its normal role in Jewish tradition. Determined to leave their past dissembling behind them, they looked to it as a definitive means of reclaiming their rightful place within the broader community of men physically, and thus irreparably, marked as Jews.

Such uncommon—and doubtless unconscious—emphasis on external manifestations was hardly the only holdover from Catholic sacramental practice that the conversos brought with them from Spain and Portugal. In fact, it did not take long for major differences of opinion to lead them to challenge the rabbis brought in from the outside to educate them in the ways of their newly adopted faith. Perhaps the most intense controversy—and one with relevance for the later scandal involving the philosopher Baruch (Benedict) Spinoza's expulsion from the community—had to do with the issue of the immortality of the soul. The Portuguese in Amsterdam were distinctive for their strong confidence in the existence of an immortal soul and, by extension, in individual salvation. These were both rather unusual positions within a religion that had few firm teachings in regard to an afterlife. The implications of this insistence—and the conflicting opinions to which it gave rise—were made clear by a public debate in the 1630s that revealed deep divisions within the community. At stake was whether the forebears of the ex-conversos who had publicly embraced Christianity—which meant both denying Judaism and practicing idolatry—would be subject to eternal punishment. The controversy pitted one rabbi, the (Ashkenazic) rationalist Mortera, against another, the (Sephardic) kabbalist Isaac Aboab da Fonseca. The former accused the latter, and by implication most of the Iberian returnees, of harboring the all-too-comfortable belief that all "Jewish souls" would receive the sort of unconditional salvation normally reserved to the righteous. That Mortera did not dispute the existence of an immortal soul—

indeed, he wrote a treatise defending this doctrine—points to the existence of a consensus over a tenet which surely struck many contemporary Jews elsewhere as being far too close to standard Christian eschatology.

As the dispute over the fate of ancestors suggests, the fact that the Iberian Jews were able to forge new lives for themselves in their new home did not lead them to forget, much less forsake, their peninsular origins. Rejudaization certainly did not cause them to give up their business ties with Spain and its empire. On the contrary, the sephardim participated intensively in the far-flung and highly diverse activities of the Spanish and Portuguese imperial economies. Their role as middlemen not only between northern and southern Europe, but also everywhere within the sprawling transatlantic trading sphere was the very foundation of the prosperity that made them such useful denizens in the eyes of their Dutch hosts. Moving back and forth obviously did not lack its risks. Still, continued involvement in the Iberian economy was seen as essential to the wellbeing of the community as a whole. Pragmatic considerations of this sort lay behind much of the Amsterdam Jews' reluctance to give up their contacts with Iberia. Not surprisingly, they continued to use Spanish and Portuguese as their languages of choice. Portuguese was preferred for daily activities and business; it was also (along with Hebrew) the official language of the synagogue. Spanish played a prominent role in education, including biblical study, which looked to the Spanish-language Ferrara Bible of 1553 as its authorized translation. Spanish was also the favored language of formal literary expression and other occasions requiring greater efforts at refinement. The various local academies founded in the second half of the seventeenth century habitually used Spanish as both a spoken and written language. It is also significant that all the literary works in Spinoza's library following his death in 1677 were in Spanish. These included several texts by the Baroque writers Quevedo, Góngora, and Gracián, a copy of *Don Quixote,* and an unnamed play by the Madrid dramatist Juan Pérez de Montalbán. The Dutch sephardim were in fact known to have performed several Golden Age plays, as in 1648, when amateurs acted out Calderón's masterpiece *La vida es sueño* for the wedding of two scions of the prominent Pinto family.

This firm attachment to Iberian language and culture raises what is perhaps the most intriguing aspect of the history of the singular phenomenon of the Amsterdam Jews: their identity. Or rather identities, for what is most striking is the way in which the members of this community saw themselves as belonging to at least three different but overlapping circles of adscription. Their most universal allegiance was to the Jewish religion and peoplehood. Then came membership in what they called the *nação,* or the "nation." This grouping was understood in an ethnic sense, as referring more restrictively to Jews of Spanish and Portuguese descent. A labile and imprecise term, it could include conversos as well as professing Jews such as themselves. Such was made manifest by the frequent inclusion of the former among the extralocal candidates for receiving dowries from the *dotar* society. Finally, there was their most specific identity as the Amsterdam congregation(s), whose members claimed leadership within the entire Iberian diaspora by virtue of their security as wealthy and respectable participants in a dynamic and expanding Atlantic and even global economy.

That the ex-conversos differed from their coreligionists elsewhere met with acknowledgment both within and outside their community. Amsterdam had quickly emerged as one of the major meeting places between early modern Sephardic and Ashkenazic Jews outside the Mediterranean area. While willing enough at the beginning to accept the leadership of Ashkenazic rabbis, as their numbers and confidence as observant Jews grew the sephardim proved increasingly reluctant to welcome immigrants from central and eastern Europe. This was in part a class issue. The wealthy Iberian merchants feared that the much poorer newcomers would become a charge on the community and urged them to move on to Jewish settlements elsewhere. Those who stayed managed to create a congregation of their own, made up mostly of Poles and Germans. Relations between the two groups at no point degenerated into open conflict, but there was substantial rivalry between them, as shown by the competition for the building of their synagogues. The sephardim saw the decision of the ashkenazim to construct a large house of worship in 1671 as a provocation, and they responded by erecting their own far more magnificent synagogue a few years later. This incident was merely one of many which illustrated the determination on the part of the Amsterdam sephardim not only to assert their local superiority but also to reaffirm their role as leaders within their half of European Judaism. This led to a highly unorthodox situation, in which a group of ex-Christians struggling (at first) to bring themselves up to the standards of normative rabbinical faith and practice nevertheless retained many of the basic habits of separateness, and even the quasi-racial language of higher lineage "honor" and reputation, that proved one of the more enduring legacies of their Iberian past.

The 1670s marked a turning point in the fortunes of the Amsterdam congregation. Yet the inauguration of the splendid new synagogue—which not only trumped an Ashkenazic community that had managed to equal them in numbers, but also displayed the degree to which their Christian hosts were willing to allow the Iberians to assert their claims to superiority—coincided with the beginning of a long-term decline in Dutch political and economic resources. In fact, the outbreak of hostilities against France in 1672 led to the temporary suspension of work on the synagogue. Holland's involvement in decades of international war severely sapped its strength, and along with other factors contributed to the growing difficulties experienced in the colonial trades. (Yet another irony here is that while their deep involvement in overseas commerce led the sephardim to be especially exposed to the effects of the downturn, the ashkenazim weathered the crisis far better thanks to their focus on the more modest sphere of local trade.) The Iberian Jews were soon in full retreat, and by the end of the eighteenth century their community had been considerably reduced in size and wealth. Above all, they were no longer able to count on immigrants from the rest of the diaspora. In fact, the arrival in 1765 of twenty-four émigrés from Portugal occasioned one of the last collective circumcision ceremonies that had been such a unique feature of the community's life. By the nineteenth and twentieth centuries the New Jews of Amsterdam—including their language, their reputation for initiative, and their stubborn pride—had become for the most part a historical memory.

But the northern European Sephardic world did not end in the Netherlands. In 1656 some two dozen Portuguese merchants founded a synagogue in London, under the name of Sha'ar Ha-Shamayim ("Gate of Heaven"). The early members were mostly New Christians, along with a small number of Jews who had publicly professed elsewhere. Many had already lived some time in London. While they held services in secret in the house of the prominent merchant Antonio Fernández Carvajal, they attended mass at the Spanish embassy and buried their dead in Christian cemeteries. Following concerted lobbying efforts by the Amsterdam rabbi Menasseh ben Israel, Oliver Cromwell gave them oral permission to open a synagogue and their own cemetery. By the 1680s the Portuguese Jewish "nation" in London numbered over four hundred members. As in Holland, assuming a new identity as practicing Jews gave rise to a certain amount of conflict, as when a number of members of the community challenged Rabbi Jacob Sasportas over the degree of observance of ritual law. Many wished to retain their dual status as Jews and Christians, and they looked upon their Judaism more as what we would call an ethnic identity than as a faith with exclusive rules of its own. Sound economic reasons for doing so—above all, continued participation in Iberian commerce—were not lacking, even if converso influence was on the wane in Madrid and the newly independent court in Lisbon. In any event, the continued involvement of conversos within the London congregation wound up intensifying the drift toward pluralism within what would eventually become one of the leading centers of Judaism in western Europe.

The final and outermost extension of the Iberian diaspora was located even farther to the west. The New World—broadly defined as the overseas possessions first of Spain and Portugal, and then of other European powers—constituted the endpoint of the Sephardic trajectory. Two foci were of particular importance. The first involved numerous far-flung networks of judaizers within the two Iberian empires. Despite specific royal legislation prohibiting New Christian migrants, an undetermined number of conversos managed to settle throughout the Americas, especially in the main trading centers of the Caribbean, Mexico, Peru, and Brazil. It is by no means clear that most of them continued to practice Judaism, although it is likely that many looked to the New World as a shelter from the sort of vigilance and pressures that made life in the peninsula uncomfortable. Once again, the key figures here were mostly from Portugal. Although some judaizers caught by the Inquisition were of Spanish origin—the most famous among these was Luis de Carvajal, who in 1596 was burned at the stake in Mexico City along with most of the members of his family—the brunt of the repression of crypto-Judaism in Hispanic America fell on members of the Portuguese Atlantic trade diaspora during the tense years of the mid-seventeenth century. Both Mexico City and Lima witnessed mass autos-da-fé of wealthy converso merchants and their families beginning in the 1630s. The fierce wave of repression appears to have forced the survivors to leave the cities or to abandon Spanish lands altogether. From that point onward few trials

were held for judaizing. As in the peninsula, the conversos either blended
in with the rest of the population or moved on to other latitudes.

The other focus of Latin American Judaism featured a different group
of *portugueses:* the very ones who had fled to Amsterdam to return to their
ancestral faith. The first public Jewish community of the hemisphere was
founded in Recife in 1630, in the wake of Holland's conquest of northeastern
Brazil. It lasted until 1654, when a Portuguese expedition managed to expel
the Dutch. A remnant of Portuguese Jews stayed on after that in the Caribbean and established outposts in Curaçao and Suriname.

As far as the overall impact of the Iberian exile is concerned, its most
direct consequence was economic in character. The diaspora from Spain
played a strategic role in the two largest trading networks of early modern
Europe. First, it contributed directly to consolidating and extending the
already existing economic ties both within and between the eastern and
western halves of the Mediterranean. Sephardic merchants did much to link
the disparate parts of the intense land and sea traffic of southern Europe. The
usefulness of their participation became increasingly visible during the most
intense period of confessional conflict between Islam and Christendom and
helps explain why many Christian rulers began to imitate the long-standing
Muslim practice of extending not only toleration but also favored treatment to Jewish agents, many if not most of whom were of Hispanic origin.
Yet while the Iberian conversos and Jews provided merely one important
element of dynamism within this highly plural construct, they contributed
centrally to creating and maintaining the second network, the transatlantic
trading sphere whose initial phase was dominated by Spain and Portugal.
Their specific role was, in fact, to facilitate the contacts between early Iberian
mercantilism and the emerging trans-oceanic powers of the Low Countries,
France, and England. Spanish and especially Portuguese New Christians
and Jews mobilized their tightly organized family networks to facilitate
the movement of an impressive variety of commodities—above all sugar,
spices, tobacco, and other plantation goods—throughout the triangle of
local economies in Africa, Europe, and the Americas. Theirs was a vital if
sometimes risky role, and while it lasted it provided substantial prosperity
and opportunities for mobility for what would prove to be the last generations of early modern Hispanic Judaism.

These and other developments in the economic sphere suggest how necessary it is not to limit the exile itself to 1492. It was a broader and lengthier process, the beginning of a chain of short- and long-range movements that permanently altered the map of Europe. Predictably, its most lasting consequences were reserved for the Jews and conversos themselves and found clear echoes in the spiritual and intellectual spheres. Removal of the sephardim from their homeland in Iberia led to an unprecedented degree of contact with their Ashkenazic coreligionists. Such encounters had taken place before, of course, in Italy, southern France, and the Balkans. Still, the expulsion and its long aftermath turned these local and sporadic contacts into more permanent coexistence at certain focal points. And while this coexistence did not lack its share of conflict between differing traditions, as in Amsterdam, far more significant was the way in which the two worlds of European Judaism made further progress in regarding themselves as members of a coherent whole. The result was, in the words of the leading student of the subject, "a more unified and integrated Jewish culture but one that was increasingly remote from that of the peoples among whom Jews lived."[4] For slowly, out of the ruins of the most thriving community of the Middle Ages, there arose a new worldview, which paradoxically turned inward as it shed its strictly local horizons for others, more European-wide in scope. And within this increasingly interconnected world the ashkenazim loomed ever larger. Apart from a few exceptions—including the most famous of the exiles, Isaac Abravanel, along with the mystic Moses Cordovero, the historians Shlomo ibn-Verga, Samuel Usque, and Yosef Ha-Kohen, and the millenarian enthusiast Menasseh ben Israel—the great figures of early modern Judaism were of central and eastern European origin. As time went by the balance tipped ever further in the latter's direction.

In retrospect, then, 1492—once again, a date that stood for something longer as well as deeper—marked a watershed: the passage from "the hegemony of the Spanish Jews" to the "German-Polish ascendance."[5] Scholars have long disagreed over the broader cultural impact of this geographic shift in the center of gravity of European Judaism. Some see it as signaling the end of the strong rationalist tradition of medieval Spain, which was now overwhelmed by more mystic tendencies hailing from the East. Others argue the opposite: that Iberian rationalism was now able to sally out of its corner and circulate in the wider world. What is more, the same could be said for kabbala, the famed body of mystical writing that had equally deep (though hardly exclusive) Spanish roots. Whatever the balance among these disparate traditions, what is beyond question is that the intellectual history of Hispanic Judaism had pretty much come to an end within the peninsula itself. Which raises a final question, one concerning the impact of the Iberian diaspora on the converts and the descendants of Jews who stayed behind.

The main point of this section has been to argue that over time, all but a very small proportion of these individuals effectively assimilated into the Christian majority. That said, there can be no question that for the shrinking remnant of holdouts, the very existence of sephardim in their new diaspora encouraged allegiance to their shared faith. Inquisitorial investigations turned up repeated evidence of interest on the part of judaizing conversos in establishing contacts with Jews from abroad, above all for purposes of instruction. The existence of letters from a Jew in Amsterdam to two nuns in a convent in the Extremaduran town of Zafra informing them of the exact dates on which to celebrate Jewish holidays (!) suggests something of the dependence of Spanish judaizers on outside help. And it is worth noting how the Sephardic settlements symbolized a freer, less controlled life for many Spaniards, not all of whom were conversos. In 1665 the Inquisition arrested an Aragonese actress named Josefa de la Torre for eating meat during Lent and indulging in scandalous sexual behavior. One witness reported that he had "heard it said [that she] has been in Livorno and entered the synagogue there and that she loved Jews very much" and that "she had said that she wished to go to Livorno to live as she pleased." Blas de Losada, also an actor and a native of Madrid, similarly claimed that he "had been in Livorno and Amsterdam and had eaten and drank with Jews and heretics" and that "he wished to return to Livorno because there he could live as he liked."[6] One cannot help wonder how many other Spaniards—Old Christians as well as New—were thinking the same thing.

CHAPTER 17

FROM HETERODOXY
TO MODERNITY?

T HE DISAPPEARANCE OF the institutions and rituals of normative
Judaism combined with Inquisitorial repression, the strength of
Catholic indoctrination, and the sheer weight of majority opinion
not only to weaken the attachment of would-be judaizers to the orthodox
forms of Jewish belief. Such pressures also moved some of these desperate
souls in altogether unexpected spiritual directions.

One might begin to chart this terrain by noting the silences as well as
the emphases that issued from this unique religious context. Even a brief
glance reveals that early modern Spanish and Portuguese Jews contributed
little to many of the key debates of Judaism held elsewhere. While this is
hardly a surprise given the circumstances, nevertheless there were certain
subjects that one might expect to have had a deep resonance among judaizing conversos, yet which seem to have produced little echo. Foremost
among these was messianism. Many Iberian Jews of the fifteenth century
trusted in the imminent appearance of the Messiah. The most notorious
antisemitic treatise of the period, Espina's *Fortress of Faith,* warned Christians that Jewish eschatological hopes were on the rise, especially following
the Muslim conquest of Constantinople in 1453, which many read as an
augury of impending judgment. Messianism, moreover, was one of the more

persistent themes in the works of the most prominent Jewish writer of the expulsion generation, Isaac Abravanel. He even provided a precise date for the much-awaited arrival, 1503. (When the End of Days did not take place, he updated his prediction to 1504, again without effect.)

Yet what is most striking is the way in which messianism receded as a perceptible current among Iberian judaizers. There were, to be sure, several cases of eschatological fervor in the first two generations of conversos. The earliest of these took place in southeastern Extremadura during the opening decade of the sixteenth century. There at least three different groups of New Christians gathered in hope of divine deliverance from persecution. The leaders who preached this message included two women, one Inés from the town of Herrera del Duque and one Mari Gómez from Chillón, near Almadén. Their avowal that both the prophet Elijah and the Messiah were en route found ready listeners, and the Inquisition punished more than thirty defendants (most of them women) for their involvement in the movement. This episode was followed in the 1530s by the even more bizarre case of David Reuveni. A "small dark man" who arrived in Venice in 1524 announced to the four winds that he had come from the "Desert of Habor" (a site mentioned in II Kings 17:6) with a mission unto both Jews and Christians. He managed to obtain an audience with the pope, whom he sought to enlist in an alliance to free the Holy Land from the Muslims. After a stay in Portugal, from whence he was expelled due to the overly enthusiastic response he provoked among the kingdom's New Christians, he returned to Italy where he was finally imprisoned and exposed as an impostor. He somehow turned up in the Extremaduran town of Llerena, where the Inquisition burned him in 1538. The same fate befell his best-known follower, Diogo Pires, a prominent converso and royal secretary who, after undergoing circumcision, changed his name to Solomon Molcho and became a kabbalist and a messianic figure on his own. What most struck contemporaries about this extraordinary tale was not only the ease with which both Reuveni and Molcho were able to arrange interviews with leading figures throughout Europe. It was also the sheer excitement their message—which combined calls for spiritual reform with plans for an unprecedented alliance between Christians and "biblical" Jews to defeat the shared enemy of Islam—generated in the Iberian peninsula as well as in Italy.

Clearly this messianic tandem struck a chord among Iberian conversos as well as in Jewish communities elsewhere. Yet apart from these and a few other instances, messianism played a much smaller role in the history of Spanish and Portuguese judaizing than one might expect. It is telling that while the main messianic movement of early modern Judaism—the tumultuous attempt of Sabbatai Zevi to proclaim himself the Messiah which ended in failure and his conversion to Islam in Istanbul in 1666—found enthusiastic adepts among sephardim throughout Europe, it is hard to find significant echoes of it among peninsular judaizers. On the whole, expectations of collective redemption through divine deliverance were at best a minor theme in early modern Hispanic Judaism. It was in fact far more characteristic of Spanish and Portuguese Christianity. Messianism and its close cousin millenarianism appeared in several guises, ranging from the mysterious *encubierto* or savior in disguise who emerged as a leader in the Germanies revolt in Valencia in 1520–23 to "Sebastianism," the lingering popular belief in the return of King Sebastian of Portugal following his death while crusading in North Africa in 1578.

Heterodox tendencies among early modern Iberian judaizers in fact moved in the opposite direction, away from religious enthusiasm and toward different varieties of skepticism. The latter label should be understood in two senses. Skepticism in the wider sense was conveyed through questioning or critical attitudes toward the truth claims of the major historical religions. More narrowly, it referred to the rejection of certain doctrines associated with these faiths. Its most specific form involved denying the central tenets of the immortality of the soul and the existence of an afterlife. This "Sadduceanism" had a long and rich history in Iberian Judaism. "There is nothing but birth and death" was a stock phrase that Christians habitually attributed to Jews. This charge was leveled in, for example, the *Alboraique* pamphlet from the 1480s, as well as in more mainstream antisemitic literature, such as Espina's encyclopedic tract. However, it was not simply a canard invented by the enemies of the Jews. Inquisitorial papers document frequent reiteration of the same phrase by suspects of judaizing. Even less pressured testimony produced abundant evidence of its popularity among Jews. Thus, statements made in Soria in the 1480s citing conversations between Christians and Jews that took place two or three decades earlier also reported the same "birth and death" cliché.

It was widely recognized that the denial of the immortality of the soul—a controversial idea that was not regarded as a binding precept in ancient or medieval Judaism—was both cause and consequence of a broader skepticism among the Jews. Abravanel himself acknowledged the existence of this sort of disbelief in his reference to those ex-Jews who "do not believe in either of the two religions [Judaism and Christianity], in the Law of God or in the laws of the nations."[1] Late medieval Spanish Judaism had earned a considerable reputation for freethinking, which drew on a wide range of sources. These included Averroism, radical Aristotelianism, and the medieval Jewish "heresy" of the Karaites. The conversos inherited this mantle and added some embroidery of their own. As far away as Germany, Martin Luther was heard to remark that all Spaniards were secret Jews, but "whereas other heretics defend their opinions obstinately, the Marranos shrug their shoulders and hold nothing for certain."[2] And in Holland, when the renowned jurist Hugo Grotius wrote in 1615 to express his (reluctant) approval of granting tolerance to the Portuguese Jews, he stipulated that first they should take an oath to demonstrate their commitment to God, as there were many "atheists and impious people" among them.[3]

What Luther called indifference and Grotius atheism was in reality a complex body of opinion. Often what was voiced was more spiritual confusion and doubt than any systematic attitude. This was obviously the case of the New Christian Francisco López Moreira, who in 1638 told the inquisitors of Santiago de Compostela that while he had practiced Judaism since the age of fourteen, "he often had doubts and did not believe in one law or the other."[4] Yet in other instances one can detect more articulated positions edging ever closer toward what is now generically referred to as rationalism. This amalgam mixed empiricism and naturalism, frequently stated in explicitly medical terms, with more unusual derivatives, such as literalist readings or even higher criticism of Scripture. The overlap with learned skepticism as it developed among Christians grew over time. While the specifically Judaic tributary to the small but rising pool of European rationalism drew on individual efforts throughout the continent, there can be no questioning the central role Iberian Jews—and conversos and ex-conversos in particular—played in this trend. One of the more visible figures in this movement was Francisco Sánchez. A New Christian of Galician-Portuguese background and a physician as well as professor of philosophy at the University of Toulouse, Sánchez won a European-wide reputation for his treatise

Quod nihil scitur ("That Nothing Is Known") of 1581. A blistering attack on Aristotelianism and Scholasticism, Sánchez's defense of empiricism and experimental science did much to clear the path for the *Discourse on Method* (1637). Descartes famously turned his initial avowal of skepticism in a fideistic direction and declared that his achievement did not question the truth of revelation but instead confirmed it. Others, however, were convinced that this brand of rationalism merely subverted the Christian faith. And among them were more than a few believers in alternatives to the Church and even to religion as a whole.

That this brand of skepticism could be turned against traditional rabbinical Judaism in addition to Christianity found eloquent illustration in the tragic story of Uriel da Costa. A well-off converso who had studied law at the University of Coimbra, Costa and much of his immediate family left their native Portugal in 1612 openly to practice Judaism in northern Europe. A brief stay in Hamburg was followed by more permanent residence in Amsterdam. There Costa's criticisms of Jewish doctrines and practices soon won him the enmity of the *mahamad,* or governing board of the community. His first book, published in 1616, led to official condemnation from the Venetian rabbi Leon da Modena. A second text in 1624 won him a *cherem* or formal ban in Amsterdam itself, which was repeated in 1633. In 1640 he accepted an offer to expiate his heresies through a public ritual of atonement. The humiliation proved too much, though, and several days later, after writing an autobiographical account of his sufferings, he committed suicide.

Although Costa's views became more radical as his isolation from his fellow Jews increased, two basic ideas formed the long-term nucleus of his dissent from traditional Judaism. The first was his disbelief in eternal life and the immortality of the soul. The second was rejection of the rabbinate as a source of religious authority. Adopting a stance similar to the Protestant critique of Catholicism, Costa stressed that Scripture—that is, written revelation and not the oral law of the rabbis—was the only legitimate guide to faith. (In his memoir he calmly remarked that he eventually understood that the Torah itself was a human invention, but apparently he did not circulate this more extreme position in public.) What brought these two deviations together was that the former was associated with the rabbinate, whose members he labeled "pharisees." Costa himself was dubbed a Sadducee, a label—one of the many used in Leon da Modena's letter of censure—that denotes a member of the rival faction known for its pronounced skepticism regarding the existence of an afterlife.

Costa depicted himself as a solitary figure in Amsterdam. Yet he did not lack for fellow believers, or rather, disbelievers. Criticism of the rabbinate and of many of the standard ritual practices associated with traditional Judaism was hardly novel. Once again, Protestant rejection of the Catholic clergy and the "superstitious" practices it promoted constituted a ready, even immediate local parallel. That the scribes had managed to elevate their Talmud above the Torah was another charge with ample precedents. In particular, it evoked the medieval Karaites—yet another of Leon da Modena's terms of abuse—who had rejected oral law while insisting on the sole authenticity of the written law. Still, Costa trod an unusually tortuous path, from being a "non-Christian Christian" to becoming a "non-Jewish Jew."[5] Starting out as a Catholic, then transforming himself into a crypto-Jewish returnee who was soon expelled from public Judaism, he ended his life as a deist who appealed to natural law instead of (as he saw it) man-made religion. Few other cases illustrate so well how one specifically Iberian Judaic emphasis—reluctance to accept the immortality of the soul—could evolve directly into the broader variant. Fewer still show how the latter could be turned against not just a single religion, but against religion in general.

The endpoint of this peculiar story was Baruch (Benedict) Spinoza. Unlike Costa, Spinoza grew up fully within Judaism. Born in Amsterdam to a well-known Portuguese family, he not only studied with Menasseh ben Israel but also learned Latin and the classics with the radical ex-Jesuit Franciscus Van Enden. In 1656, when he was twenty-three, he was subjected to the same sort of *cherem* that had been leveled against Costa, although this time no public ceremony was involved. Still, the ban was a harsh one, and unlike Costa's, it was never lifted. For the rest of his life he eked out an existence outside the Jewish community, first in Amsterdam and then, after 1661, in Rijnsburg, a village near Leiden, where he worked as a lens grinder. As his philosophical writings began to circulate he became an increasingly controversial if respected figure. Since he limited his direct criticism of revealed religion to Judaism, and to the Jews' self-understanding as the chosen people of God, the Christian authorities left him alone. Yet contemporary readers did not have to be too perspicacious to sense how effortlessly his critique of the Old Testament could be applied to the New. It was equally easy—and for many readers, quite shocking—to see how philosophy could be fully detached from religion, whose imperatives were now reduced to a few basic rules of ethics.

The essence of the "Spinozist revolt" that was foreshadowed by Costa in the 1620s and brought to fruition beginning in the 1650s was threefold. Its bases included the "denial of all revealed religion, the claim that God did not exist other than 'philosophically,' that is as a First Cause which did not interfere in the affairs of men, and a thoroughgoing materialism which denied the immortality of the soul."[6] That all this formed part of a trajectory is suggested by the significant affinities and connections between the two legendary nonconformists (although, popular legend to the contrary, they never met). Also strengthening the impression that a collective effort was at work here was the involvement of other individuals of converso background. An especially key figure, who in many ways served as a bridge between the two generations of Costa and Spinoza, was Juan de Prado. A New Christian physician of Portuguese origin, Prado left Spain in 1653 and began a lengthy period of spiritual as well as geographical wandering that took him to Rome, Hamburg, Amsterdam, and Antwerp, where he died (apparently as a professed Christian) in 1669. While in Amsterdam he won a reputation for freethinking. In 1658 he was placed under a ban following an investigation that revealed his hostility toward oral law and rabbinical norms, along with his doubts about the status of the Jews as the Chosen People and the doctrine of the immortality of the soul. Prado's case is particularly revealing not only because he had apparently absorbed some of his skepticism while studying medicine at Alcalá and Toledo during the 1620s and 1630s (his earliest expression of deist opinions dates to 1643). It also shows many affinities with developments elsewhere, such as the "erudite libertinism" that was on the rise throughout Europe in the first half of the seventeenth century. There were firm limits to Prado's originality as a thinker, but that this cosmopolitan character was in direct contact with Spinoza clearly makes his evolution all the more suggestive.

As for its being an endpoint: from the point of the view of the converso tradition under examination here, Spinoza's achievement was to take the main emphases of Costa and others like him—rejection of oral law and the afterlife, along with a historicist approach to religion—in an even more universalist and philosophical direction. With unprecedented thoroughness he moved this form of rationalism completely beyond the scope of Judaism or of any religion that could not be reduced strictly to an ethical system. That Spinoza's new dispensation had its personal and much of its intellectual roots in Judaism can hardly be disputed. That its future depended in any way on Judaism was something Spinoza himself did his best to make sure would not take place.

Having reached this juncture, one last question remains: how crucial a role did the Iberian background play in this admittedly idiosyncratic path to modern rationalism? Many byways led in the same direction. Can a precedence of sorts be claimed for this one? And if so, on what grounds?

It was a commonplace in this period as in others that rivalry among religions exposes their truth claims to public competition and that this in turn gives rise to situations in which skepticism and even atheism can emerge. One text from the early modern era which rehearses precisely a situation of this sort was the "Colloquium of the Seven" the French philosopher Jean Bodin wrote toward the end of his life. This highly controversial work—so controversial, in fact, that it could not be printed, although it circulated widely in manuscript form—consisted of a dialogue among a handful of men, each of whom argued for the merits of his respective religion. The Jew (one "Salomon Barcassius") and a deist ("Diego Toralba") won the day, defeating the unusual coalition of the Catholic, Lutheran, and Calvinist. This was an unlikely outcome, even for someone like Bodin who, while he died within Catholicism, was a notorious dabbler in kabbala and other esoteric pursuits. Yet—and this is the deeper matter at issue here—was it so unlikely that an alliance of Judaism and deism should prevail? And that the deist should bear such a transparently Spanish name?

The sequence looks something like this. The starting point was the rationalism and skepticism that formed a prominent, though far from exclusive, current of late medieval Iberian Judaism. They were epitomized by the Sadducean denial of the immortality of the soul, which even major spokesmen for orthodoxy such as Maimonides could defend only by moving it in a rationalist direction and by uncoupling it from the closely related belief in the resurrection of the dead. The prolonged experience of conversion and public adherence to Christianity then led crypto-Judaism into a markedly "internalist" direction. The result was an unprecedented accent on individualism and on a subjectivist understanding of faith that stressed inner intention and attachment at the expense of outward conformity. The assumption of essentially new identities as public Jews outside the peninsula then brought new difficulties of its own. It not only meant confronting the demanding practice of Judaism in daily life after long experience of private criticism of Catholic ritualism. It also meant submitting to a new form of authority, the rabbinate, whose legitimacy seemed to rest on a questionable equivalence of oral law with Torah or written law. For conversos who grew up essentially as Nicodemites—that is, publicly behaving as Catholics yet privately subjecting the Church to many of the same sort of criticisms leveled by Protestants—the rabbis' pretense to authority was hard to distinguish from that of the Catholic clergy. Even more damaging was the perceived impossibility of justifying such claims on the basis of reason and natural law—something their Scholastic education in the peninsula had taught them to do. A final ingredient—once again, discernibly rooted in the spiritual and physical experience of migration across religious and other frontiers—was the replacement of Jewish separatism by a universalism which forcefully moved ethics to the center of a religious identity whose theological contents proved increasingly—and perhaps even deliberately—vague and lacking in precision.

It would be misleading—and above all far too simplistic—to see all this as a well-defined pathway that led from skepticism in the strict sense to its broader catchment, or from the rejection of specific doctrines to the rejection of religion as a whole. But that there was a logic of sorts by which Hispanic Judaism moved via concrete historical experience toward the Spinozist synthesis is not that unlikely. In fact, spokesmen for the orthodox majority suggested as much. In 1663–64 Isaac Orobio de Castro—an ex-converso now living in Amsterdam who knew Prado well—wrote an illuminating reply to critics of rabbinical authority. In the prologue to his *Invective against [Juan de] Prado,* Orobio differentiates between two types of conversos who had reached Holland to live as Jews. He opposes those who, while profoundly ignorant of the tenets of Judaism, obey the rabbis, to those who after studying in Spanish and Portuguese universities and "full of vanity, pride, and arrogance" reject orthodox teachings and "fall in the abysm of apostasy and heresy."[7] He then goes on to differentiate three types of dissenters from the faith: atheists who deny Scripture; believers who accept written law, but not its oral counterpart; and those who accept both but reject rabbinical regulation as superfluous and lacking in legitimacy. Reading this schema in reverse order reveals a clear progression that begins by questioning "clerical" authority, moves on to growing doubts about oral and then written law, and culminates in the dismissal of religion altogether. This was precisely the line along which Uriel da Costa had evolved and which appears to encapsulate the final phase in the Iberian drift toward philosophical rationalism.

Yet central as these Hispanic origins were, one should not lose from sight the other necessary ingredient in this mix: the atmosphere of religious and intellectual toleration in seventeenth-century Holland that allowed this heterodoxy to take root and flourish. To be sure, much of this transigence was far from disinterested. Some Protestant divines spread news of heterodoxy among the Portuguese as a means of facilitating the much-awaited conversion of the Jews. This seems to have been the stance of Philip van Limborch, the supporter of Uriel da Costa who was responsible for circulating his autobiography (an act of generosity that apparently did not preclude his tampering with the text). A number of "liberal" Protestants from the Netherlands and even further afield similarly had contact with Spinoza; indeed, they constituted the most visible exception to his fabled intellectual and personal isolation. Whatever their motives, though, the existence of a haven safe enough for Jewish heterodoxy as well as orthodoxy was vital to the development of this particular filament within European deistic rationalism.

Overheated statements have been made on behalf of this process and the context in which it took place—so much so that before departing this question some words of caution and, above all, due proportion are needed. It has been argued that the Portuguese community in seventeenth-century Amsterdam gave rise both to "New Jews" and—however reluctantly—to the "first modern Jews." By this is meant that Holland served as the birthplace not only of a crucial strand of modern critical thought but also of a precocious effort to live religion as a culture instead of as a sum of firm dogmas. Another variant of this thesis downplays the role of Amsterdam as the crucible for the formation of "modern Jews." Insisting that skepticism was not the only path to modernity, it places its emphasis instead on the converso experience in general. This generic *marranismo* had as its leading trait an unstable mixture of beliefs and practices from various religious traditions, which fostered attitudes of irony, skepticism, mental reservation, and interiority. The existential reality of this divided existence similarly encouraged judaizers to define themselves as Jews less in terms of adherence to specific doctrines than as bearers of a common memory held together by shared ethnic identity. In such circumstances, it comes as little surprise to find some judaizers subjecting the claims of their ancestral religion to the same rationalist criteria by which they found wanting Christian beliefs such as the Incarnation and the Trinity.

These are bold assertions, and some of them would find it hard to stand their ground. Two caveats in particular should be kept in mind. First, the vast majority of Amsterdam's "New Jews" did not second the skeptical-deist trajectory outlined here. Their integration into orthodox Judaism went fairly smoothly and in the end sustained a community that was modern in some senses but also conservative and traditional in many others. Despite their undoubted relevance for the intellectual future of Europe, Spinoza and others like him represented a numerically insignificant part of this broader collective. They were, to put it baldly, a minority (skeptics and rationalists) of a minority (judaizers and returnees to Judaism) of a minority (Iberian conversos).

Moreover, one should always keep in mind the infinite variety of the New Christian experience and the ease with which it ended up producing often radically different outcomes. It is certainly appropriate to underline the elements within the admittedly unusual, even unique history of crypto-Judaism that led Costa, Prado, Spinoza, and others to break the cake of custom in regard to institutional religion's role as intellectual authority and basis of political community. Yet one must also recognize that the very same experience of dissimulation, syncretism, and the like which moved some judaizers toward universalism could lead others in the opposite direction, toward greater affirmation of separatist identity. This new, internal exile produced not only dissenters from orthodoxy. It also engendered militant traditionalists, such as Orobio de Castro, whose campaigns against Prado, Spinoza, and others were just as rooted in the converso dilemma as was their way of thinking. In a related vein, conditions that have been read as leading some New Christians to deny the immortality of the soul led others toward an intense preoccupation with individual salvation that surprised their rabbis. At work here was not just the lingering influence of Catholic theology but also a more pressing worry: the ultimate fate of their forebears and kinsmen back in Iberia whose lack of public profession cast grave doubts on their status as Jews.

In the end, it is misleading to speak of *the* Iberian Jewish path to modernity. That there was *an* Iberian Jewish path to modernity cannot be gainsaid. That it deserves recognition as one means among many by which Europe reached the Enlightenment is equally true. What perhaps most merits emphasis is that this was an important piece of Spanish history whose denouement took place outside Spain itself. Within the latter the converso world had melted into oblivion. Apart from a last gasp of trials in the 1720s—predictably, almost all the defendants were of Portuguese origin—Judaism within Spain had become literally vestigial. It lived on as a memory, or more precisely myth, reduced to polemical uses. As history, Spanish Judaism had moved elsewhere. Or as one elegy to a distant offshoot of this exile put it, "Gone are the living, but the dead remain."[8]

TWO HISTORIES,
PARALLEL AND DIFFERENT

A T FIRST GLANCE, what overwhelms are the similarities. Both the Jews and Muslims of Spain were the objects of collective violence. In both cases violence was accompanied by exclusion and followed by expulsion. And in both instances the victor was the same: a self-confident, militant Christianity, now determined to mark a new course by disowning its former willingness, however grudging, to tolerate followers of different dogmas. The result was the creation of two new social categories within a Spain that grasped for union on a variety of levels. What brought conversos as well as moriscos into being was largely though not exclusively the same mechanism: obligatory baptism. Yet the recourse to force damaged the project from the very beginning, by sowing the fatal seed of doubt in the minds of everyone it touched. And to say that the Christian society's unwillingness to acknowledge that what it wrought was a moral and spiritual failure is not just a reading backward into time of present-day sensibilities. As the ample discourse surrounding both groups of New Christians shows, principled and courageous theologians could be found opposing the acceptance of the validity of coercion, even in regard to something as powerful as a sacrament. Unfortunately, too few of their contemporaries bothered to listen.

Much the same origins, then, launched the unfortunate histories of these minorities. Yet historical comparison does not search only for similarities. It also hearkens to differences. When looking for divergences in the paths taken, one needs to look toward the end, at the radically different fates of the two groups. The Muslims suffered not one but two expulsions: the first, beginning in 1500, as Muslims and the second, beginning in 1609, as moriscos widely suspected of being crypto-Muslims. The Jews were expelled once, in 1492. Thereafter their descendants were absorbed into Christian society. This was a long, drawn-out process and fraught with numerous difficulties. But the fact that the conversos were never expelled, that they eventually assimilated into the Christian mainstream while the moriscos did not, constitutes the single greatest divergence between the two lineages of New Christians.

This divergence was not an accident, nor was it the product of a single moment in time. Instead, it had deep roots in the past. The difference between conversion and conquest had been the principal divergence between the histories of Jews and Muslims in medieval Spain. While the Jews, who were already long accustomed to Christian rule, were subjected to relentless pressure to be baptized beginning in the later fourteenth century, the Muslims were divided among those—at first a minority—who lived in Christian society as mudéjares and those who had yet to be brought in the fold. The latter were the object of protracted military measures which culminated in the elimination in 1492 of the last surviving redoubt of Islam in the peninsula: the Nasrid kingdom of Granada. Yet even after this turning point the factor of force continued to differentiate Muslims and their nominally Christian descendants from the conversos. Rightly or wrongly, the moriscos were seen as a military threat. They won their reputation for rebellion in 1500 in the Alpujarras south of Granada, in the mid-1520s in the Sierra de Espadán in Valencia, and in 1569 once again in the Alpujarras. Above all, they were seen as having other armies on their side: the hosts of Islam, ranging from the corsairs of North Africa to the powerful navies of the Ottoman Sultanate. All these were potential and on occasion real allies. The conversos, however, had no such outside help to turn to. Seen in this light, it is hardly an accident that early modern Spain produced much more formal discourse about the moriscos than the conversos. The former were a problem of state, and policy—involving, in the end, truly drastic measures—was required to solve the "morisco problem." The conversos raised no such strategic concerns. There were, in fact, no converso revolts, excepting one or two conspiracies during the first decades of the Inquisition. The low-level, judicial violence of the Holy Office was enough to keep such a diverse and disorganized group in check. Thus, to the extent there was a "converso problem," it was dealt with on a spiritual level and required neither armies nor galleys.

A second issue inviting comparison involves the social profile of the two categories. The most visible factor marking them as groups was their socioeconomic characteristics. For far too long historians have lumped all moriscos together into a single profile: poor, uneducated, rural-bound, immobile. Recent research has done much to change this stereotype. We now know that a small but energetic elite developed among them. Its members were drawn not just from the surviving remnants of the aristocratic lineages of Granada. Rather, it emerged in virtually all areas of morisco settlement and comprised individuals who distinguished themselves as intermediaries with Old Christian superiors and as organizers of collective resources, including public and private credit, the distribution of taxes, and the like. That said, there is no gainsaying that in terms of location and professional activity, the vast majority of moriscos did live up to the stereotype. Not only did they live in the countryside. In Valencia and Granada in particular, and also in Aragon, they eked out an existence in agriculture and tended to group together in the sort of isolated settlements that facilitated a high degree of social cohesion. Elsewhere—above all, in Castile proper—their profile was somewhat different. Here one finds substantially closer contact with the Old Christian population and a broader occupational range, including artisans and specialists in local and medium-range transport and other services. In the end, however, this latter, more broadly based experience was confined to a minority. Even making allowances for greater diversity among the ex-Muslims and the imperative need not to approach them as a homogeneous bloc, the older image of the rural morisco still holds its ground.

The social configuration of the conversos also conformed to a stereotype. The descendants of the Jews were by and large city dwellers. They also held a much wider range of occupational berths, reaching from artisans and shopkeepers upward into the mercantile and professional strata. They constituted, in other words, a middling class. What is more, not a few among their

numbers managed to make their way upward into the elite. The gap between
the relative possibilities for social mobility was dramatic. The conversos
found it much less difficult than the moriscos to take the two classic paths
of social advancement: investing capital in local office and/or recourse to
Latin education and higher studies (particularly law at the universities) that
would facilitate entry into royal and ecclesiastical administration. An interesting study has highlighted the differences between converso and morisco
medical professionals who fell afoul of the Inquisition.[1] One finds not only
a striking contrast between the university-trained converso physicians and
the impoverished, lower-class morisco folk healers who possessed virtually
no formal education. There is also the fact that the conversos were all tried
for judaizing, whereas the moriscos were charged with various magical
practices. The former were clearly in the medical and social mainstream,
while the latter were marginalized thanks to, inter alia, their distance from
academic medicine. That one finds virtually no moriscos in the universities
and thus on the pathway that led to employment in the early modern state
or Church is one of the most clamorous differences between the two groups
and goes a long way in explaining their divergent fates.

What was at work here? Muslim community versus Jewish individualism?
Surely one can find a better key than this tired cliché with which to unlock
the differences between the two sets of New Christians. The principal draw-
back of this opposition from the perspective of social history is the blithe
way in which it ignores a number of crucial variables. One of these was the
intermediate level of the family. Vague notions of conversos' living out their
lives as deracinated individuals remove from sight the unshakable fact of
the rooting of virtually all forms of comportment and conviction in larger
aggregates, especially those of kinship. This was nowhere truer than in the
case of the crypto-Jews, for whom both the immediate domestic circle and
the broader network of lineage stepped in as substitutes when the collective
institutions and figures of normative Judaism disappeared. Much the same
can be said of the morisco family, with one proviso. Given the frequent
historiographic tendency to depict Muslims as impossible to pry loose from
their broader (and often idealized) collectivities, it should also be recognized
that families were the strongest contributors to differentiation and internal
conflict, as well as solidarity, within morisco society, as well as elsewhere.

That said, it is true that conversos and moriscos lived their lives in broadly different ways and that the relative degree of group solidarity was one of the most perceptible differences between them. Baldly stated, the moriscos were much more successful in maintaining a communal identity—and this despite the fact that there surely was more morisco assimilation into Old Christian society than used to be believed. When trying to explain this fact it is hard to detach causes from consequences. One thus wonders: was the greater physical isolation of the moriscos the result of their own separatism or was it imposed by Old Christians who wished to have as little contact with them as possible? What can be more reliably asserted is, first, that during the crucial early decades of the exposure of the former Muslims to Christianity they received scant and certainly insufficient attention from ecclesiastical authorities. (Once again, one sees here a crucial difference with the conversos, for whom the Inquisition was expressly created, and which reserved its greatest violence for its opening phase.) And second, that the tenacity with which the moriscos held on to their customs and rituals was not necessarily motivated by religious reasons. Only tangentially linked to Islam were practices such as foodways, dress, music, dance, and, more than anything else, language—precisely the habits that the morisco leader Núñez Muley insisted (in vain) were cultural in character and thus doctrinally neutral. A combination of an urban lifestyle in close proximity to Old Christians and the vigilance of the Inquisition had led the conversos early on to relinquish any similar signs of distinctiveness. This lower profile reduced the sense of difference between this set of converts and the rest of society and, once again, helped smooth the way to their integration.

Even in the instrument most specifically designed to prevent such assimilation—the blood purity statutes—one can detect a similar bifurcation of efforts at discrimination. The laws of limpieza provide the most telling evidence of the tendency of early modern Spaniards to conceive of Judaism and Islam in ethnic as well as religious terms. Not surprisingly, the letter of the law was evenhanded in barring descendants of both Jews and Muslims from a wide range of official roles and positions in Christian society. That they were applied far more frequently in the case of the former than the latter reflected, once again, the far greater social mobility of the conversos. After all, very few moriscos applied to the Colegios Mayores of the universities or tried to claim a place for themselves on city councils, within cathedral chapters, or in the military orders. Still, it is quite suggestive that when formal exceptions to these rules were made, they always favored the moriscos. This was seen most clearly in the case of the old Muslim elite of the kingdom of Granada, many of whose members were promoted to positions of prominence in the new municipal and ecclesiastical administrations. Even more telling is the fact that they kept their posts without renouncing their Muslim aristocratic heritage even as the blood purity laws proliferated. This fact, along with the ease with which they intermarried with Granada's Old Christian families, suggests that while the descendants of Muslims were generally despised and discriminated against as humble, impoverished members of a racial minority, their blood—and especially that of their nobles—was seen as less "contaminating" and "dishonorable" than that of Jews. In the words of the Aragonese humanist Antonio Agustín,

> It is a greater infamy to descend from Jews than from Moors. Thus we see in some noble lineages that it matters little if they have some Moorish ancestors, whereas those who have even a drop of Jewish blood are pointed out, and cannot join the military orders, enter the university colleges or hold bishoprics.[2]

The Muslims' impressive past (and present) as warriors played a crucial role here. But a sense of broader redeemability was also involved. It is significant that when the moriscos were finally expelled the wife of the viceroy of Valencia and other local notables kidnapped scores of children from their families in order to keep them in Spain and raise them as Christians. That nothing similar attended the expulsions of the Jews a century before—children were seized, but only as a form of blackmail to keep their parents from departing—suggests that the common mental and social framework of early modern racialism could accommodate a certain amount of nuance when it came to defining degrees of exclusivity.

There is no avoiding this strange irony: that the group that contemporary racism defined as *most* irreducible, *most* contaminating, and *most* polluting was the one which wound up assimilated. So blatant a contradiction raises all sorts of questions regarding the relation between official ideologies and political and military realities, the weight of popular as opposed to learned imagery within political praxis, and the role of sheer chance in what have long been presented as inevitable historical trajectories. It also brings into the open what was perhaps the greatest contrast between—and paradox within—these two parallel but different histories. Readers today will be familiar with the names of many early modern Spaniards of Jewish descent. Their ranks include a doctor of the Church, St. Teresa of Avila, and poets of the stature of Luis de León, to name just two New Christians made famous by their writings. It is doubtful that a single morisco will come to mind, despite the fact that by the early sixteenth century there were many more New Christians of Muslim than of Jewish ancestry. The reason why is simple enough: a substantial though by no means dominant portion of the members of early modern Spain's cultural and religious elites had some sort of Jewish familial past. The paradox is while many of these figures are known today to have been conversos, it is questionable whether the same knowledge was shared by early modern Spaniards. Teresa's case illustrates this well. While historians have uncovered the firmest possible evidence of her converso background—her maternal grandfather had in fact been penanced by the Toledo Inquisition for judaizing—there is not a single documented *contemporary* reference to her being of Jewish descent. This fact was surely known to many people both in her native Avila and beyond. But it was an *invisible* fact as far as the historical record of her own time is concerned. This curious situation is yet another reminder—certain surface impressions to the contrary—of the extent to which the descendants of Spain's Jews had become assimilated. Had it been otherwise, the fate of the conversos surely would have resembled more closely that which befell the moriscos.

NOTES

PREFACE

1. I am similarly indebted to all three for kindly keeping me supplied with copies of their own work. Other colleagues who have suggested references and given or sent me their publications include Manuel Barrios, Jaime Contreras, Baltasar Cuart, María Antonia Garcés, Lu Ann Homza, Kim Lynn, Natalia Muchnik, José Pardo Tomás, Felipe Pereda, Fernando Rodríguez Mediano, Bernard Vincent, and Alison Weber.

CHAPTER TWO

1. Luis del Mármol Carvajal, *Historia de la rebelión y castigo de los moriscos del Reino de Granada,* intro. Angel Galán (Málaga, 2004), p. 63.

2. L. P. Harvey, *Muslims in Spain, 1500 to 1614* (Chicago, 2005), p. 296, citing Pascual Boronat y Barrachina (1901).

3. Cited in Francisco Márquez Villanueva, *El problema morisco (desde otras laderas)* (Madrid, 1998), p. 229.

4. Cited in Antonio Domínguez Ortiz and Bernard Vincent, *Historia de los moriscos: Vida y tragedia de una minoría* (Madrid, 1979), p. 161.

5. Fray Jaime Bleda, *Corónica de los moros de España* (Valencia, 1618), p. 1027, cited in James Casey, *Early Modern Spain: A Social History* (London, 1999), p. 228.

6. Gerardo Moraleja Pinilla, *Historia de Medina del Campo* (Medina del Campo, 1971), p. 175, as cited in Alberto Marcos Martín, "Medina del Campo 1500–1800: An Historical Account of Its Decline," in I. A. A. Thompson and Bartolomé Yun Casalilla, eds., *The Castilian Crisis of the Seventeenth Century: New Perspectives on the Economic and Social History of*

Seventeenth-Century Spain (Cambridge, 1994), p. 235. For Capmany, see his *Ideari,* ed. Emili Giralt i Raventós, trans. from the Spanish by Joan-Lluís Marfany (Barcelona, 1965), p. 48.

7. Cited in James M. Cox, "Recovering Literature's Lost Ground through Autobiography," in James Olney, ed., *Autobiography: Essays Theoretical and Critical* (Princeton, NJ, 1980), p. 139.

8. Cited in David Mitchell, *Travellers in Spain: An Illustrated Anthology* (London, 1990), p. 17.

CHAPTER THREE

1. Pedro de Valencia, *Tratado acerca de los moriscos de España (Manuscrito del siglo XVII),* ed. Joaquín Gil Sanjuan (Málaga, 1997), p. 74.

2. Bernardo Pérez de Chinchón, *Antialcorano, Diálogos christianos, conversión y evangelización de moriscos,* ed. Francisco Pons Fuster (Alicante, 2000), p. 382.

3. Cited in Mercedes García Arenal, *Inquisición y moriscos: Los procesos del tribunal de Cuenca* (Madrid, 1978), p. 143.

4. Cited in García Arenal, *Inquisición y moriscos,* p. 30.

5. Archivo Histórico Nacional (Madrid)/Inquis., lib. 731, ff. 253v.–254r. For Pedro de León's remarks, see *Grandeza y miseria en Andalucía: Testimonio de una encrucijada histórica (1578-1616),* ed. Pedro Herrera Puga (Granada, 1981), p. 104.

6. Serafín de Tapia, "Carta de un morisco de Arévalo a un amigo cristiano viejo escrita desde el destierro en el sur de Francia," document appended to his "Los moriscos de Castilla la Vieja, ¿una identidad en proceso de disolución?" *Sharq al-Andalus,* vol. 12, 1995, pp. 194–95.

CHAPTER FOUR

1. The Spanish original of the chapter title is "Christianos aparentes y moros verdaderos": from Francisco Bermúdez de Pedraza, *Historia eclesiástica, principios, y progressos de la ciudad, y religión católica de Granada* (Granada, 1638), p. 238, as cited in Pedro Longás, *La vida religiosa de los moriscos* (Madrid, 1915), p. lii.

2. Pedro de Medina, *Obras. Libro de grandezas y cosas memorables de España: Libro de la verdad,* ed. Angel González Palencia (Madrid, 1944), p. 184.

3. Mármol, *Historia de la rebelión,* p. 63.

4. Cited in García Arenal, *Inquisición y moriscos,* p. 102.

5. Ahmad ibn-Qasim Al-Hajari, *Kitab Nasir al-din ala 'L'Qawn al-Kafirin (The Supporter of Religion against the Infidel),* ed. P. S. Van Koningsveld, Q. Al-Samarrai, and H. G. A. Wiegers (Madrid, 1997), p. 64.

6. Cited in García Arenal, *Inquisición y moriscos,* p. 103.

7. "Que en lo exterior fingiesen cristiandad, y en lo interior fuesen moros," as cited in Domínguez Ortiz and Vincent, *Historia de los moriscos,* p. 147.

8. Cited in Longás, *Vida religiosa,* pp. 305-7.

9. Al-Hajari, *Kitab Nasir al-din,* pp. 121-122.

CHAPTER FIVE

1. Pedro de Valencia, *Tratado*, p. 87.

2. Cited in García Arenal, *Inquisición y moriscos*, pp. 15–18.

3. Cited in Daniel Eisenberg, "Cisneros y la quema de los manuscritos granadinos," *Journal of Hispanic Philology*, vol. 16, 1992, p. 115.

4. Deborah E. Harkness, *The Jewel House: Elizabethan London and the Scientific Revolution* (New Haven, 2007), p. 87.

5. Pedro de Valencia, *Tratado*, p. 134.

6. Lope de Vega, "Los Tellos de Meneses I," in his *Obras dramáticas escogidas*, ed. Eduardo Juliá Martínez (Madrid, 1935), vol. III, p. 5.

7. Cited in García Arenal, *Inquisición y moriscos*, p. 51.

8. Bermúdez de Pedraza, *Historia eclesiástica*, p. 187, as cited in Casey, *Early Modern Spain*, p. 224.

9. Cited in García Arenal, *Inquisición y moriscos*, p. 94. For the Caffor testimony, see Stephen Haliczer, *Inquisition and Society in the Kingdom of Valencia, 1478–1834* (Berkeley, 1990), p. 63.

CHAPTER SIX

1. Harvey, *Muslims in Spain*, p. 192.

CHAPTER SEVEN

1. Cited in Luis de la Cueva, *Diálogos de las cosas notables de Granada y lengua española y algunas cosas curiosas*, ed. José Mondéjar (Granada, 1993), p. xxxviii.

CHAPTER EIGHT

1. Cited in Nabil Matar, ed./trans. from the Arabic, *In the Lands of the Christians: Arab Travel Writing in the Seventeenth Century* (New York, 2003), pp. 113–89.

CHAPTER NINE

1. Sebastián de Covarrubias Horozco, *Tesoro de la lengua castellana o española* (Madrid, 1674), f. 190v.

2. Cited in David Nirenberg, "Mass Conversion and Genealogical Mentalities: Jews and Christians in Fifteenth-Century Spain," *Past and Present*, no. 174, February 2002, pp. 3–41 [9].

3. Cited in Nirenberg, "Mass Conversion," p. 13.

4. *La relación de Villena de 1575: Edición comentada y apéndice documental*, ed. José María Soler García, 2nd ed. (Alicante, 1974), pp. 20–21.

5. Cited in Jocelyn N. Hillgarth, *The Mirror of Spain, 1500–1700: The Formation of a Myth* (Ann Arbor, 2000), p. 165, from Bodin's *Colloquium Heptaplomeres* and Mendieta's *Historia Eclesiástica Indiana*, vol. I. For Abravanel, see Leo W. Schwarz, ed./trans. from the Hebrew et al., *Memoirs of My People through a Thousand Years* (Philadelphia, 1960), p. 46.

6. Cited in Hillgarth, *Mirror of Spain*, p. 164.

CHAPTER ELEVEN

1. Cited in Michael Alpert, *Criptojudaísmo e Inquisición en los siglos XVII y XVIII: La Ley en la que quiere vivir y morir* (Barcelona, 2001), p. 36.

CHAPTER TWELVE

1. *A un hombre de gran nariz: Soneto*, in Francisco de Quevedo, *Antología poética*, ed. Eldemira Martínez Fuertes (Madrid, 2005), p. 92.

2. Cited in George Mariscal, *Contradictory Subjects: Quevedo, Cervantes, and Seventeenth-Century Spanish Culture* (Ithaca, 1991), p. 44.

3. Cited in José Maria Madurell Marimon, "La cofradía de la Santa Trinidad, de los conversos de Barcelona," *Sefarad*, vol. 18, 1958, pp. 60–82 [74].

4. Cited in Hillgarth, *Mirror of Spain*, p. 238.

5. Cited in Hillgarth, *Mirror of Spain*, p. 315.

6. Miriam Bodian, *Hebrews of the Portuguese Nation: Conversos and Community in Early Modern Amsterdam* (Bloomington, 1997), p. 11.

7. Nirenberg, "Mass Conversion," p. 7.

8. Luis Hurtado de Toledo, "Toledo: Memorial de algunas cosas notables que tiene la Imperial Ciudad de Toledo (1576)," in Carmelo Viñas and Ramón Paz, eds., *Relaciones histórico-geográfico-estadísticas de los pueblos de España hechas por iniciativa de Felipe II: Reino de Toledo* (Madrid, 1951), pt. 3, pp. 481–576 [512].

9. *Fontes Iudaeorum Regni Castellae. II. El Tribunal de la Inquisición en el Obispado de Soria (1486–1502)*, ed. Carlos Carrete Parrondo (Salamanca-Granada, 1985), pp. 120 and 57.

10. Cited in Constance Hubbard Rose, *Alonso Núñez de Reinoso: The Lament of a Sixteenth-Century Exile* (Rutherford, NJ, 1971), p. 65.

11. Cited in Hugh Thomas, ed., *Madrid: A Travellers' Companion* (London, 1988), p. 169.

CHAPTER THIRTEEN

1. Cited in Pilar Huerga Criado, *En la raya de Portugal: Solidaridad y tensiones en la comunidad judeoconversa* (Salamanca, 1994), p. 136.

2. Cited in Henry Kamen, *The Spanish Inquisition: A Historical Revision, 3rd ed.* (London, 1997), p. 237.

3. Cited in Jorge Antonio Catalá Sanz, *Rentas y patrimonios de la nobleza valenciana en el siglo XVIII* (Madrid, 1995), p. 108.

4. Cited in Antonio Domínguez Ortiz, *Los judeoconversos en la España Moderna* (Madrid, 1978), pp. 130 and 134n.

5. David Nirenberg, "Race, Religion, and Miscegenation in Late Medieval Spain," unpublished manuscript of a seminar presented at Stanford University, April 1997, p. 25.

6. Angela Selke, *El Santo Oficio de la Inquisición: Proceso del Fr. Francisco Ortiz, 1529–1532* (Madrid, 1968), p. 85.

7. Juan Antonio Llorente, *Noticia autobiográfica*, ed. Antonio Márquez (Madrid, 1982), p. 69.

8. Linda Martz, "Relations between Conversos and Old Christians in Early Modern Toledo: Some Different Perspectives," in Mark D. Meyerson and Edward D. English, eds., *Christians, Muslims, and Jews in Medieval and Early Modern Spain: Interaction and Cultural Change* (Notre Dame, 1999), pp. 220–40 [220].

9. Cited in Jaime Contreras, "Criptojudaísmo en la España moderna: Clientelismo y linaje," *Areas*, vol. 9, 1988, pp. 75–100 [87].

10. Cited in Kamen, *The Spanish Inquisition*, p. 248.

11. The converso playwright Antonio Enríquez Gómez, as cited in I. S. Révah, "Un pamphlet contre l'Inquisition d'Antonio Enríquez Gómez: La seconde partie de 'La Política Angélica' (Rouen, 1647)," *Revue des Études Juives*, vol. 121, 1962, p. 145.

CHAPTER FOURTEEN

1. "Para cumplir con las gentes," as cited in Huerga, *En la raya de Portugal*, p. 197.

2. Cited in Francisco Cantera Burgos, "Fernando de Pulgar y los conversos," *Sefarad*, vol. 4, 1944, pp. 295–348 [345].

3. Cited in Jaime Contreras and Gustav Henningsen, "Forty-Four Thousand Cases of the Spanish Inquisition, 1540–1700: Analysis of a Historical Data Bank," in Gustav Henningsen, John Tedeschi, and Charles Amiel, eds., *The Inquisition in Early Modern Europe: Studies on Sources and Methods* (Dekalb, 1986), pp. 100–129 [124].

4. Cited in Hillgarth, *Mirror of Spain*, p. 195.

CHAPTER FIFTEEN

1. Cited in Huerga, *En la raya de Portugal*, pp. 188–89.

2. José Faur, "Four Classes of Conversos: A Typological Study," *Revue des Etudes Juives*, vol. 149, 1990, pp. 113–24.

3. *Dietari de Jeroni Soria*, ed. Francisco de P. Momblanch Gonzálbez (Valencia, 1960), p. 41.

4. Cited in Alpert, *Criptojudaísmo*, pp. 104–11.

5. Santa Teresa de Jesús, *Libro de las fundaciones*, ed. Antonio Comas (Madrid, 1967), p. 117.

6. *Marrano Poets of the Seventeenth Century: An Anthology of the Poetry of João Pinto Delgado, Antonio Enríquez Gómez and Miguel de Barrios*, ed./trans. from the Spanish by Timothy Oelman (Rutherford, NJ, 1982), pp. 74–83.

CHAPTER SIXTEEN

1. *Relación del cautiverio y libertad de Diego Galán, natural de la villa de Consuegra y vecino de la ciudad de Toledo*, ed. Miguel Angel de Bunes and Matías Barchino (Toledo, 2001), p. 97.

2. Rabbi Isaac Uziel, quoted in Steven Nadler, *Spinoza: A Life* (Cambridge, 2001), p. 11.

3. Steven Nadler, *Rembrandt's Jews* (Chicago, 2003), p. 171.

4. Jonathan I. Israel, *European Jewry in the Age of Mercantilism*, 3rd ed. (London, 1998), p. 25.

5. Simon Dubnow, *Jewish History; An Essay in the Philosophy of History*, trans. from the German by Henrietta Szold (Philadelphia, 1927), pp. 114 and 134.

6. Archivo Histórico Nacional (Madrid)/Inquisición, lib. 735, ff. 14r.–v. and 17r.–18v.

CHAPTER SEVENTEEN

1. This phrase from Abravanel's commentary on Ezekiel 5:6 is cited in Faur, "Four Classes of Conversos," p. 122.

2. Cited in Roland H. Bainton, *Hunted Heretic: The Life and Death of Michael Servetus, 1511–1553* (Boston, 1960), p. 10.

3. Cited in Yirmiyahu Yovel, *Spinoza and Other Heretics*, vol. I: *The Marrano of Reason* (Princeton, NJ, 1989), p. 10.

4. Cited in Huerga, *En la raya de Portugal*, p. 172.

5. Yovel, *Spinoza*, p. 43.

6. Israel, *European Jewry*, p. 178.

7. Cited in Wim Klever, "Spinoza 'corruptor' de Prado o la teoría de Gebhardt y Révah invertido," in Atilano Domínguez, ed., *Spinoza y España* (Cuenca, 1994), p. 218.

8. Henry Wadsworth Longfellow, "The Jewish Cemetery at Newport" (1852).

EPILOGUE

1. Luis García-Ballester, "The Inquisition and Minority Medical Practitioners in Counter-Reformation Spain: Judaizing and Morisco Practitioners, 1560–1610," in Ole Peter Grell and Andrew Cunningham, eds., *Medicine and the Reformation* (London, 1993), pp. 156–91.

2. Agustín, *Diálogo de las armas y linajes de la nobleza de España*, VI, cited in Antonio Domínguez Ortiz, "Caro Baroja y los moriscos granadinos: Con unas reflexiones sobre la nobleza de los cristianos nuevos," *Cuadernos Hispanoamericanos*, no. 533–34, November–December 1994, pp. 227–35 [234].

SELECT BIBLIOGRAPHY

E XPLANATORY NOTE: WHILE originally written in English, this book first appeared in Spanish translation, as *Historias paralelas: Judeo-conversos y moriscos en la España moderna* (Madrid: Akal, 2011). Two unusual features marked this version. First, the footnotes to the text were limited strictly to sources of direct quotations. This self-denying ordinance was made possible by the second anomaly, the inclusion of a lengthy (164 pages!) bibliographic essay, in which I commented at leisure not only on the sorts of sources that are available for studying the moriscos and conversos, but also on the main arguments and currents of the rich historical writing available on both groups. There seemed to be little reason to duplicate what was largely a Spanish-language bibliography in English. Thus any reader looking for detailed further information on both primary sources and secondary bibliography is invited to consult the original edition.

My decision to retain the same system of footnotes does raise one question, though. As I noted in the Preface, this is resolutely a work of synthesis. As such, it depends vitally on the research of historians and other scholars from various disciplines and generations. The long, discursive bibliography of the Spanish version specifically acknowledged my borrowings in a way this reduced version cannot. I have distinguished works on which I have relied in particular with an asterisk; readers thus can easily see which texts have played an especially important role in my interpretation. Making sure that credit is received where it is due is a fundamental professional obligation, and if any reader harbors doubts about the provenance of any information, I once again strongly urge him or her to consult the Spanish version. That said, the following evidently is not a comprehensive listing of all relevant works. Rather, with a student audience largely in mind, I have focused almost exclusively on titles in English, along with some in Spanish. I decided to present the works of each section below in alphabetical order according to author or, infrequently, title.

PREVIOUS STUDIES OF MORISCOS AND CONVERSOS

Edwards, John. "Mission and Inquisition among Conversos and Moriscos in Spain, 1250–1550." *Studies in Church History,* vol. 21, 1984, pp. 139–51.

Gutwirth, Eleazar. "Hispano-Jewish Attitudes to the Moors in the Fifteenth Century." *Sefarad,* vol. 49, 1989, pp. 237–62.

Ingram, Kevin, ed. *The Conversos and Moriscos in Early Modern Spain and Beyond.* Volume One: *Departures and Change.* Leiden, 2009.

Kagan, Richard L., and Abigail Dyer, eds. *Inquisitorial Inquiries: The Brief Lives of Secret Jews and Other Heretics.* Baltimore, 2004.

Kamen, Henry. "Strategies of Survival: Minority Cultures in the Western Mediterranean." In John A. Marino, ed. *Early Modern History and the Social Sciences: Testing the Limits of Braudel's Mediterranean.* Kirksville, MO, 2002 (pp. 205–22).

Méchoulan, Henri. *El honor de Dios: Indios, judíos y moriscos en el Siglo de Oro.* Barcelona, 1981 [orig. ed. 1979].

Melammed, Renée Levine. "Judeo-conversas and Moriscas in Sixteenth-Century Spain: A Study of Parallels." *Jewish History,* vol. 24, 2010, pp. 155–68.

Muchnik, Natalia. "Judeoconversos y moriscos frente a la Diáspora." In Mercedes García-Arenal and Gerard A. Wiegers, eds. *Los moriscos: Expulsión y diáspora. Una perspectiva internacional.* Valencia-Granada-Zaragoza, 2013 (pp. 415–40).

Stuczynski, Claude B. "Two Minorities Facing the Iberian Inquisition: The 'Marranos' and the 'Moriscos.'" *Hispania Judaica,* vol. 3, 2000, pp. 127–43.

PART I. THE *MORISCOS* AND THE END OF MUSLIM SPAIN
General

Barceló, Carmen, and Ana Labarta. *Archivos moriscos. Textos árabes de la minoría islámica valenciana, 1401–1608.* Valencia, 2009.

*Bernabé Pons, Luis F. *Los moriscos. Conflicto, expulsión y diáspora*. Madrid, 2009.

Bunes Ibarra, Miguel Angel de. *Los moriscos en el pensamiento histórico. Historio-grafía de un grupo marginado.* Madrid, 1983.

Candau Chacón, María Luisa. *Los moriscos en el espejo del tiempo. Problemas históricos e historiográficos.* Huelva, 1998.

Carrasco, Rafael. *Deportados en nombre de Dios: La expulsión de los moriscos. Cuarto centenario de una ignominia.* Barcelona, 2009.

Chejne, Anwar G. *Islam and the West: The Moriscos. A Cultural and Social History.* Albany, 1983.

Domínguez Ortiz, Antonio. *Moriscos: La mirada de un historiador.* Ed. Bernard Vincent. Granada, 2009.

*Domínguez Ortiz, Antonio, and Bernard Vincent. *Historia de los moriscos: Vida y tragedia de una minoría.* Madrid, 1979.

Echevarría Arsuaga, Ana. *Los moriscos.* Málaga, 2010.

García-Arenal, Mercedes. *Los moriscos.* Madrid, 1975.

*Harvey, L. P. *Muslims in Spain, 1500 to 1614.* Chicago, 2005.

*Márquez Villanueva, Francisco. *El problema morisco (desde otras laderas).* Madrid, 1998.

Temimi, Abdeljelil, ed. *Bibliographie générale d'études morisques.* Zaghouan, Tunisia, 1990.

*Vincent, Bernard. *El río morisco.* Trans. from the French by Antonio Luis Cortés Peña. Valencia-Granada-Zaragoza, 2006.

Monographs

Caro Baroja, Julio. *Los moriscos del Reino de Granada: Ensayo de historia social.* Madrid, 1976 [orig. ed. 1953].

Dadson, Trevor J. *Los moriscos de Villarrubia de los Ojos (siglos XV–XVIII). Historia de una minoría asimilada, expulsada y reintegrada.* Madrid-Frankfurt, 2006; summary in "The Assimilation of Spain's Moriscos: Fiction or Reality?" *Journal of Levantine Studies,* vol. 1, no. 2, Winter 2011, pp. 11–30.

*García-Arenal, Mercedes. *Inquisición y moriscos. Los procesos del tribunal de Cuenca.* Madrid, 1978.

Halperín Donghi, Tulio. *Un conflicto nacional: Moriscos y cristianos viejos en Valencia.* Valencia, 1980 [orig. ed. 1955–57].

Lapeyre, Henri. *Geografía de la España morisca.* Valencia, 1986 [orig. ed. 1959].

Tapia Sánchez, Serafín de. *La comunidad morisca de Avila.* Salamanca, 1991.

CHAPTER ONE.

THE DECLINE OF COEXISTENCE

Barton, Simon, and Richard Fletcher, eds./trans. *The World of El Cid: Chronicles of Spanish Reconquest. Selected Sources.* Manchester, 2000.

Burns, Robert I. *Muslims, Christians and Jews in the Medieval Kingdom of Valencia: Societies in Symbiosis.* Cambridge, 1984.

Catlos, Brian A. *The Victors and the Vanquished: Christians and Muslims of Catalonia and Aragon, 1050–1300.* Cambridge, 2004.

Constable, Olivia Remie, ed. *Medieval Iberia: Readings from Christian, Muslim, and Jewish Sources.* Philadelphia, 1997.

Dodds, Jerrilyn D., María Rosa Menocal, and Abigail Krasner Balbale. *The Arts of Intimacy: Christians, Jews, and Muslims in the Making of Castilian Culture.* New Haven, CT, 2008.

Glick, Thomas F. *Islamic and Christian Spain in the Early Middle Ages: Comparative Perspectives on Social and Cultural Formation.* Princeton, NJ, 1979.

———. *From Muslim Fortress to Christian Castle: Social and Cultural Change in Medieval Spain.* Manchester, 1995.

Harvey, L. P. *Islamic Spain, 1250–1500.* Chicago, 1990.

Lomax, Derek W. *The Reconquest of Spain.* London, 1978.

Lowney, Chris. *A Vanished World: Muslims, Christians, and Jews in Medieval Spain.* Oxford, 2006.

Mann, Vivian, et al., eds. *Convivencia: Jews, Muslims, and Christians in Medieval Spain.* New York, 1992.

Menocal, María Rosa. *The Ornament of the World: How Muslims, Jews, and Christians Created a Culture of Tolerance in Medieval Spain.* Boston-New York, 2002.

Meyerson, Mark D. *The Muslims of Valencia in the Age of Fernando and Isabel: Between Coexistence and Crusade.* Berkeley-Los Angeles, 1991.

Meyerson, Mark D., and Edward D. English, eds. *Christians, Muslims, and Jews in Medieval and Early Modern Spain: Interaction and Cultural Change.* Notre Dame, 1999.

Miller, Kathryn A. *Guardians of Islam: Religious Authority and Muslim Communities in Late Medieval Spain.* New York, 2008.

*Nirenberg, David. *Communities of Violence: Persecution of Minorities in the Middle Ages.* Princeton, NJ, 1996.

Tartakoff, Paola. *Between Christian and Jew: Conversion and Inquisition in the Crown of Aragon, 1250–1391.* Philadelphia, 2012.

Watt, W. Montgomery, with Pierre Cachia. *A History of Islamic Spain.* Garden City, NY, 1967.

CHAPTER TWO.
RISE AND FALL OF THE MORISCOS: A POLITICAL HISTORY

Ardit, Manuel. "The Expulsion of the Moriscos from the Catalan Countries: Ideology and History." *Catalan Historical Review*, vol. 2, 2009, pp. 65–81.

Barrios Aguilera, Manuel. *La suerte de los vencidos: Estudios y reflexiones sobre la cuestión morisca.* Granada, 2009.

Benítez Sánchez-Blanco, Rafael. *Heroicas decisiones: La Monarquía Católica y los moriscos valencianos.* Valencia, 2001.

Boronat y Barrachina, Pascual. *Los moriscos españoles y su expulsión.* 2 vols. Valencia, 1901.

Coleman, David. *Creating Christian Granada: Society and Religious Culture in an Old-World Frontier City, 1492–1600.* Ithaca, 2003.

Edwards, John. "Christian Mission in the Kingdom of Granada, 1492–1568." *Renaissance and Modern Studies*, vol. 31, 1987, pp. 20–33.

Ehlers, Benjamin. *Between Christians and Moriscos: Juan de Ribera and Religious Reform in Valencia, 1568–1614.* Baltimore, 2006.

Eisenberg, Daniel. "Cisneros y la quema de los manuscritos granadinos." *Journal of Hispanic Philology*, vol. 16, 1992, pp. 107–24.

El Alaoui, Youssef. *Jésuites, morisques et indiens. Étude comparative des méthodes d'évangélisation de la Compagnie de Jésus d'après les traités de José de Acosta (1588) et d'Ignacio de las Casas (1605–1607).* Paris, 2006.

Fuchs, Barbara. *Mimesis and Empire: The New World, Islam, and European Identities.* Cambridge, 2001.

García-Arenal, Mercedes, and Gerard A. Wiegers, eds. *Los moriscos: Expulsión y diáspora. Una perspectiva internacional.* Valencia-Granada-Zaragoza, 2013.

Griffin, Nigel. "'Un muro invisible': Moriscos and Cristianos viejos in Granada." In *Medieval and Renaissance Studies on Spain and Portugal in Honour of P. E. Russell.* Oxford, 1981 (pp. 133–53).

Magnier, Grace. *Pedro de Valencia and the Catholic Apologists of the Expulsion of the Moriscos: Visions of Christianity and Kingship.* Leiden, 2010.

Martín Casares, Aurelia. *La esclavitud en la Granada del siglo XVI. Género, raza y religión.* Granada, 2000.

Moliner Prada, Antonio, ed. *La expulsión de los moriscos.* Barcelona, 2009.

*Monter, E. William. *Frontiers of Heresy: The Spanish Inquisition from the Basque Lands to Sicily.* Cambridge, 1990.

*Pastore, Stefania. *Il Vangelo e la spada: L'Inquisizione di Castiglia e i suoi critici, 1460–1598.* Rome, 2003.

CHAPTER THREE.

IMAGES AND REALITIES

An Early Modern Dialogue with Islam: Antonio de Sosa's Topography of Algiers, 1612. Ed. María Antonia Garcés. Trans. from the Spanish by Diana de Armas Wilson. Notre Dame, 2011.

Bennassar, Bartolomé, and Lucile Bennassar. *Los cristianos de Alá. La fascinante aventura de los renegados.* Trans. from the French by José Luis Gil Aristu. Madrid, 1989.

Brodman, James W. *Ransoming Captives in Crusader Spain: The Order of Merced on the Christian-Islamic Frontier.* Philadelphia, 1986.

Bunes, Miguel Angel de. *La imagen de los musulmanes y el norte de Africa en la España de los siglos XVI y XVII: Los caracteres de una hostilidad.* Madrid, 1989.

Camamis, George. *Estudios sobre el cautiverio en el Siglo de Oro.* Madrid, 1977.

Cardaillac, Louis. *Moriscos y cristianos. Un enfrentamiento polémico, 1492–1640.* Trans. from the French by Mercedes García-Arenal; preface, Fernand Braudel. Madrid, 1979.

Carrasco Urgoiti, María Soledad. *The Moorish Novel: 'El Abencerraje' and Pérez de Hita.* Boston, 1976.

Echevarría, Ana. *The Fortress of Faith: The Attitude toward Muslims in Fifteenth-Century Spain.* Leiden, 1999.

Friedman, Ellen G. *Spanish Captives in North Africa in the Early Modern Age.* Madison, 1983.

Fuchs, Barbara. *Exotic Nation: Maurophilia and the Construction of Early Modern Spain.* Philadelphia, 2009.

*Garcés, María Antonia. *Cervantes in Algiers: A Captive's Tale.* Nashville, 2002.

García-Arenal, Mercedes, and Miguel Angel de Bunes Ibarra. *Los españoles y el norte de Africa, S. XV–XVIII.* Madrid, 1992.

García-Arenal, Mercedes, Miguel Angel de Bunes, and Victoria Aguilar. *Repertorio bibliográfico de las relaciones entre la Península Ibérica y el Norte de Africa, siglos XV–XVI.* Madrid, 1989.

Hess, Andrew C. "The Moriscos: An Ottoman Fifth Column in Sixteenth-Century Spain." *American Historical Review,* vol. 74, 1968, pp. 1–25.

———. *The Forgotten Frontier: A History of the Sixteenth-Century Ibero-African Frontier.* Chicago, 1978.

López-Baralt, Luce. *Islam in Spanish Literature: From the Middle Ages to the Present.* Trans. from the Spanish by Andrew Hurley. Leiden, 1992.

Mas, Albert. *Les turcs dans la littérature espagnole du Siècle d'Or.* 2 vols. Paris, 1967.

Perceval, José María. *Todos son unos. Arquetipos, xenofobia y racismo. La imagen del morisco en la Monarquía Española durante los siglos XVI y XVII.* Almería, 1997.

Schwartz, Stuart B. *All Can Be Saved: Religious Tolerance and Salvation in the Iberian Atlantic World.* New Haven, CT, 2008.

Sweet, James H. "The Iberian Roots of American Racist Thought." *William and Mary Quarterly,* vol. 54, 1997, pp. 143–66.

Taylor, Bruce. "The Enemy Within and Without: An Anatomy of Fear on the Spanish Mediterranean Littoral." In William G. Naphy and Penny Roberts, eds. *Fear in Early Modern Society.* Manchester, 1997 (pp. 78–99).

CHAPTER FOUR.

"CHRISTIANS IN APPEARANCE BUT MUSLIMS UNDERNEATH"

*García-Arenal, Mercedes. "El problema morisco: Propuestas de discusión." *Al-Qantara,* vol. 13, no. 2, 1992, pp. 491–503.

Longás, Pedro. *La vida religiosa de los moriscos.* Madrid, 1915 (facs. ed. by Darío Cabanelas, Granada, 1998).

Pereda, Felipe. *Las imágenes de la discordia: Política y poética de la imagen sagrada en la España del cuatrocientos.* Madrid, 2007.

Perry, Mary Elizabeth. *The Handless Maiden: Moriscos and the Politics Of Religion in Early Modern Spain.* Princeton, NJ, 2005.

Surtz, Ronald E. "Morisco Women, Written Texts, and the Valencia Inquisition." *Sixteenth Century Journal,* vol. 32, 2001, pp. 421–33.

Tueller, James B. "The Assimilating Morisco: Four Families in Valladolid prior to the Expulsion of 1610." *Mediterranean Studies,* vol. 7, 1998, pp. 167–77.

Vincent, Bernard. "The Moriscos and Circumcision." In Anne J. Cruz and Mary Elizabeth Perry, eds. *Culture and Control in Counter-Reformation Spain.* Minneapolis, 1992 (pp. 78–92).

CHAPTER FIVE.

COMMUNITIES AND INDIVIDUALS

García Ballester, Luis. *Medicine in a Multicultural Society: Christian, Jewish and Muslim Practitioners in the Spanish Kingdoms, 1222–1610.* Aldershot, 2001.

López-Morillas, Consuelo. "Language and Identity in Late Spanish Islam." *Hispanic Review,* vol. 63, no. 2, 1995, pp. 193–210.

*Núñez Muley, Francisco. *A Memorandum for the President of the Royal Audience and Chancery Court of the City and Kingdom of Granada*. Ed. and trans. from the Spanish by Vincent Barletta. Chicago, 2007.

CHAPTER SIX. *MORISCO* EXPRESSION

Barletta, Vincent. *Covert Gestures: Crypto-Islamic Literature as Cultural Practice in Early Modern Spain*. Minneapolis, 2005.

López-Baralt, Luce. "The Moriscos." In María Rosa Menocal, Raymond P. Scheindlin, and Michael Sells, eds. *The Cambridge History of Arabic Literature: The Literature of Al-Andalus*. Cambridge, 2000 (pp. 472–87).

Mateos Paramio, Alfredo, and Juan Carlos Villaverde Amieva. *Memoria de los moriscos: Escritos y relatos de una diáspora cultural*. Madrid, 2010.

Tratado [Tafsira]: Mancebo de Arévalo. Ed. María Teresa Narváez Córdova. Madrid, 2003.

Wiegers, Gerard. *Islamic Literature in Spanish and Aljamiado*. Leiden, 1994.

CHAPTER SEVEN. A FINAL BOW

*Barrios Aguilera, Manuel, and Mercedes García-Arenal, eds. *Los Plomos del Sacromonte: Invención y tesoro*. Valencia-Granada-Zaragoza, 2006.

———. *¿La historia inventada? Los libros plúmbeos y el legado sacromontano*. Granada, 2008.

*García-Arenal, Mercedes, and Fernando Rodríguez Mediano. *Un oriente español: Los moriscos y el Sacromonte en tiempos de Contrarreforma*. Madrid, 2010.

*Harris, A. Katie. *From Muslim to Christian Granada: Inventing a City's Past in Early Modern Spain*. Baltimore, 2007.

Matar, Nabil. "The Mary of the Sacromonte." *Muslim World*, vol. 95, no. 2, 2005, pp. 199–215.

Woolard, Kathryn A. "Bernardo de Aldrete and the Morisco Problem: A Study in Early Modern Spanish Language Ideology." *Comparative Studies in Society and History*, vol. 44, no. 3, 2002, pp. 446–80.

CHAPTER EIGHT. AFTERMATH

Bahri, Raja Yassine. "Los moriscos después de la expulsión: Vivir en el exilio." *Torre de los Lujanes*, no. 67, 2010, pp. 219–32.

Epalza, Mikel de. *Los andalusíes y sus éxodos hacia Marruecos en los siglos XVI–XVII*. Alicante, 1991.

———. *Los moriscos antes y después de la expulsión*. Madrid, 1992.

García-Arenal, Mercedes. *La diáspora de los andalusíes*. Barcelona, 2003.

Tratado de los dos caminos, por un morisco refugiado en Túnez (Ms. S2 de la Colección Gayangos, Biblioteca de la Real Academia de la Historia). Eds. Álvaro Galmés de Fuentes, Juan Carlos Villaverde Amieva, and Luce López-Baralt. Madrid-Oviedo, 2005.

PART II. FROM JEWS TO CHRISTIANS

General

*Alpert, Michael. *Criptojudaismo e Inquisición en los siglos XVII y XVIII. La Ley en la que quiere vivir y morir*. Barcelona, 2001.

Baer, Yitzhak. *A History of the Jews in Christian Spain*. 2 vols. Philadelphia, 1961–66.

Bethencourt, Francisco. *The Inquisition: A Global History, 1478–1834*. Trans. from the French by Jean Birrell. Cambridge, 2009 [orig. ed. 1995].

*Caro Baroja, Julio. *Los judíos en la España moderna y contemporánea*. 3 vols. Madrid, 1961–62.

*Domínguez Ortiz, Antonio. *Judeoconversos en la España Moderna*. Madrid, 1978 [orig. ed. 1955].

Gerber, Jane S. *The Jews of Spain: A History of the Sephardic Experience*. New York, 1992.

Gitlitz, David M. *Secrecy and Deceit: The Religion of the Crypto-Jews*. Philadelphia-Jerusalem, 1996.

*Hillgarth, Jocelyn N. *The Mirror of Spain, 1500–1700: The Formation of a Myth*. Ann Arbor, 2000.

*Israel, Jonathan I. *European Jewry in the Age of Mercantilism*, 3rd ed. London, 1985.

———. *Diasporas within a Diaspora: Jews, Crypto-Jews, and the World Maritime Empires, 1540–1740*. Boston, 2002.

*Kamen, Henry. *The Spanish Inquisition: A Historical Revision*. London, 1997.

*Márquez Villanueva, Francisco. *De la España judeoconversa: Doce estudios*. Barcelona, 2006.

*Melammed, Renée Levine. *Heretics or Daughters of Israel? The Crypto-Jewish Women of Castile*. Oxford, 1999.

*———. *A Question of Identity: Iberian Conversos in Historical Perspective*. Oxford, 2004.

*Netanyahu, Benzion. *The Marranos of Spain from the Late 14th to the Early 16th Century, According to Contemporary Hebrew Sources*. Ithaca, 1999 [orig. ed. 1966].

*————. *The Origins of the Inquisition in Fifteenth-Century Spain.* New York, 2001 [orig. ed. 1995].

*————. *Toward the Inquisition: Essays on Jewish and Converso History in Late Medieval Spain.* Ithaca, 1997.

*Pastore, Stefania. *Un'eresia spagnola. Spiritualità conversa, alumbradismo e Inquisizione, 1449–1559.* Florence, 2004.

See also the ample bibliography in Rachel Simon, *Sources for Sephardic Studies: A Library Research Guide,* at http://www.huc.edu/sephardic/media/LibraryResearchGuide.pdf (last accessed 25 January 2013).

Monographs

Anaya Hernández, Luis Alberto. *Judeoconversos e Inquisición en las Islas Canarias, 1492–1605.* Las Palmas, 1996.

Bel Bravo, María Antonia. *El auto de fe de 1593. Los conversos granadinos de origen judío.* Granada, 1988.

López Belinchón, Bernardo. *Honra, libertad y hacienda. Hombres de negocios y judíos sefardíes.* Alcalá de Henares, 2001.

Contreras, Jaime. *El Santo Oficio de la Inquisición de Galicia (poder, sociedad y cultura).* Madrid, 1982 (esp. pp. 588–608).

*————. *Sotos contra Riquelmes: Regidores, inquisidores y criptojudíos.* Madrid, 1992.

Coronas Tejada, Luis. *Conversos and Inquisition in Jaén.* Jerusalem, 1988.

Dedieu, Jean-Pierre. *L'administration de la foi: L'Inquisition de Tolède, XVIe–XVIIIe siècles.* Madrid, 1989.

Gil, Juan. *Los conversos y la Inquisición sevillana: Ensayo de prosopografía.* 8 vols. Seville, 2001–3.

Gómez-Menor, José. *Cristianos nuevos y mercaderes de Toledo.* Toledo, 1970.

*Huerga Criado, Pilar. *En la raya de Portugal. Solidaridad y tensiones en la comunidad judeoconversa.* Salamanca, 1994.

*Kaplan, Yosef. *From Christianity to Judaism: The Story of Isaac Orobio de Castro.* Trans. from the Hebrew by Raphael Loewe. Oxford, 2004 [orig. ed. 1982].

Martz, Linda. *A Network of Converso Families in Early Modern Toledo: Assimilating a Minority.* Ann Arbor, 2003.

Muchnik, Natalia. *Une vie marrane: Les pérégrinations de Juan de Prado dans l'Europe du XVIIe siècle.* Paris, 2005.

*Pulido Serrano, Juan Ignacio. *Injurias a Cristo: Religión, política y antijudaísmo en el siglo XVII.* Alcalá de Henares, 2002.

Schreiber, Markus. *Marranen in Madrid 1600–1670.* Stuttgart, 1994.

*Yerushalmi, Yosef Hayim. *From Spanish Court to Italian Ghetto: Isaac Cardoso. A Study in Seventeenth-Century Marranism and Jewish Apologetics.* Seattle, 1981 [orig. ed. 1971].

CHAPTER NINE.

CREATING *CONVERSOS*, 1391–1492

Abulafia, David. *1492: The Expulsion from Spain and Jewish Identity.* London, 1992.

Assis, Yom Tov, and Yosef Kaplan, eds. *Jews and Conversos at the Time of the Expulsion.* Jerusalem, 1999.

Benito Ruano, Eloy. *Los orígenes del problema converso.* Madrid, 2001 [orig. ed. 1976].

Beinart, Haim. "The Judaizing Movement in the Order of San Jerónimo in Castile." *Scripta Hierosolymitana,* vol. 7, 1961, pp. 167–92.

———. *The Expulsion of the Jews from Spain.* Trans. from the Hebrew by Jeffrey M. Green. Portland, 2002 [orig. ed. 1994–96].

Gampel, Benjamin R. *The Last Jews on Iberian Soil: Navarrese Jewry, 1479–1498.* Berkeley–Los Angeles, 1989.

Gerli, E. Michael. "Social Crisis and Conversion: Apostasy and Inquisition in the Chronicles of Fernando del Pulgar and Andrés Bernáldez." *Hispanic Review,* vol. 70, 2002, pp. 147–67.

Haliczer, Stephen. "The Castilian Urban Patriciate and the Jewish Expulsion of 1480–92." *American Historical Review,* vol. 78, no. 1, 1973, pp. 35–62.

Hinojosa Montalvo, José. *The Jews of the Kingdom of Valencia: From Persecution to Expulsion, 1391–1492.* Trans. from the Spanish by Stephanie Nakache. Jerusalem, 1993.

Kamen, Henry. "The Mediterranean and the Expulsion of Spanish Jews in 1492." *Past and Present,* no. 119, 1988, pp. 30–55.

Lawee, Eric. *Isaac Abarbanel's Stance toward Tradition: Defense, Dissent, and Dialogue.* Albany, 2001.

MacKay, Angus. "Popular Movements and Pogroms in Fifteenth-Century Castile." *Past and Present,* no. 55, 1972, pp. 33–67.

———. "The Hispanic-Converso Predicament." *Transactions of the Royal Historical Society,* 5th ser., vol. 35, 1985, pp. 159–79.

Meyerson, Mark D. "Aragonese and Catalan Jewish Converts at the Time of Expulsion." *Jewish History,* vol. 6, no. 1–2, 1992, pp. 131–49.

———. *A Jewish Renaissance in Fifteenth-Century Spain.* Princeton, NJ, 2004.

Monsalvo Antón, José María. *Teoría y evolución de un conflicto social: El antisemitismo en la Corona de Castilla en la Baja Edad media.* Madrid, 1985.

Netanyahu, Benzion. *Don Isaac Abravanel: Statesman and Philosopher.* Ithaca, 1998 [orig. ed. 1953].

Nirenberg, David. "Mass Conversion and Genealogical Mentalities: Jews and Christians in Fifteenth-Century Spain." *Past and Present,* no. 174, February 2002, pp. 3–41.

———. "La generación de 1391: Conversión masiva y crisis de identidad." In José I. Fortea, Juan E. Gelabert, and Tomás A. Mantecón, eds. *Furor et rabies: Violencia, conflicto y marginación en la Edad Moderna.* Santander, 2002 (pp. 313–38).

Oron, Michal. "Autobiographical Elements in the Writings of Kabbalists from the Generation of the Expulsion." *Mediterranean Historical Review,* vol. 6, no. 2, December 1991, pp. 102–11.

Rábade Obradó, María del Pilar. *Una élite de poder en la Corte de los Reyes Católicos. Los judeoconversos.* Madrid, 1993.

Raphael, David, ed. *The Expulsion 1492 Chronicles: An Anthology of Medieval Chronicles Relating to the Expulsion of the Jews from Spain and Portugal.* North Hollywood, 1992.

Ray, Jonathan. *The Sephardic Frontier: The Reconquista and the Jewish Community in Medieval Iberia.* Ithaca, 2006.

Rosenstock, Bruce. *New Men: Conversos, Christian Theology, and Society in Fifteenth-Century Castile.* London, 2002.

Roth, Norman. *Conversos, Inquisition, and the Expulsion of the Jews from Spain.* Madison, 1995.

Shepard, Sanford. "The Present State of Ritual Crime in Spain." *Judaism,* vol. 17, Winter 1968, pp. 68–78.

Starr-Lebeau, Gretchen. *In the Shadow of the Virgin: Inquisitors, Friars, and Conversos in Guadalupe, Spain.* Princeton, NJ, 2003.

Suárez Fernández, Luis (ed.). *Documentos acerca de la expulsión de los judíos.* Valladolid, 1964.

Wolff, Philippe. "The 1391 Pogrom in Spain: Social Crisis or Not?" *Past and Present,* no. 50, 1971, pp. 4–18.

CHAPTER TEN.

VIGILANCE THROUGH VIOLENCE

Beinart, Haim, ed. *Records of the Trials of the Spanish Inquisition in Ciudad Real.* 4 vols. Jerusalem, 1974–85.

Dedieu, Jean-Pierre. "Los cuatro tiempos de la Inquisición." In Bartolomé Bennassar, ed. *Inquisición española: Poder político y control social.* Barcelona, 1981 (pp. 15–39).

Fontes Iudaeorum Regni Castellae. VII. El tribunal de la Inquisición de Sigüenza, 1492–1505. Ed. Carlos Carrete Parrondo and María Fuencisla García Casar. Salamanca, 1997.

Henningsen, Gustav, and Jaime Contreras. "Forty-Four Thousand Cases of the Spanish Inquisition, 1540–1700: Analysis of a Historical Data Bank." In Gustav Henningsen, John Tedeschi, and Charles Amiel, eds. *The Inquisition in Early Modern Europe: Studies on Sources and Methods.* Dekalb, 1986 (pp. 100–129).

CHAPTER ELEVEN.
NEW CHRISTIANS IN A NEW SPAIN

Arrizabalaga, Jon. "The World of Iberian Converso Practitioners, from Lluís Alcanyís to Isaac Cardoso." In Víctor Navarro Brotóns and William Eamon, eds. *Más allá de la Leyenda Negra: España y la Revolución Científica/Beyond the Black Legend: Spain and the Scientific Revolution.* Valencia, 2007 (pp. 307–22).

Barreto Xavier, Ângela. "*Conversos* and *Novamente Convertidos:* Law, Religion, and Identity in the Portuguese Kingdom and Empire." *Journal of Early Modern History,* vol. 15, 2011, pp. 255–87.

Boyajian, James C. *Portuguese Bankers at the Court of Spain, 1626–1650.* New Brunswick, 1983.

Carrasco, Rafael. "Preludio al 'siglo de los portugueses': La Inquisición de Cuenca y los judaizantes lusitanos del siglo XVI." *Hispania,* vol. 47, 1987, pp. 503–59.

Casado Alonso, Hilario. "De la judería a la Grandeza de España: La trayectoria de la familia de mercaderes de los Bernuy, siglos XIV–XIX." *Bulletin of the Society for Spanish and Portuguese Historical Studies,* vol. 22, no. 2, Spring 1997, pp. 9–27.

Cohen, Martin. *The Canonization of a Myth: Portugal's 'Jewish Problem' and the Assembly of Tomar, 1629.* Cincinnati, 2002.

Greyerz, Kaspar von. "Portuguese Conversos on the Upper Rhine and the Converso Community of Sixteenth-Century Europe." *Social History,* vol. 14, no. 1, 1989, pp. 59–82.

Martz, Linda. "Relations between Conversos and Old Christians in Early Modern Toledo: Some Different Perspectives." In Meyerson and English, *Christians, Muslims, and Jews* (pp. 220–40).

Révah, I. S. *Uriel da Costa et les marranes de Porto.* Ed. Carsten L. Wilke. Paris, 2004.

Rodrigues da Silva Tavim, José Alberto. "In the Shadow of Empire: Portuguese Jewish Communities in the Sixteenth Century." In Liam Matthew Brockey, ed. *Portuguese Colonial Cities in the Early Modern World.* Aldershot, 2008 (pp. 17–39).

Ruderman, David B. "The Community of Converso Physicians: Race, Medicine, and the Shaping of a Cultural Identity." In his *Jewish Thought and Scientific Discovery in Early Modern Europe*. New Haven, CT, 1995 (pp. 273–309).

Salomon, H. P. "The 'Monitório do Inquisidor Geral' of 1536: Background and Sources of Some 'Judaic' Customs Listed Therein." *Arquivos do Centro Cultural Português. Homenagem a Léon Bourdon*, vol. 17, 1982, pp. 41–64.

———, with J. De Lange. *Portrait of a New Christian: Fernão Alvares Melo, 1569–1632*. Paris, 1982.

Saraiva, António José. *The Marrano Factory: The Portuguese Inquisition and Its New Christians, 1536–1765*. Trans. from the Portuguese by H. P. Salomon and I. S. D. Sassoon. Leiden, 2001 [orig. ed. 1956].

Sarrión Mora, Adelina. *Médicos e Inquisición en el siglo XVII*. Cuenca, 2006.

Selke, Angela S. *The Conversos of Majorca: Life and Death in a Crypto-Jewish Community in Seventeenth-Century Spain*. Jerusalem, 1986.

Studnicki-Gizbert, Daviken. *A Nation upon the Ocean Sea: Portugal's Atlantic Diaspora and the Crisis of the Spanish Empire, 1492–1640*. Oxford, 2007.

CHAPTER TWELVE.
THE PERSISTENCE OF ANTISEMITISM

Bataillon, Marcel. *Erasmo y España: Estudios sobre la historia espiritual del siglo XVI*. Trans. from the French by Antonio Alatorre. Mexico City, 1966 [orig. ed. 1937] (pp. 738–49).

Edwards, John. "Religious Faith and Doubt in Late Medieval Spain: Soria, circa 1450–1500." *Past and Present*, no. 120, 1988, pp. 3–25.

Ettinghausen, Henry. "La sátira antijudía de Quevedo." In Carlos Vaíllo and Ramón Valdés, eds. *Estudios sobre la sátira española en el Siglo de Oro*. Madrid, 2006 (pp. 59–79).

Gutwirth, Eleazar. "From Jewish to Converso Humour in Fifteenth-Century Spain." *Bulletin of Hispanic Studies*, vol. 67, 1990, pp. 253–64.

Hobson, Anthony. *Renaissance Book Collecting: Jean Grolier and Diego Hurtado de Mendoza, Their Books and Bindings*. Cambridge, 1999.

Ginio, Alisa Meyuhas. "The Conversos and the Magic Arts in Alonso de Espina's *Fortalitium Fidei*." *Mediterranean Historical Review*, vol. 5, 1990, pp. 169–82.

Nirenberg, David. "Race and the Middle Ages: The Case of Spain and Its Jews." In Margaret R. Greer, Walter D. Mignolo, and Maureen Quilligan, eds. *Rereading the Black Legend: The Discourses of Religious and Racial Difference in the Renaissance Empires*. Chicago, 2007 (pp. 71–87).

Pardo Tomás, José. "Physicians' and Inquisitors' Stories? Circumcision and Crypto-Judaism in Sixteenth-Eighteenth-Century Spain." In Florike Egmond and Robert Zwijnenberg, eds. *Bodily Extremities: Preoccupations with the Human Body in Early Modern European Culture.* Aldershot, 2003 (pp. 168–94).

Praag, J. A. van. "Los *Protocolos de los sabios de Sión* y la *Isla de los monopantos* de Quevedo." *Bulletin Hispanique,* vol. 51, 1949, pp. 169–73.

Yerushalmi, Yosef Hayim. *Assimilation and Racial Anti-Semitism: The Iberian and the German Models.* New York, 1982.

CHAPTER THIRTEEN.

REJECTION AND ASSIMILATION: A POROUS PURITY

Beusterien, John. "Blotted Genealogies: A Survey of the libros verdes." *Bulletin of Hispanic Studies (Liverpool),* vol. 78, no. 2, April 2001, pp. 183–97.

Contreras Contreras, Jaime. "Aldermen and Judaizers: Cryptojudaism, Counter-Reformation, and Local Power." In Cruz and Perry, *Culture and Control* (pp. 93–123).

———. "Conflicto social y estatutos de limpieza en la obra de Cervantes." *Torre de los Lujanes,* no. 56, July 2005, pp. 87–103.

———. "Linajes y cambio social: La manipulación de la memoria." *Historia Social,* vol. 21, 1995, pp. 105–24.

Cuart Moner, Baltasar. *Colegiales mayores y limpieza de sangre durante la Edad Moderna.* Salamanca, 1991.

"Diálogo entre Lain Caluo, i Nuño Rasura, jueces de Castilla i veçinos de Vijueces, sobre el estado de la ciudad de Burgos que al pressente tiene, y antiguamente tuuo." Ed. R. Foulché-Delbosc. *Revue Hispanique,* vol. 10, 1903, pp. 160–83.

Homza, Lu Ann. "How to Harass an Inquisitor-General: The Polyphonic Law of Friar Francisco Ortiz." In John A. Marino and Thomas Kuehn, eds. *A Renaissance of Conflicts: Visions and Revisions of Law and Society in Italy and Spain.* Toronto, 2004 (pp. 299–336).

Ingram, Kevin. "Diego Velázquez's Secret History: The Family Background the Painter was at Pains to Hide in His Application for Entry into the Military Order of Santiago." *Boletín del Museo del Prado,* vol. 17, no. 35, 1999, pp. 69–85.

Kamen, Henry. "Limpieza and the Ghost of Américo Castro: Racism as a Tool of Literary Analysis." *Hispanic Review,* vol. 64, no. 1, 1996, pp. 19–29.

Martínez, María-Elena. *Genealogical Fictions: Limpieza de Sangre, Religion, and Gender in Colonial Mexico.* Stanford, 2008.

Maryks, Robert Aleksander. *The Jesuit Order as a Synagogue of Jews: Jesuits of Jewish Ancestry and Purity-of-Blood Law in the Early Society of Jesus.* Leiden, 2009.

Pike, Ruth. *Linajudos and Conversos in Seville: Greed and Prejudice in Sixteenth- and Seventeenth-Century Spain.* New York, 2000.

*Sicroff, Albert A. *Los estatutos de limpieza de sangre. Controversias entre los siglos XV y XVII.* Trans. from the French by Mauro Armiño. Madrid, 1985 [orig. ed. 1960].

Soria Mesa, Enrique. "Genealogía y poder: Invención de la memoria y ascenso social en la España Moderna." *Estudis,* vol. 30, 2004, pp. 21–55.

CHAPTER FOURTEEN.
JUDAIZING AND THE IMPOSSIBILITY OF ORTHODOXY

Amiel, Charles. "Los ritos judíos en los edictos de fe ibéricos." In Carlos Barros, ed. *Xudeus e Conversos na Historia.* Santiago de Compostela, 1994 (vol. I, pp. 205–24).

Bodian, Miriam. *Dying in the Law of Moses: Crypto-Jewish Martyrdom in the Iberian World.* Bloomington, 2007.

Carrete Parrondo, Carlos. *Hebraistas judeoconversos en la universidad de Salamanca, siglos XV–XVI.* Salamanca, 1983.

The Enlightened: The Writings of Luis de Carvajal, El Mozo. Ed. and trans. from the Spanish by Seymour B. Liebman. Miami, 1967.

Chinchilla, Rosa Helena. "The Brief Revival of Hebrew Studies by Christian Humanists in Spain, 1503–1527." *Journal of Hispanic Philology,* vol. 20, nos. 1–2–3, Fall 1995–Winter/Spring 1996, pp. 30–45.

Edwards, John. "Was the Spanish Inquisition Truthful?" *Jewish Quarterly Review,* vol. 87, 1997, pp. 351–66.

Edwards, John H. "Male and Female Religious Experience among Spanish New Christians, 1450–1500." In Waddington and Williamson, *Expulsion of the Jews* (pp. 41–52).

Faur, José. "Four Classes of Conversos: A Typological Study." *Revue des Études Juives,* vol. 149, 1990, pp. 113–24.

Giles, Mary E., ed. *Women in the Inquisition: Spain and the New World.* Baltimore, 1998.

Gitlitz, David. "Hybrid Conversos in the *Libro llamado el Alboraique*." *Hispanic Review,* vol. 60, 1992, pp. 1–17.

Lazar, Moshe. "Scorched Parchments and Tortured Memories: The 'Jewishness' of the Anussim (Crypto-Jews)." In Mary Elizabeth Perry and Anne J. Cruz, eds., *Cultural Encounters: The Impact of the Inquisition in Spain and the New World.* Berkeley, 1991 (pp. 176–206).

Regev, Sahul. "The Attitude towards the Conversos in 15th–16th Century Jewish Thought." *Revue des Études Juives,* vol. 156, no. 1–2, 1997, pp. 117–34.

Wachtel, Nathan. *The Faith of Remembrance: Marrano Labyrinths*. Trans. from the French by Nikki Halpern, foreword Yosef Kaplan. Philadelphia, 2012 [orig. ed. 2001].

Zagorin, Perez. "The Marranos and Crypto-Judaism." In his *Ways of Lying: Dissimulation, Persecution, and Conformity in Early Modern Europe*. Cambridge MA, 1990 (pp. 38–62).

CHAPTER FIFTEEN.
IDENTITY AND CREATIVITY

Arrizabalaga, Jon. "The Ideal Medical Practitioner in Counter-Reformation Castile: The Perception of the Converso Physician Henrique Jorge Henriques (c. 1555–1622)." In Samuel S. Kottek and Luis García-Ballester, eds. *Medicine and Medical Ethics in Medieval and Early Modern Spain: An Intercultural Approach*. Jerusalem, 1996 (pp. 61–91).

Castro, Américo. *The Spaniards: An Introduction to Their History*. Trans. from the Spanish by Willard F. King and Selma Margaretten. Berkeley-Los Angeles, 1971 [orig. ed. 1966].

Egido, Teófanes. *El linaje judeo-converso de Santa Teresa. Pleito de hidalguía de los Cepeda*. Madrid, 1986.

Gilman, Stephen. *The Spain of Fernando de Rojas: The Intellectual and Social Landscape of "La Celestina."* Princeton, NJ, 1972.

Girón-Negrón, Luis M. "'Your Dove-Eyes among your Hairlocks': Language and Authority in Fray Luis de León's *Respuesta que desde su prisión da a sus émulos*." *Renaissance Quarterly*, vol. 54, no. 4.1, Winter 2001, pp. 1197–1250.

Glick, Thomas F., and Oriol Pi-Sunyer. "Acculturation as an Explanatory Concept in Spanish History." *Comparative Studies in Society and History*, vol. 11, Spring 1969, pp. 136–54.

Gómez, Jesús. "El diálogo *Contra Iudaeos* de Vives y su tradición medieval." *Criticón*, vol. 41, 1988, pp. 67–85.

Graizbord, David L. *Souls in Dispute: Converso Identities in Iberia and the Jewish Diaspora, 1580–1700*. Philadelphia, 2003.

Homza, Lu Ann. *Religious Authority in the Spanish Renaissance*. Baltimore, 2000 (esp. pp. 77–112).

Márquez, Antonio. *Literatura e Inquisición en España, 1478–1834*. Madrid, 1980.

Marrano Poets of the Seventeenth Century: An Anthology of the Poetry of João Pinto Delgado, Antonio Enríquez Gómez and Miguel de Barrios. Ed. and trans. from the Spanish by Timothy Oelman. Rutherford, NJ, 1982.

Olivari, Michele. *Entre el trono y la opinión: La vida política castellana en los siglos XVI y XVII.* Trans. from the Italian by Jesús Villanueva. Valladolid, 2004 [orig. ed. 2002].

Pinta Llorente OSA, Miguel de la, and José María de Palacio y de Palacio, eds. *Procesos inquisitoriales contra la familia judía de Juan Luis Vives. I. Proceso contra Blanquina March, madre del humanista.* Madrid, 1964.

Pinto Delgado, João. *The Poem of Queen Esther.* Trans. from the Spanish by David R. Slavitt. New York, 1999.

Pardo Tomás, José. *El médico en la palestra: Diego Mateo Zapata (1664–1745), y la ciencia moderna en España.* Valladolid, 2004.

Roth, Norman. *Dictionary of Iberian Jewish and Converso Authors.* Salamanca, 2008.

Thompson, Colin. *The Strife of Tongues: Fray Luis de León and the Golden Age of Spain.* Cambridge, 1988.

Yovel, Yirmiyahu. *Spinoza and Other Heretics. Vol. I: The Marrano of Reason.* Princeton, NJ, 1989.

———. *The Other Within: The Marranos, Split Identity and Emerging Modernity.* Princeton, NJ, 2009.

CHAPTER SIXTEEN.
DIASPORA WITHIN THE DIASPORA

Antunes, Cátia. *Globalisation in the Early Modern Period: The Economic Relationship between Amsterdam and Lisbon, 1640–1705.* Amsterdam, 2004.

Artigas, María del Carmen. ed. *Antología sefaradí: 1492–1700. Respuesta literaria de los hebreos españoles a la expulsión de 1492.* Madrid, 1997.

———. *Segunda antología sefaradí: Continuidad cultural, 1600–1730.* Madrid, 2006.

Beinart, Haim, ed. *Moreshet Sepharad: The Sephardi Legacy.* 2 vols. Jerusalem, 1992.

Benbassa, Esther, and Aron Rodrigue. *The Jews of the Balkans: The Judeo-Spanish Community, 15th to 20th Centuries.* Oxford, 1995.

———. *Sephardi Jewry: A History of the Judeo-Spanish Community, 14th–20th Centuries.* Berkeley–Los Angeles, 2000.

*Bodian, Miriam. *Hebrews of the Portuguese Nation: Conversos and Community in Early Modern Amsterdam.* Bloomington, 1997.

Boer, Harm den. *La literatura sefardí de Amsterdam.* Alcalá de Henares, 1996; also 2005 CD-Rom "Spanish and Portuguese Printing in the Northern Netherlands, 1584–1825."

Brunelle, Gayle K. "Migration and Religious Identity: The Portuguese of Seventeenth-Century Rouen." *Journal of Early Modern History,* vol. 7, no. 3–4, 2003, pp. 283–311.

Cohen, Martin. "Don Gregorio López: Friend of the Secret Jew. A Contribution to the Study of Religious Life in Early Colonial Mexico." *Hebrew Union College Annual*, vol. 38, 1967, pp. 259–84.

Contreras, Jaime, Bernardo José García García, and Ignacio Pulido, eds. *Familia, religión y negocio: El sefardismo en las relaciones entre el mundo ibérico y los Países Bajos en la Edad Moderna*. Madrid, 2003.

Escobar Quevedo, Ricardo. *Inquisición y judaizantes en la América española*. Bogotá, 2008.

García-Arenal, Mercedes, and G. A. Wiegers. *A Man of Three Worlds: Samuel Pallache, a Moroccan Jew in Catholic and Protestant Europe*. Trans. from the Spanish by Martin Beagles, foreword David Nirenberg and Richard Kagan. Baltimore, 2003 [orig. ed. 1999].

Goldish, Mark. "Jews, Christians and Conversos: Rabbi Solomon Aailion's Struggle in the Portuguese Community of London." *Journal of Jewish Studies*, vol. 45, 1994, pp. 227–57.

Graizbord, David L. "Becoming Jewish in Early Modern France: Documents on Jewish Community-Building in Seventeenth-Century Bayonne and Peyrehorade." *Journal of Social History*, vol. 40, no. 1, Fall 2006 (pp. 147–80).

Israel, Jonathan. "Duarte Nunes da Costa (Jacob Curiel) of Hamburg: Sephardi Nobleman and Communal Leader, 1585–1664." *Studia Rosenthaliana*, vol. 21, 1987, pp. 14–34.

———. *Empires and Entrepots: The Dutch, the Spanish Monarchy and the Jews, 1585–1713*. London, 1990.

Israel, Jonathan I. "Lopo Ramirez (David Curiel) and the Attempt to Establish a Sephardi Community in Antwerp in 1653–1654." *Studia Rosenthaliana*, vol. 28, 1994, pp. 99–119.

Israel, Jonathan, and Stuart Schwartz. *The Expansion of Tolerance: Religion in Dutch Brazil, 1624–1654*. Amsterdam, 2007.

Juhasz, Esther, ed. *Sephardi Jews in the Ottoman Empire: Aspects of Material Culture*. Jerusalem, 1990.

Kagan, Richard L., and Philip D. Morgan, eds. *Atlantic Diasporas: Jews, Conversos, and Crypto-Jews in the Age of Mercantilism, 1500–1800*. Baltimore, 2008.

Kaplan, Yosef. "The Jewish Profile of the Spanish-Portuguese Community of London during the Seventeenth Century." *Judaism*, vol. 41, 1992, pp. 229–40.

———. "Wayward New Christians and Stubborn New Jews: the Shaping of a Jewish Identity." *Jewish History*, vol. 8, 1994, pp. 27–41.

———. *Judíos nuevos en Amsterdam: Estudio sobre la historia social e intelectual del judaísmo sefardí en el siglo XVII*. Barcelona, 1996.

Kaplan, Yosef, Henri Méchoulan, and Richard H. Popkin, eds. *Menasseh Ben Israel and His World.* Leiden, 1989.

Kedourie, Elie, ed. *Spain and the Jews: The Sephardi Experience 1492 and After.* London, 1992.

Levy, Avigdor. *The Sephardim in the Ottoman Empire.* Princeton, NJ, 1992.

Lieberman, Julia R. "Between Tradition and Modernity: The Sephardim of Livorno." In Stanislao G. Pugliese, ed. *The Most Ancient of Minorities: The Jews of Italy.* Westport, CT, 2002 (pp. 67–76).

Mark, Peter, and José da Silva Horta. *The Forgotten Diaspora: Jewish Communities in West Africa and the Making of the Atlantic World.* Cambridge, 2011.

Mazower, Mark. *Salonica, City of Ghosts: Christians, Muslims and Jews, 1430–1950.* London, 2004.

Méchoulan, Henri, ed. *Los judíos de España, historia de una diáspora, 1492–1992.* Madrid, 1993.

Mott, Margaret. "Leonor de Cáceres and the Mexican Inquisition." *Journal of the History of Ideas* vol. 62, no. 1, 2001, pp. 81–98.

*Nadler, Steven. *Spinoza: A Life.* Cambridge, 2001.

———. *Spinoza's Heresy: Immortality and the Jewish Mind.* Oxford, 2001.

———. *Rembrandt's Jews.* Chicago, 2003.

Pereyra, Abraham Israel. *Hispanidad y judaísmo en tiempos de Espinoza: Edición de* La certeza del camino *de Abraham Pereyra.* Ed. Henry Méchoulan. Salamanca, 1981.

Pullan, Brian. *The Jews of Europe and the Inquisition of Venice, 1550–1670.* New York, 1997.

Quiroz, Alonso W. "The Expropriation of Portuguese New Christians in Spanish America, 1635–1649." *Ibero-Amerikanisches Archiv,* vol. 11, no. 1, 1985, pp. 407–65.

Ray, Jonathan. *After Expulsion: 1492 and the Making of Sephardic Jewry.* New York, 2012.

Roth, Cecil. *Doña Gracia of the House of Nasi.* Philadelphia, 1948.

———. *The House of Nasi: The Duke of Naxos.* Philadelphia, 1948.

Rozen, Minna. *The Jewish Community of Istanbul—The Formative Years, 1453–1566.* Leiden, 2002.

Salomon, H. P., ed. "The 'De Pinto' Manuscript: A Seventeenth-Century Marrano Family History." *Studia Rosenthaliana,* vol. 9, no. 1, 1975, pp. 1–62.

Salomon, Herman Prins, and Aron di Leone Leoni. "Mendes, Benveniste, de Luna, Micas, Nasi: The State of the Art." *Jewish Quarterly Review,* vol. 88, 1998, pp. 135–211.

*Segre, Renata. "Sephardic Settlements in Sixteenth-Century Italy: A Historical and Geographic Survey." *Mediterranean Historical Review,* vol. 6, 1991, pp. 112–37.

Silverblatt, Irene. *Modern Inquisitions: Peru and the Colonial Origins of the Civilized World.* Durham, NC, 2004.

Snyder, Saskia Coenen. "'Madness in a Magnificent Building': Gentile Responses to Jewish Synagogues in Amsterdam, 1670–1730." In Glenn Clark, Judith Owens, and Greg T. Smith, eds. *City Limits: Perspectives on the Historical European City.* Montreal-Kingston, 2010 (pp. 273–99).

Stow, Kenneth. *Theater of Acculturation: The Roman Ghetto in the Sixteenth Century.* Seattle, 2001.

Swetschinski, Daniel M. *Reluctant Cosmopolitans: The Portuguese Jews of Seventeenth-Century Amsterdam.* Oxford, 2000.

Toniolo, Alberta. "Los sefarditas españoles y la sedería italiana en la primera edad moderna." *Revista de Historia Industrial,* vol. 12, 1997, pp. 43–74.

*Trivellato, Francesca. *The Familiarity of Strangers: The Sephardic Diaspora, Livorno, and Cross-Cultural Trade in the Early Modern Period.* New Haven, CT, 2009.

Uchmany, Eva Alexandra. *La vida entre el judaísmo y el cristianismo en la Nueva España, 1580–1606.* Mexico City, 1992.

Zeldes, Nadia. *'The Former Jews of This Kingdom': Sicilian Converts after the Expulsion, 1492–1516.* Leiden, 2003.

CHAPTER SEVENTEEN.

FROM HETERODOXY TO MODERNITY?

Costa, Uriel da. *Espejo de una vida humana. Exemplar humanae vitae.* Ed. and trans. from the Latin by Gabriel Albiac. Madrid, 1985.

Eliav-Feldon, Miriam. "Invented Identities: Credulity in the Age of Prophecy and Exploration." *Journal of Early Modern History,* vol. 3, no. 3, 1999, pp. 203–32.

Ferry, Barbara, and Debbie Nathan. "Mistaken Identity? The Case of New Mexico's 'Hidden Jews.'" *Atlantic Monthly,* December 2000, pp. 85–95.

Idel, Moshe. *Messianic Mystics.* New Haven, CT, 1998 (esp. pp. 126–211).

*Israel, Jonathan I. *Radical Enlightenment: Philosophy and the Making of Modernity, 1650–1750.* Oxford, 2000.

Kaplan, Yosef. *An Alternative Path to Modernity: The Western Sephardi Diaspora in the Seventeenth Century.* Leiden, 2000.

López Belinchón, Bernardo J. "Los criptojudíos españoles y Sabbatai Zevi." In Alfredo Alvar, Jaime Contreras, and José Ignacio Ruiz, eds. *Política y Cultura en la Época Moderna: Cambios dinásticos, milenarismos, mesianismos y utopías.* Alcalá, 2004 (pp. 697–704).

Popkin, Richard H. *The History of Skepticism from Erasmus to Descartes.* New York, 1968.

Popkin, Richard, and Mark Goldish, eds. *Millenarianism and Messianism in Early Modern European Culture. I. Jewish Messianism in the Early Modern Period.* Dordrecht, 2001.

Shepard, Sanford. "The Background of Uriel da Costa's Heresy: Marranism, Skepticism, Karaism." *Judaism,* vol. 20, 1971, pp. 341–50.

Valensi, Lucette. "Reflexiones sobre historias relacionadas: Esperanzas mesiánicas en el imperio otomano, Portugal y Brasil durante el siglo XVII." In Roger Chartier and Antonio Feros, eds. *Europa, América y el mundo: Tiempos históricos.* Madrid, 2006 (pp. 67–83).

EPILOGUE.

TWO HISTORIES, PARALLEL AND DIFFERENT

Pulido Serrano, Juan Ignacio. "La expulsión frustrada. Proyectos para la erradicación de la herejía judaica en la Monarquía Hispana." In Francisco José Aranda, ed. *La declinación de la Monarquía hispánica.* Cuenca, 2004 (pp. 891–904).

INDEX

Abravanel, Isaac, 64, 77, 120, 149, 152, 154
Abulafia, Meir ha-Levi, 71
Acosta, Cristóbal, 128
Agustín, Antonio, 168
Albaicín (Muslim quarter of Granada), 12, 14, 16–17
alcabala (tax), 85
Alcázar, Baltasar, 128
Alemán, Mateo, 32, 97, 128
alfaquíes. See clerics, role of
Alfasi, Isaac ben Jacob, 71
Alfonso, Pedro, 129
Alhambra palace, 12, 17
aljamas (Jewish quarters), 70, 72
aljamiado literature, 37–38, 48–53
Alpujarras revolt (1568–70), 8, 12, 16, 48, 164
alumbrados, 81, 127
Amsterdam: crucible for modern Jews, as, 160–61; Jewish identity in, 144–45; limitations for sephardic Jews, in, 141–42; New Jews and, 142–44; printing in, 140–41; Sephardic diaspora and, 139–46; Spinoza in, 156–57; synagogues in, 140, 145–46. *See also* Holland

Andalusia: architectural styles in, 47; book burning in, 12; clothing differences in, 44; Costa in, 155–56; descendants of moriscos in, 65; expulsion of Jews from, 75; expulsion of moriscos from, 61–63; forced conversions in, 8; Jewish riots and, 70, 73
antisemitism, 70, 92–97, 111, 115–16, 142
Antonio, Nicolás, 58–59
Aragon: blood purity in, 103–4; expulsion of moriscos from, 61; forced conversions in, 8, 13; moriscos in, 14, 18–19, 30
Arévalo, 32, 50
Arias Montano, Benito, 57, 96
Aristotelianism, 54
Arroyuelos (Extremadura), 120–21
Asher ben Jehiel, 71
Ashkenazim: Amsterdam, in, 139–40, 145–46; ascendancy of, 149; immortal soul controversy and, 143–45; Italy in, 134, 135; Talmud Torah and, 140
atheism, 154, 158
autos-da-fé, 89, 97, 121, 147
Avalos, Gaspar de, 13

Medina, Pedro de, 34
Medina del Campo, 23
Menasseh ben Israel, 141, 146, 149, 156
Mendieta, Jerónimo de, 78
messianism, 151–53
Mexico, 78, 147
Modena, Leon da, 155
Molcho, Solomon, 152
Moncada, Sancho de, 23
Mondéjar, Marquis of, 17–18
Montemayor, Jorge de, 128
"Moorish novels," 32, 48
moriscos: 1568 revolt of, 16–18; Andalusia
in, 14–15; baptism, effect on, 11, 13, 22,
36, 163; blood purity statue, effect on,
167–68; Catholic church and, 7, 19,
21–22, 25, 26; characteristics of, 44–46;
circumcision and, 15, 39; creativity of,
47–53; crypto-Islamic behavior and,
34–40; Cuenca Inquisition and, 30,
35–36, 42, 45; demographic impact of,
23; ecclesiastical authorities and, 167;
economic impact of, 23–24; expulsion
of in 1492, 2, 21, 22, 75–79, 133–34, 149;
expulsions of (1492 and 1609-14), 2,
18–19, 21–25, 60–65, 164; fate of, 60–65;
forced conversion of, 126; ghettos, in,
19; group solidarity and, 42–44, 166–67;
healers/magicians, as, 28–29, 42–43,
166; marriage practices and, 43–44;
Old Christians and, 7–9, 26–28, 29–31;
Ottoman Empire, relationship with, 17,
19, 20, 28, 62, 164; pirates, as, 19–20, 26,
29, 62, 164; religious impact of, 22; rites,
maintaining of, 36–38; segregation of,
29–31, 35; sense of community among,
41–44; socioeconomic characteristics of,
165; traditional images of, 26–29;
Valencia, in, 14–15. See also Muslims
Morocco, 20, 61–63, 135
Mortera, Saul Levi, 139, 143–44
"Mosaic heresy," 74

mudéjares, 10–12, 30, 45, 164. See also
Muslims
Murcia, 30, 61, 90
Muslims: beliefs and practices of, 15;
Capitulations of Santa Fe and, 11; con-
verts to Christianity (see moriscos);
creativity of, 47–53; expulsion of (1492),
2, 21, 22, 75–79, 133–34, 149; expulsions
of (1492 and 1609-1614), 2, 18–19, 21–25,
60–65, 164; Inquisition and, 15–16;
North Africa, in, 135–36; Ottoman
Empire, in, 135–37; parallel history of
Jews and, 163–69

Nahmanides of Girona, 71
Naples, 134–35
Nasi, Joseph, 136–37
Nasrid kingdom. See Granada
Navarre, 8, 57, 134
Neve Shalom ("Oasis of Peace"), 139.
See also synagogues
New Christians: diaspora of, 133–48;
moriscos, attitudes towards, 26–27;
New Jews, struggle to become, 142–44;
New World, in, 147–48; Old Christians,
relations with, 12, 15, 88–89; See also
conversos; moriscos
Nicodemites, 159
Nissim ben Reuben Gerondi, 70
North Africa: aide source for moriscos, as,
17, 26, 164; Jewish resettlement area, as,
74, 84–54, 135–36; morisco resettlement
area, as, 12, 14, 22, 61–63; prison and
slavery stronghold, as, 29, 35
Núñez de Reinoso, Alonso, 97
Núñez Muley, Francisco, 45–46, 108, 167

Old Christians: moriscos and, 7–9, 23,
26–28, 30–31; New Christians, relations
with, 12, 15, 88–89
Olivares, count-duke of, 85, 90–91, 106, 128
On Making Peace (Vives), 129